HELLBOY™

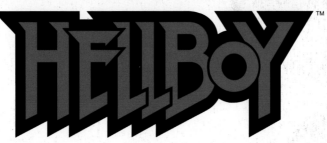

THE RIGHT HAND *of* DOOM

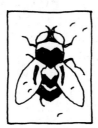

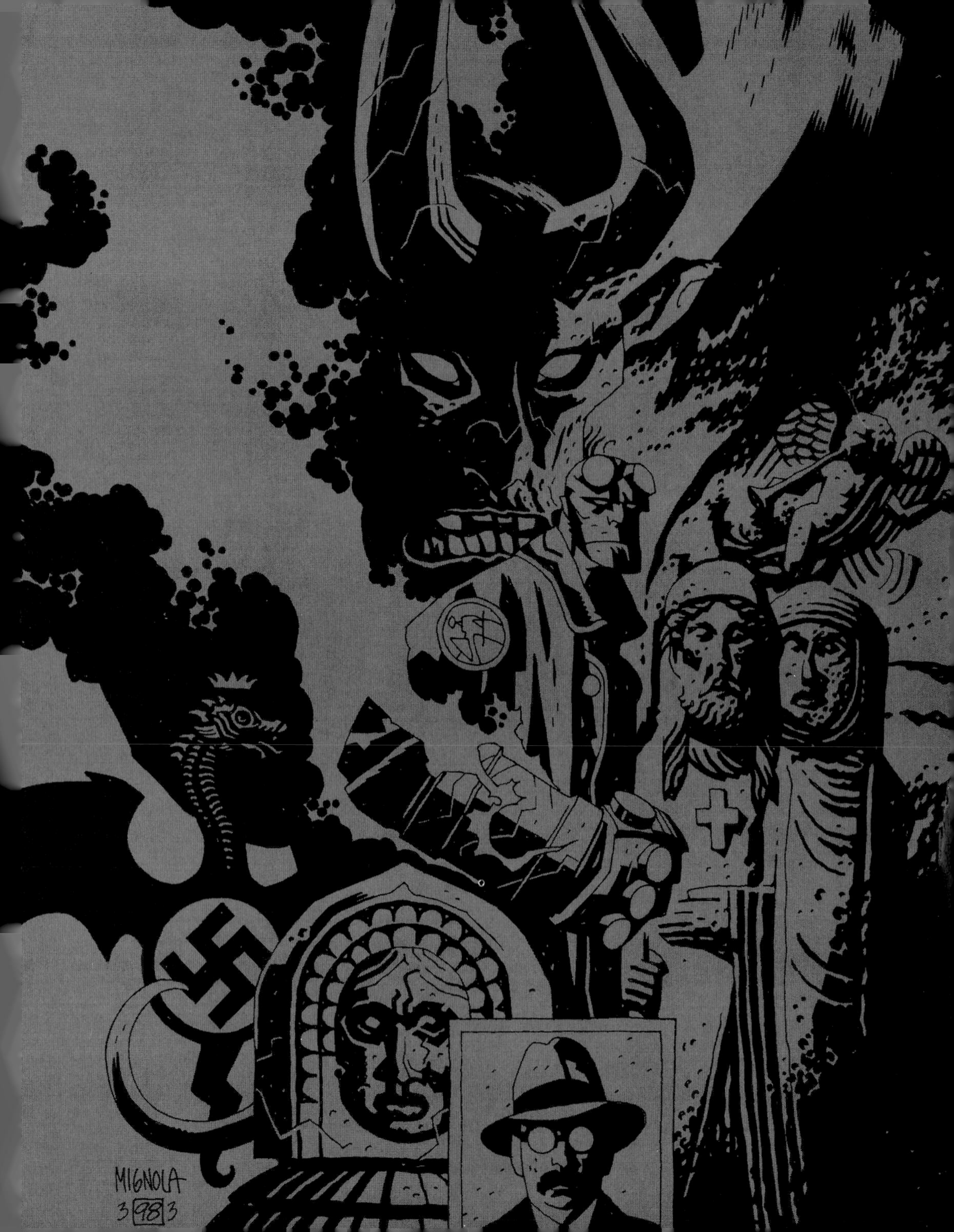
MIGNOLA
3 98 3

HELLBOY

THE RIGHT HAND *of* DOOM

by
MIKE MIGNOLA

Colored by
DAVE STEWART

Lettered by
PAT BROSSEAU

✠

Edited by
SCOTT ALLIE

Hellboy logo designed by
KEVIN NOWLAN

Collection designed by
MIKE MIGNOLA & CARY GRAZZINI

Published by
MIKE RICHARDSON

DARK HORSE BOOKS™

NEIL HANKERSON ✠ *executive vice president*

TOM WEDDLE ✠ *vice president of finance*

RANDY STRADLEY ✠ *vice president of publishing*

CHRIS WARNER ✠ *senior books editor*

SARA PERRIN ✠ *vice president of marketing*

MICHAEL MARTENS ✠ *vice president of business development*

ANITA NELSON ✠ *vice president of sales & licensing*

DAVID SCROGGY ✠ *vice president of product development*

DALE LaFOUNTAIN ✠ *vice president of information technology*

DARLENE VOGEL ✠ *director of purchasing*

KEN LIZZI ✠ *general counsel*

Published by Dark Horse Books
A division of Dark Horse Comics, Inc.
10956 SE Main St.
Milwaukie, OR 97222
www.darkhorse.com

First Edition: April 2000
Second Edition: November 2003
ISBN: 1-59307-093-4

This volume collects stories from the Dark Horse comic books *Dark Horse Presents* #151,
Dark Horse Presents Annual 1998, *Dark Horse Presents Annual 1999*, *Gary Gianni's The MonsterMen*,
Abe Sapien: Drums of the Dead, and *Hellboy: Box Full of Evil* #1 and #2.

10 9 8 7

PRINTED IN CHINA

PART ONE
THE EARLY YEARS

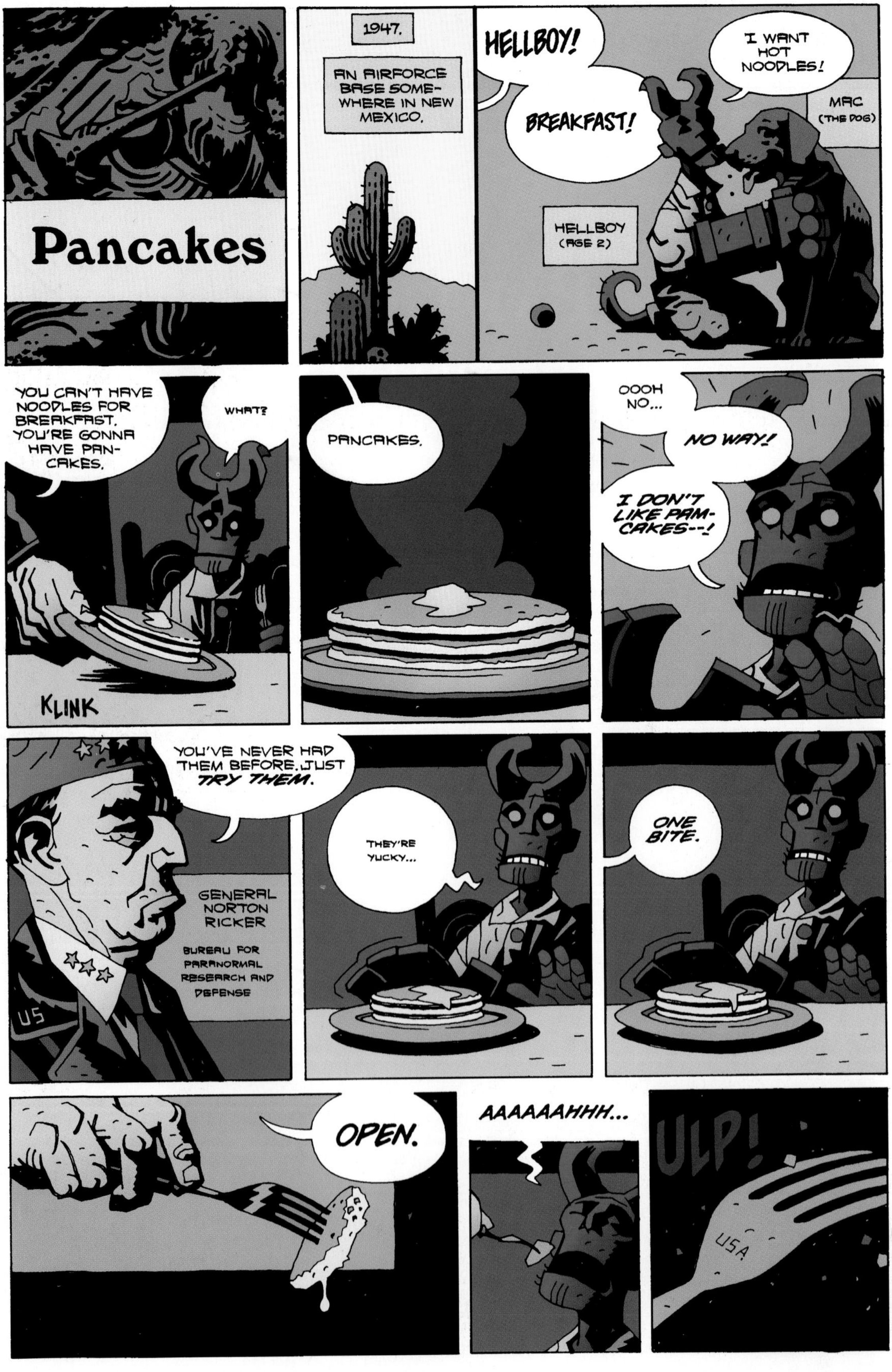
Pancakes
1947.
AN AIRFORCE BASE SOMEWHERE IN NEW MEXICO.
HELLBOY!
BREAKFAST!
I WANT HOT NOODLES!
MAC (THE DOG)
HELLBOY (AGE 2)
YOU CAN'T HAVE NOODLES FOR BREAKFAST. YOU'RE GONNA HAVE PANCAKES.
WHAT?
KLINK
PANCAKES.
OOOH NO...
NO WAY!
I DON'T LIKE PANCAKES--!
YOU'VE NEVER HAD THEM BEFORE. JUST TRY THEM.
GENERAL NORTON RICKER
BUREAU FOR PARANORMAL RESEARCH AND DEFENSE
US
THEY'RE YUCKY...
ONE BITE.
OPEN.
AAAAAAHHH...
ULP!
USA

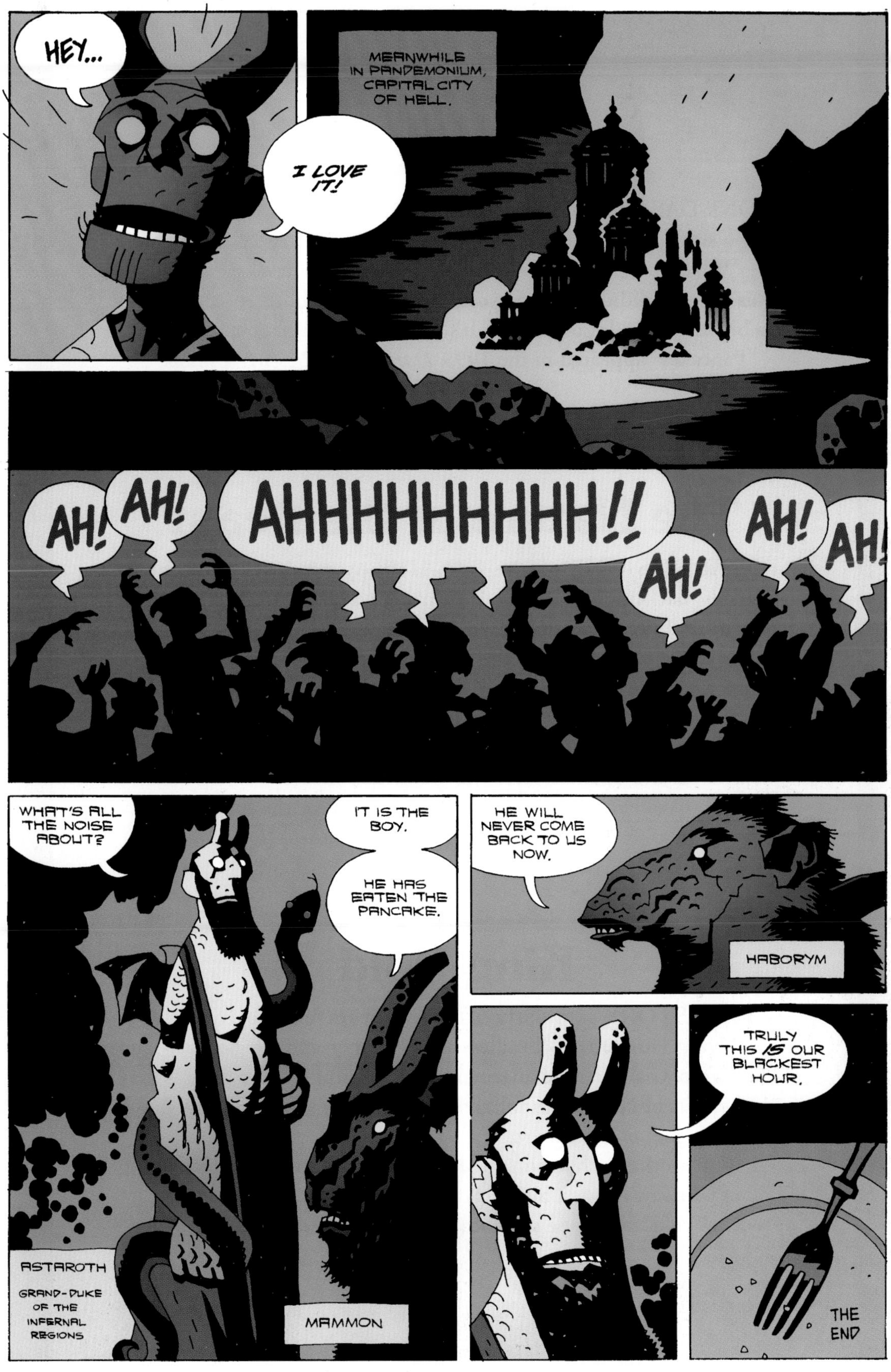
HEY...
I LOVE IT!
MEANWHILE IN PANDEMONIUM, CAPITAL CITY OF HELL.
AH!
AH!
AHHHHHHHHH!!
AH!
AH!
AH!
WHAT'S ALL THE NOISE ABOUT?
IT IS THE BOY.
HE HAS EATEN THE PANCAKE.
ASTAROTH
GRAND-DUKE OF THE INFERNAL REGIONS
MAMMON
HE WILL NEVER COME BACK TO US NOW.
HABORYM
TRULY THIS IS OUR BLACKEST HOUR.
THE END

Pancakes

ONE DAY SOMEONE at Dark Horse asked if I was interested in doing a story about young Hellboy. I wasn't, but instead of saying no I said, "What about two pages of Hellboy eating pancakes?" I thought it was a riot. I didn't expect anyone else to like it, but it turned out to be a big hit with a lot of readers. It's nice when that happens.

"Pancakes" appeared in the 1999 *Dark Horse Presents Annual.*

✠

The Nature of the Beast

THIS WAS ONE of the first Hellboy stories I thought of (probably back in 1994), but I didn't get around to putting it on paper until 1999. The story is built around a sixth-century English folktale about Saint Leonard the Hermit. He was wounded fighting a dragon and wherever his blood fell lilies-of-the-valley sprang up. The lilies are supposedly still there, halfway between Horsham and Pease Pottage in West Sussex.

"The Nature of the Beast" was published in *Dark Horse Presents* #151 and, like "Pancakes," appears here in color for the first time.

✠

King Vold

THIS STORY is mostly a combination of two folktales— "The Flying Huntsman" (headless King Volmer and his hounds) and "The Green Giant" (dead mermaid and burning gold coins). There are other bits of Norwegian folklore thrown in to show just how much weird stuff goes on over there.

I want to thank that unnamed fan that gave me that great photo book of Norway. It was a big help.

"King Vold" was done specifically for this collection.

The Nature of the Beast

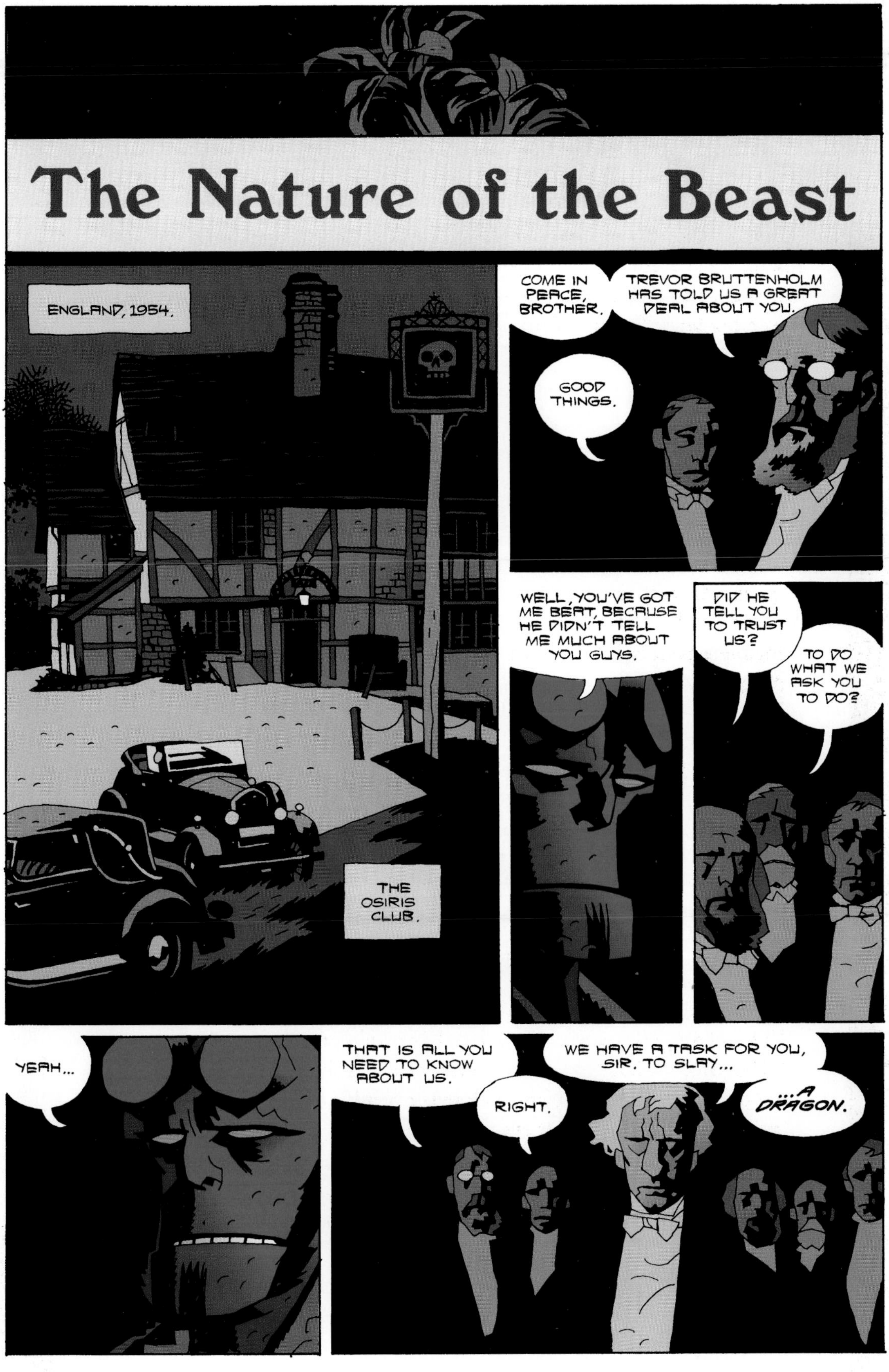
ENGLAND, 1954.
THE OSIRIS CLUB.
COME IN PEACE, BROTHER.
TREVOR BRUTTENHOLM HAS TOLD US A GREAT DEAL ABOUT YOU.
GOOD THINGS.
WELL, YOU'VE GOT ME BEAT, BECAUSE HE DIDN'T TELL ME MUCH ABOUT YOU GUYS.
DID HE TELL YOU TO TRUST US?
TO DO WHAT WE ASK YOU TO DO?
YEAH...
THAT IS ALL YOU NEED TO KNOW ABOUT US.
RIGHT.
WE HAVE A TASK FOR YOU, SIR. TO SLAY...
...A DRAGON.

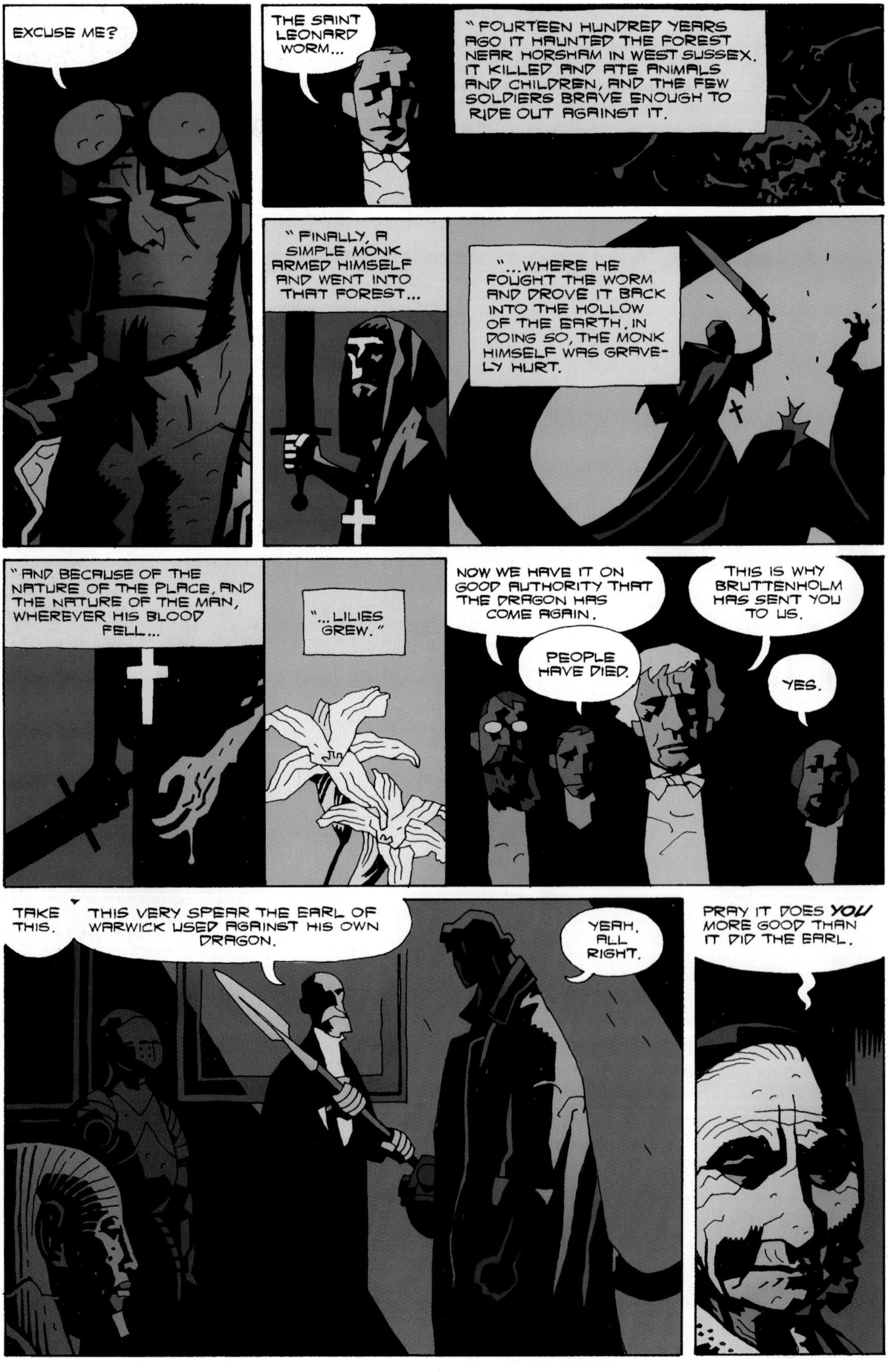
EXCUSE ME?
THE SAINT LEONARD WORM...
"FOURTEEN HUNDRED YEARS AGO IT HAUNTED THE FOREST NEAR HORSHAM IN WEST SUSSEX. IT KILLED AND ATE ANIMALS AND CHILDREN, AND THE FEW SOLDIERS BRAVE ENOUGH TO RIDE OUT AGAINST IT.
"FINALLY, A SIMPLE MONK ARMED HIMSELF AND WENT INTO THAT FOREST...
"...WHERE HE FOUGHT THE WORM AND DROVE IT BACK INTO THE HOLLOW OF THE EARTH. IN DOING SO, THE MONK HIMSELF WAS GRAVELY HURT.
"AND BECAUSE OF THE NATURE OF THE PLACE, AND THE NATURE OF THE MAN, WHEREVER HIS BLOOD FELL...
"...LILIES GREW."
NOW WE HAVE IT ON GOOD AUTHORITY THAT THE DRAGON HAS COME AGAIN.
PEOPLE HAVE DIED.
THIS IS WHY BRUTTENHOLM HAS SENT YOU TO US.
YES.
TAKE THIS.
THIS VERY SPEAR THE EARL OF WARWICK USED AGAINST HIS OWN DRAGON.
YEAH, ALL RIGHT.
PRAY IT DOES *YOU* MORE GOOD THAN IT DID THE EARL.

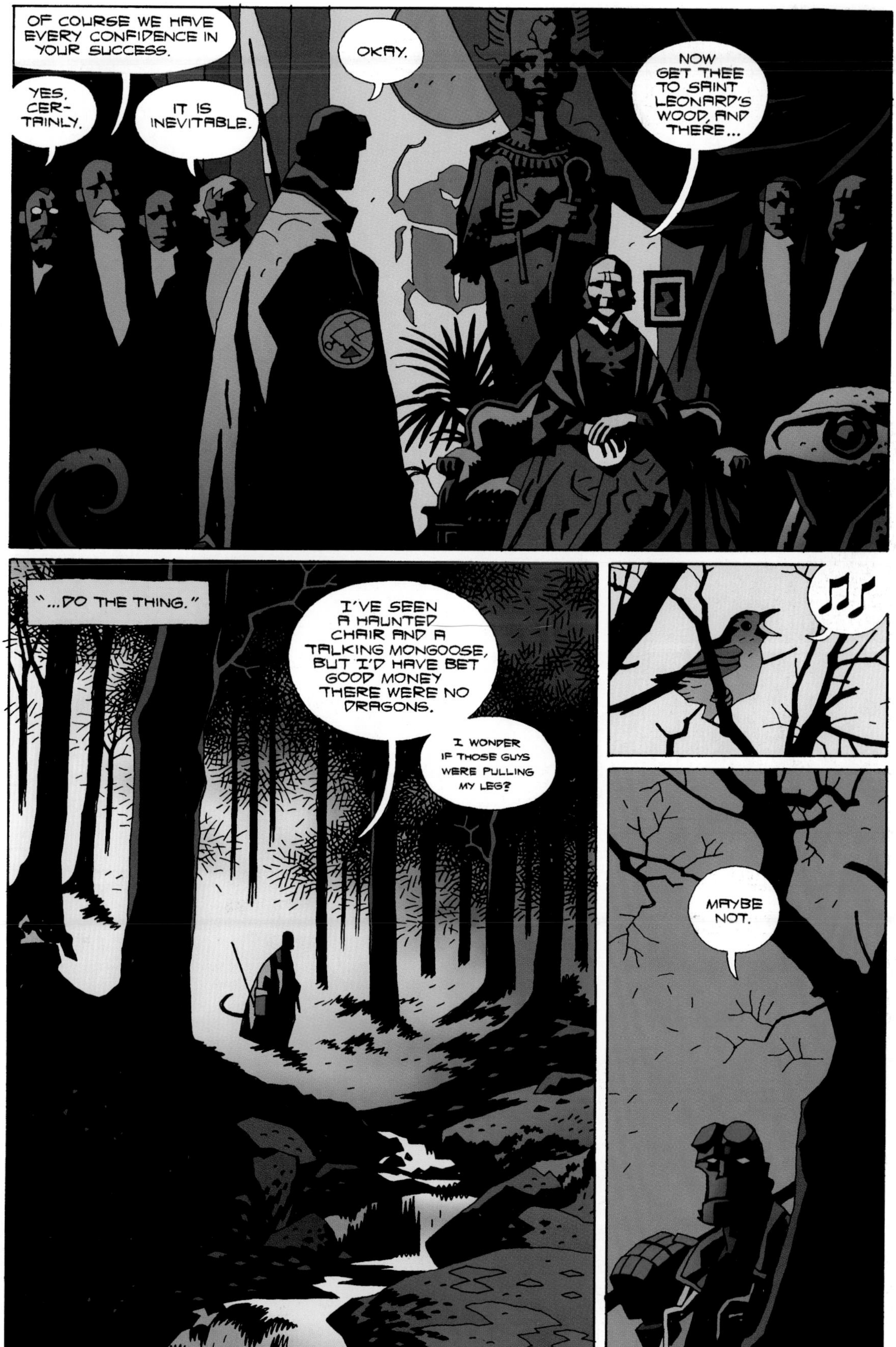

OF COURSE WE HAVE EVERY CONFIDENCE IN YOUR SUCCESS.
YES. CER-TAINLY.
IT IS INEVITABLE.
OKAY.
NOW GET THEE TO SAINT LEONARD'S WOOD, AND THERE...
"...DO THE THING."
I'VE SEEN A HAUNTED CHAIR AND A TALKING MONGOOSE, BUT I'D HAVE BET GOOD MONEY THERE WERE NO DRAGONS.
I WONDER IF THOSE GUYS WERE PULLING MY LEG?
♫♪
MAYBE NOT.

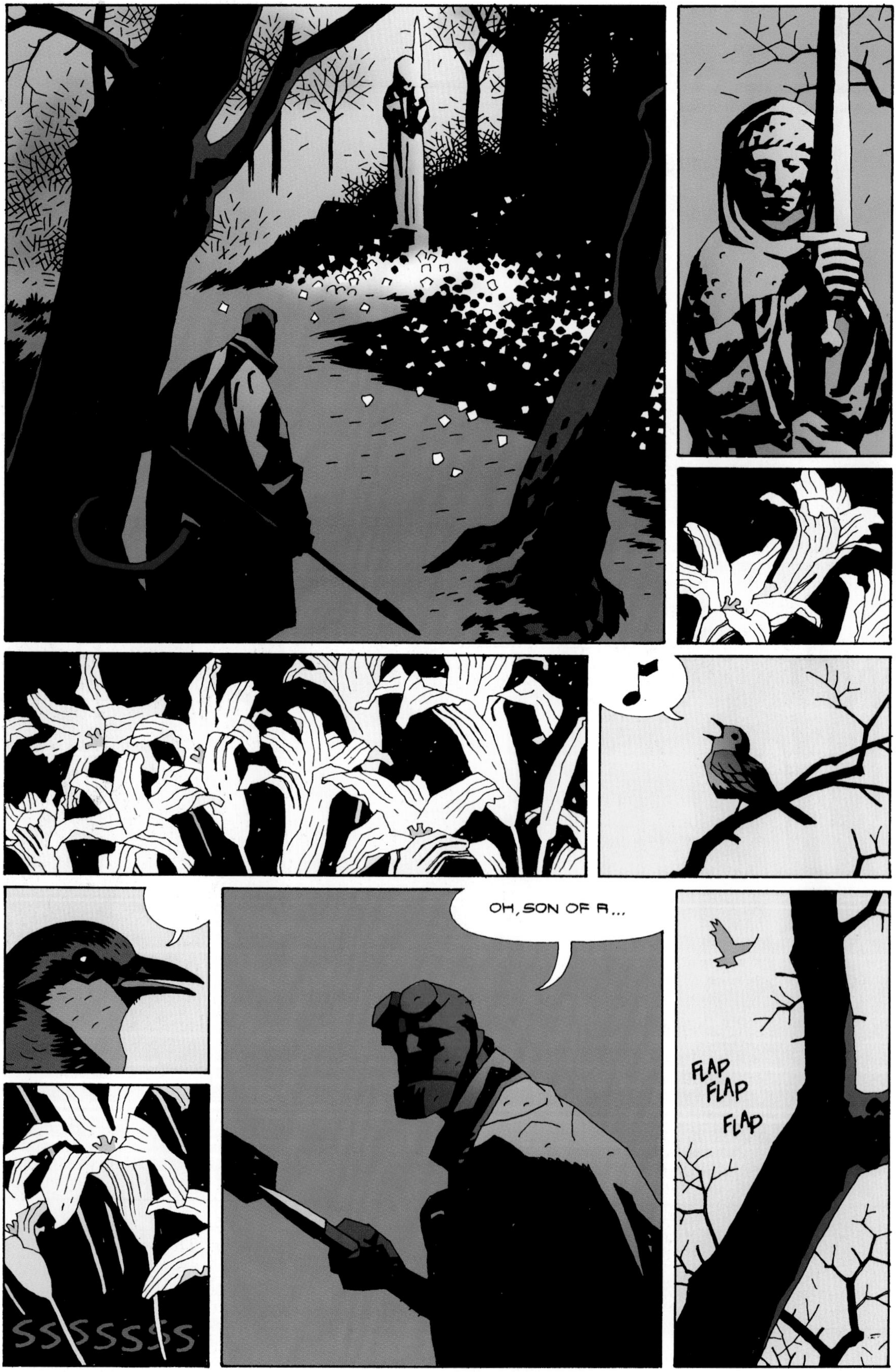

OH, SON OF A...
FLAP
FLAP
FLAP
SSSSSSS

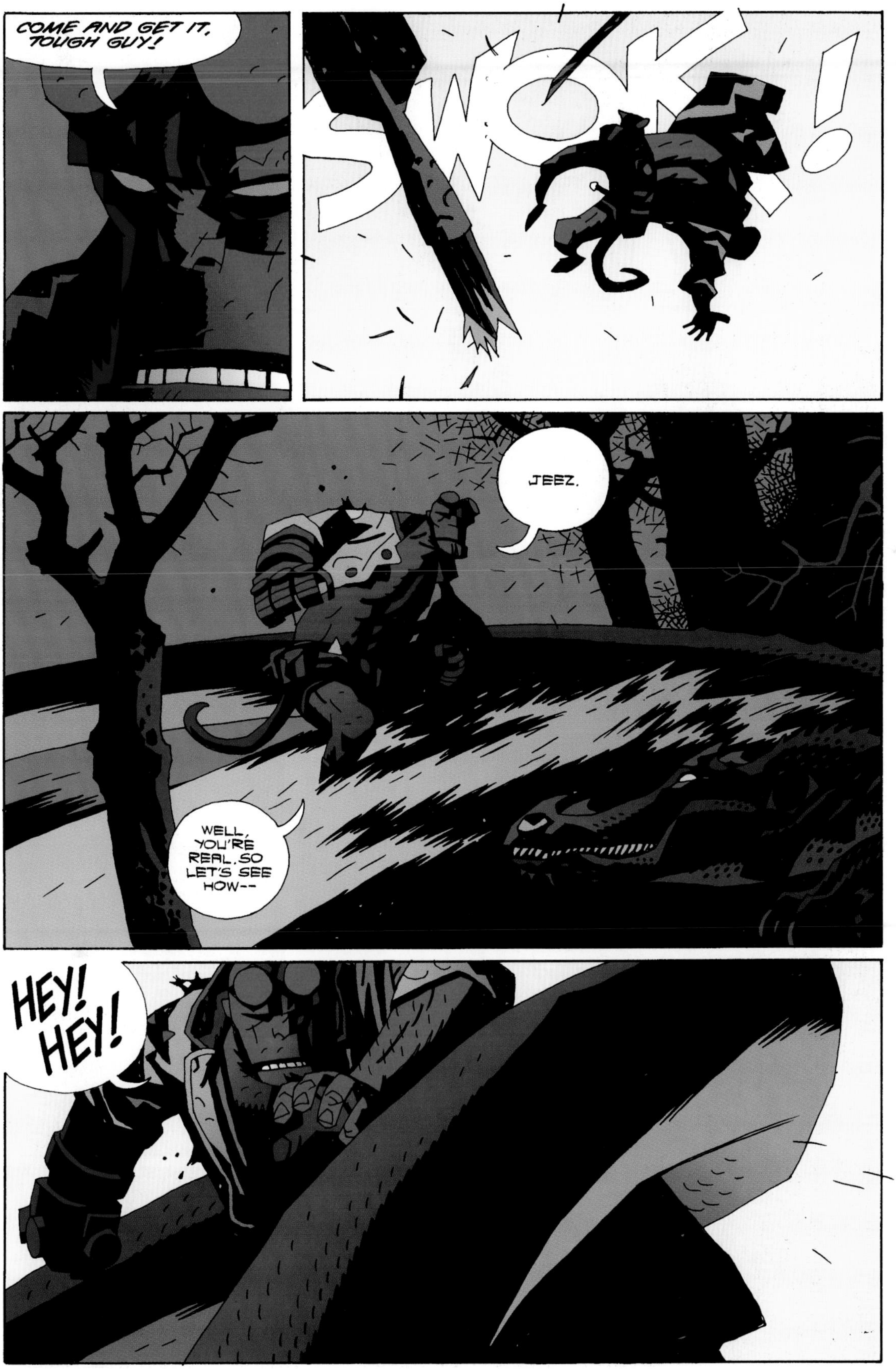
COME AND GET IT, TOUGH GUY!
SWOK!
JEEZ.
WELL, YOU'RE REAL, SO LET'S SEE HOW--
HEY! HEY!

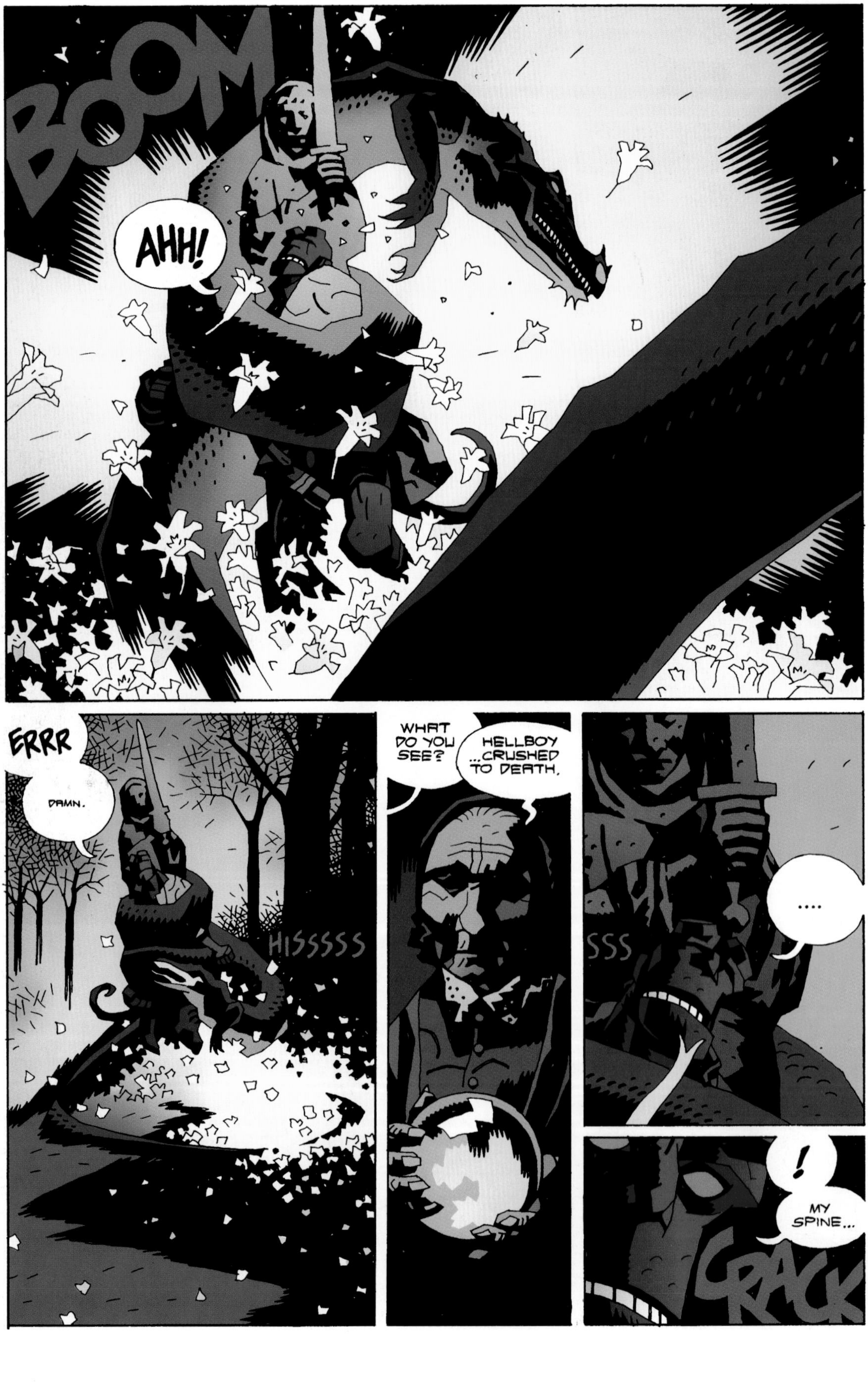
BOOM!
AHH!
ERRR
DAMN.
HISSSSS
WHAT DO YOU SEE?
HELLBOY ...CRUSHED TO DEATH.
SSS
....
!
MY SPINE...
CRACK

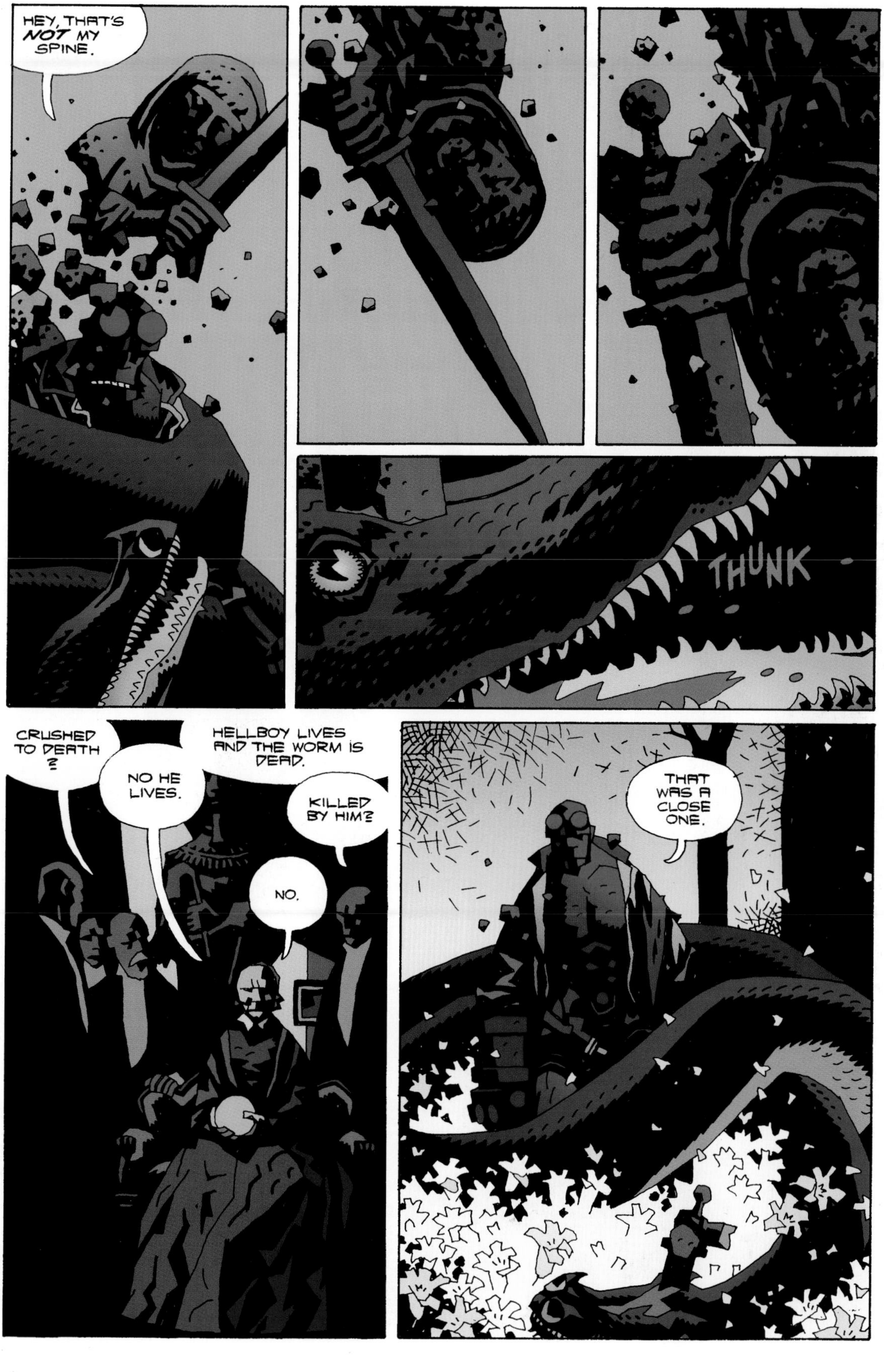
HEY, THAT'S NOT MY SPINE.
THUNK
CRUSHED TO DEATH?
NO HE LIVES.
HELLBOY LIVES AND THE WORM IS DEAD.
KILLED BY HIM?
NO.
THAT WAS A CLOSE ONE.

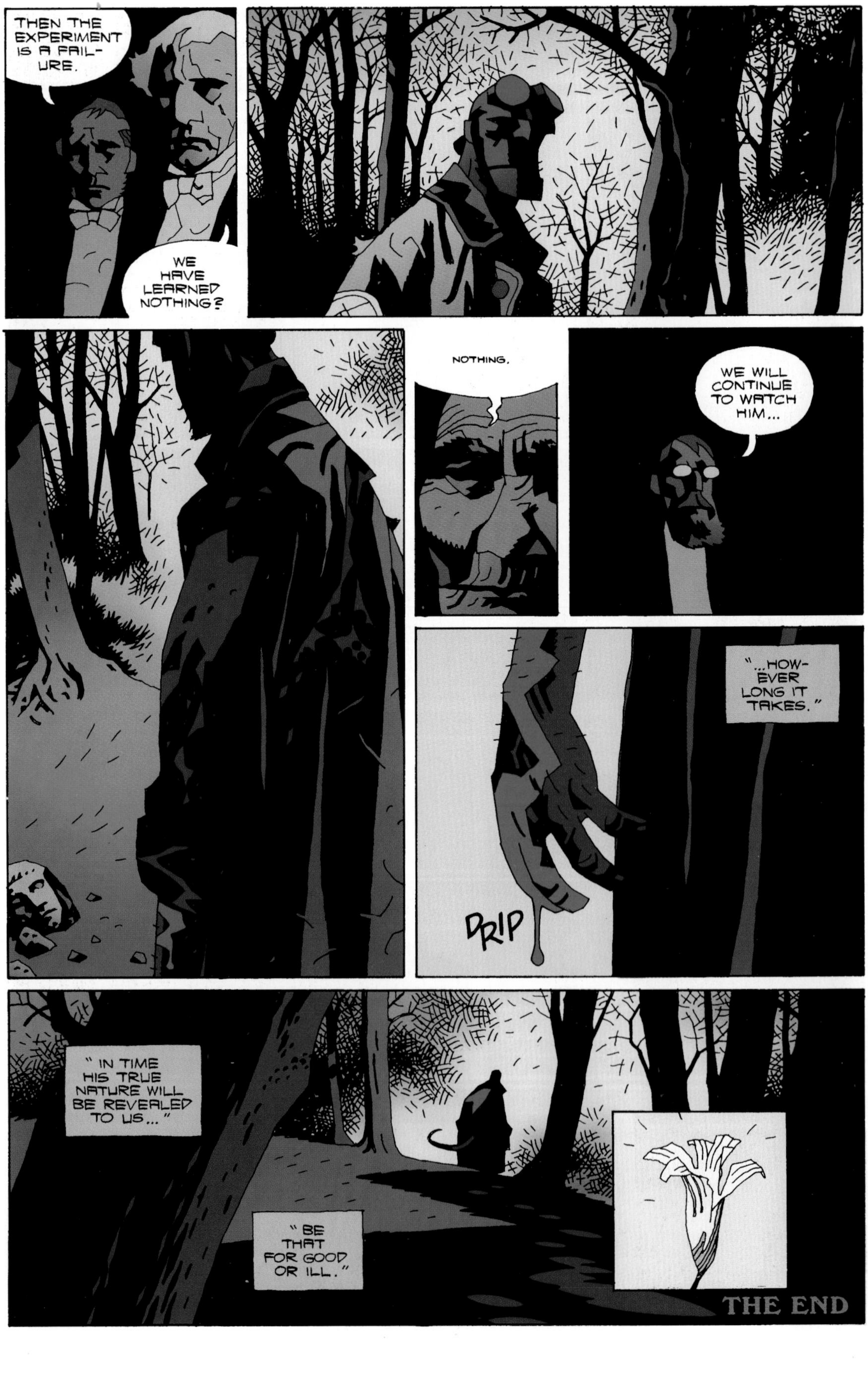
THEN THE EXPERIMENT IS A FAIL- URE.
WE HAVE LEARNED NOTHING?
NOTHING.
WE WILL CONTINUE TO WATCH HIM...
"...HOW- EVER LONG IT TAKES."
DRIP
" IN TIME HIS TRUE NATURE WILL BE REVEALED TO US..."
" BE THAT FOR GOOD OR ILL."
THE END

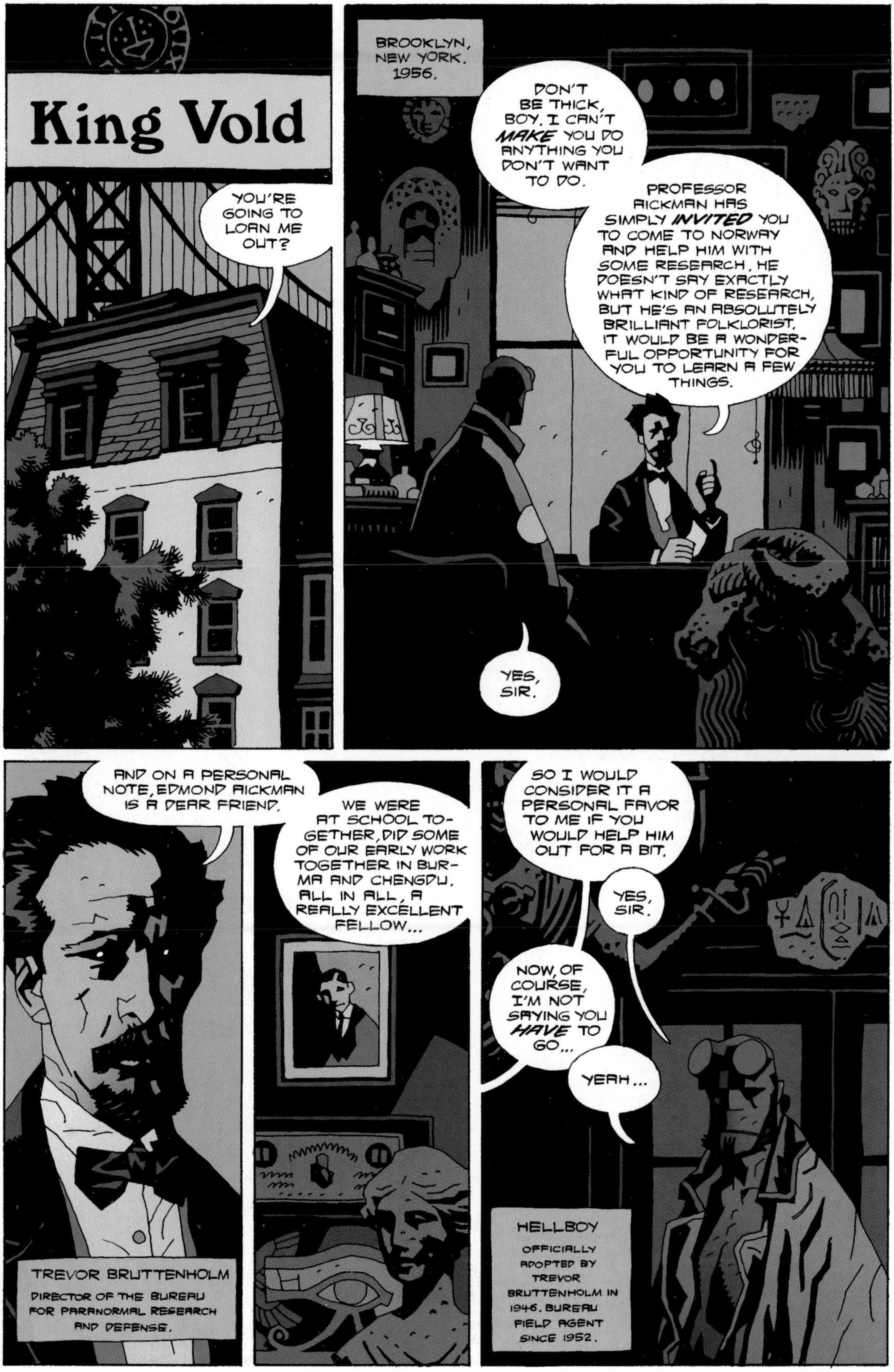
King Vold
YOU'RE GOING TO LOAN ME OUT?
BROOKLYN, NEW YORK. 1956.
DON'T BE THICK, BOY. I CAN'T MAKE YOU DO ANYTHING YOU DON'T WANT TO DO.
PROFESSOR AICKMAN HAS SIMPLY INVITED YOU TO COME TO NORWAY AND HELP HIM WITH SOME RESEARCH. HE DOESN'T SAY EXACTLY WHAT KIND OF RESEARCH, BUT HE'S AN ABSOLUTELY BRILLIANT FOLKLORIST. IT WOULD BE A WONDERFUL OPPORTUNITY FOR YOU TO LEARN A FEW THINGS.
YES, SIR.
AND ON A PERSONAL NOTE, EDMOND AICKMAN IS A DEAR FRIEND.
TREVOR BRUTTENHOLM
DIRECTOR OF THE BUREAU FOR PARANORMAL RESEARCH AND DEFENSE.
WE WERE AT SCHOOL TOGETHER, DID SOME OF OUR EARLY WORK TOGETHER IN BURMA AND CHENGDU. ALL IN ALL, A REALLY EXCELLENT FELLOW...
SO I WOULD CONSIDER IT A PERSONAL FAVOR TO ME IF YOU WOULD HELP HIM OUT FOR A BIT.
YES, SIR.
NOW, OF COURSE, I'M NOT SAYING YOU HAVE TO GO...
YEAH...
HELLBOY
OFFICIALLY ADOPTED BY TREVOR BRUTTENHOLM IN 1946. BUREAU FIELD AGENT SINCE 1952.

YEAH, ALL RIGHT.

GOOD BOY.

ONE WEEK LATER...

NORWAY.

" YOU SEE THAT HOUSE THERE? YEARS AGO LIGHTNING SMASHED THAT CHIMNEY, AND A TROLL FELL OUT.

" ELEVEN PEOPLE SAW IT. *THAT'S* A MATTER OF PUBLIC RECORD.

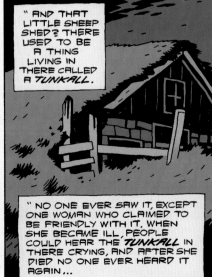

" AND THAT LITTLE SHEEP SHED? THERE USED TO BE A THING LIVING IN THERE CALLED A *TUNKALL.*

" NO ONE EVER SAW IT, EXCEPT ONE WOMAN WHO CLAIMED TO BE FRIENDLY WITH IT. WHEN SHE BECAME ILL, PEOPLE COULD HEAR THE *TUNKALL* IN THERE CRYING, AND AFTER SHE DIED NO ONE EVER HEARD IT AGAIN...

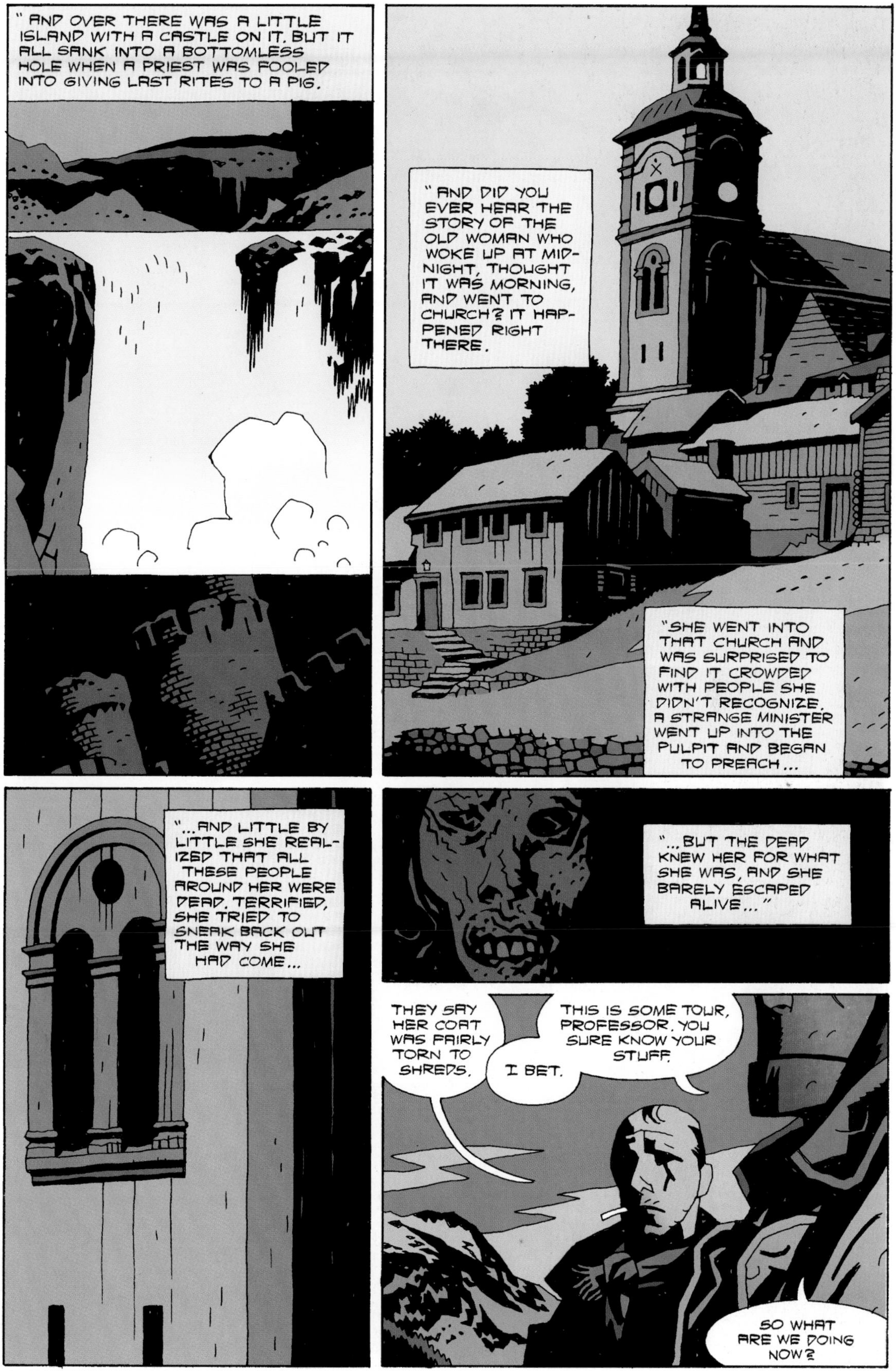
"AND OVER THERE WAS A LITTLE ISLAND WITH A CASTLE ON IT. BUT IT ALL SANK INTO A BOTTOMLESS HOLE WHEN A PRIEST WAS FOOLED INTO GIVING LAST RITES TO A PIG.
"AND DID YOU EVER HEAR THE STORY OF THE OLD WOMAN WHO WOKE UP AT MID-NIGHT, THOUGHT IT WAS MORNING, AND WENT TO CHURCH? IT HAP-PENED RIGHT THERE.
"SHE WENT INTO THAT CHURCH AND WAS SURPRISED TO FIND IT CROWDED WITH PEOPLE SHE DIDN'T RECOGNIZE. A STRANGE MINISTER WENT UP INTO THE PULPIT AND BEGAN TO PREACH...
"...AND LITTLE BY LITTLE SHE REAL-IZED THAT ALL THESE PEOPLE AROUND HER WERE DEAD. TERRIFIED, SHE TRIED TO SNEAK BACK OUT THE WAY SHE HAD COME...
"...BUT THE DEAD KNEW HER FOR WHAT SHE WAS, AND SHE BARELY ESCAPED ALIVE..."
THEY SAY HER COAT WAS FAIRLY TORN TO SHREDS.
I BET.
THIS IS SOME TOUR, PROFESSOR. YOU SURE KNOW YOUR STUFF.
SO WHAT ARE WE DOING NOW?

WAITING FOR KING VOLD.

OH.

KING WHO?

KING VOLD, THE FLYING HUNTS- MAN.

LEGEND HAS IT THAT IN LIFE HE USED TO SAY, "GOD CAN KEEP HEAVEN FOR HIM- SELF LONG AS I GO HUNTING IN GURRE."

OUCH.

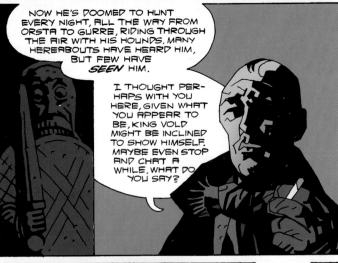

NOW HE'S DOOMED TO HUNT EVERY NIGHT, ALL THE WAY FROM ORSTA TO GURRE, RIDING THROUGH THE AIR WITH HIS HOUNDS. MANY HEREABOUTS HAVE HEARD HIM, BUT FEW HAVE SEEN HIM.

I THOUGHT PER- HAPS WITH YOU HERE, GIVEN WHAT YOU APPEAR TO BE, KING VOLD MIGHT BE INCLINED TO SHOW HIMSELF, MAYBE EVEN STOP AND CHAT A WHILE. WHAT DO YOU SAY?

I'M GONNA END UP HAVING TO FIGHT THIS GUY, AREN'T I?

FIGHT?

CERTAINLY NOT.

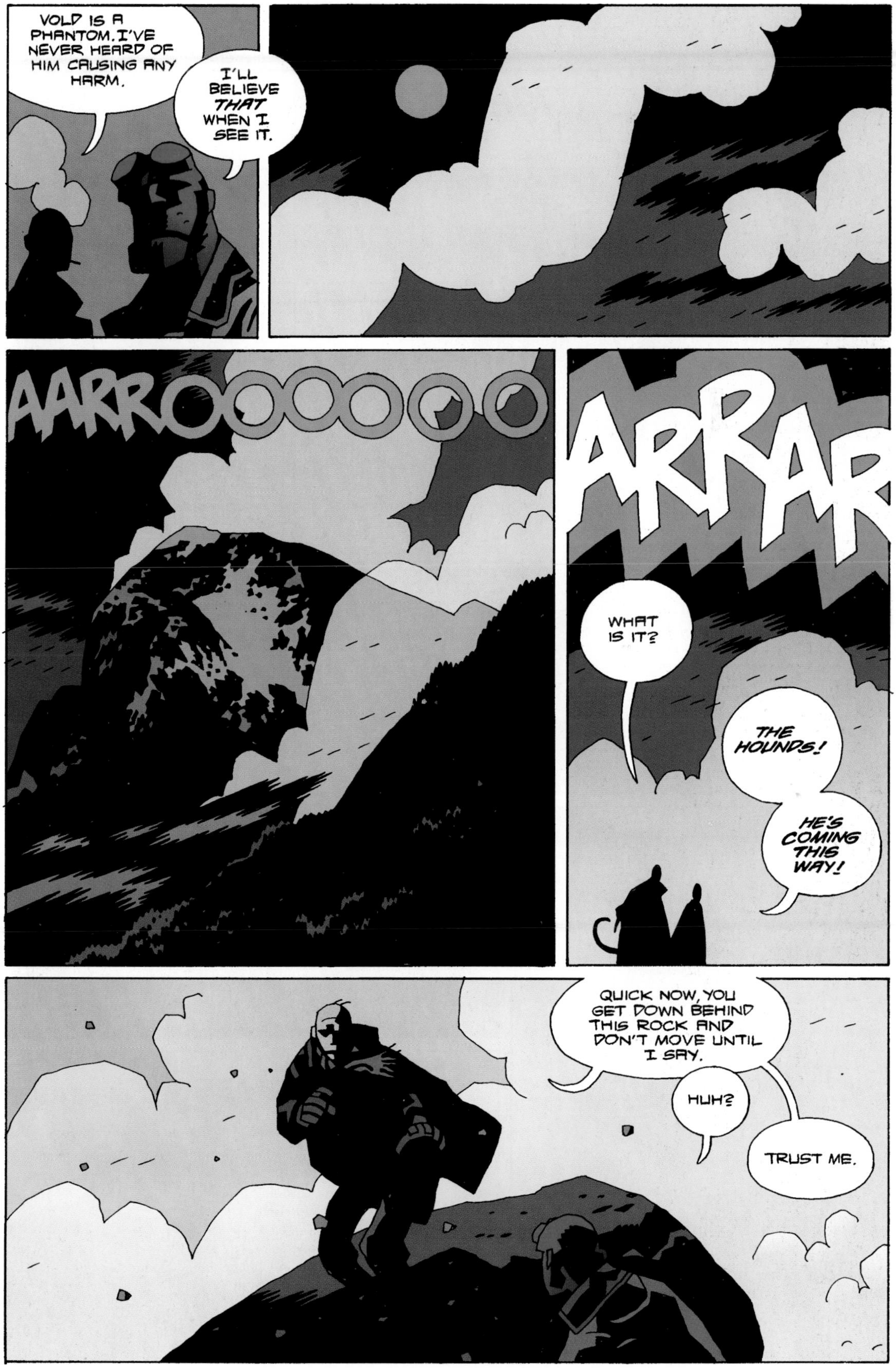
VOLD IS A PHANTOM. I'VE NEVER HEARD OF HIM CAUSING ANY HARM.
I'LL BELIEVE *THAT* WHEN I SEE IT.
AARROOOOOOO
ARRAR
WHAT IS IT?
THE HOUNDS!
HE'S COMING THIS WAY!
QUICK NOW, YOU GET DOWN BEHIND THIS ROCK AND DON'T MOVE UNTIL I SAY.
HUH?
TRUST ME.

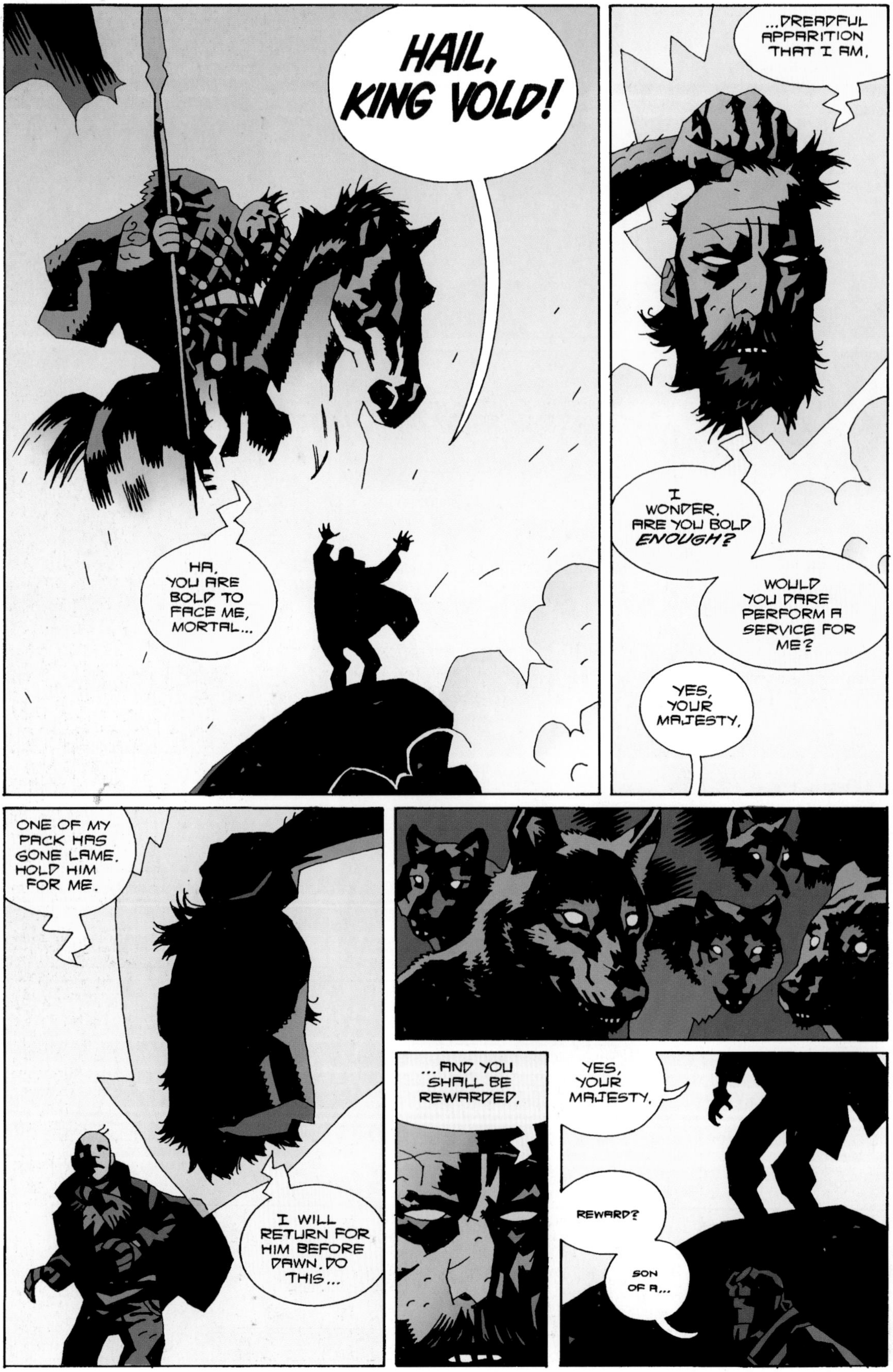
HAIL, KING VOLD!
HA, YOU ARE BOLD TO FACE ME, MORTAL...
...DREADFUL APPARITION THAT I AM.
I WONDER. ARE YOU BOLD *ENOUGH?*
WOULD YOU DARE PERFORM A SERVICE FOR ME?
YES, YOUR MAJESTY.
ONE OF MY PACK HAS GONE LAME. HOLD HIM FOR ME.
I WILL RETURN FOR HIM BEFORE DAWN. DO THIS...
...AND YOU SHALL BE REWARDED.
YES, YOUR MAJESTY.
REWARD?
SON OF A...

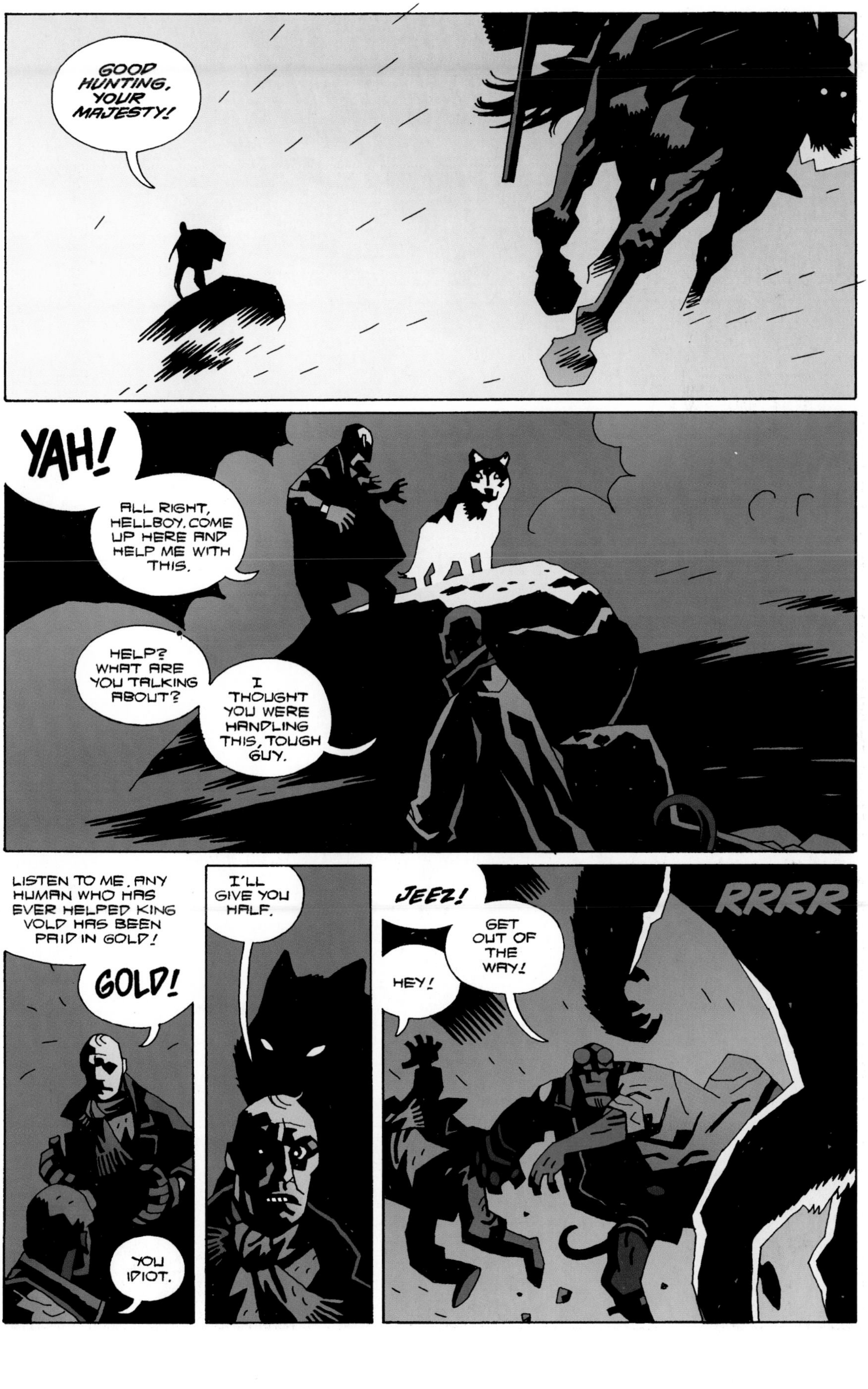
GOOD HUNTING, YOUR MAJESTY!
YAH!
ALL RIGHT, HELLBOY. COME UP HERE AND HELP ME WITH THIS.
HELP? WHAT ARE YOU TALKING ABOUT?
I THOUGHT YOU WERE HANDLING THIS, TOUGH GUY.
LISTEN TO ME. ANY HUMAN WHO HAS EVER HELPED KING VOLD HAS BEEN PAID IN GOLD!
GOLD!
YOU IDIOT.
I'LL GIVE YOU HALF.
JEEZ!
GET OUT OF THE WAY!
HEY!
RRRR

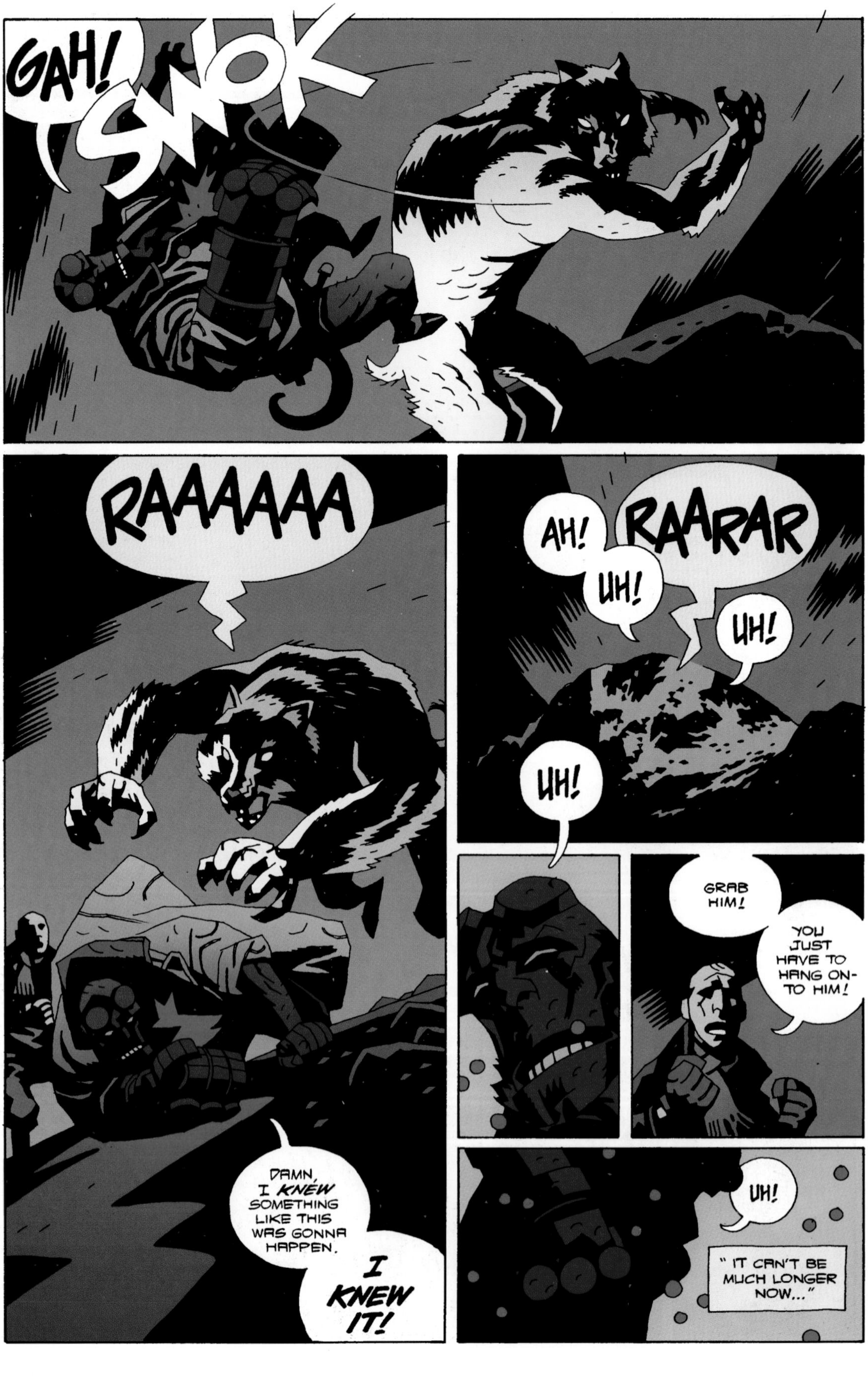
GAH!
SNOK
RAAAAAA
DAMN, I KNEW SOMETHING LIKE THIS WAS GONNA HAPPEN.
I KNEW IT!
AH!
RAARAR
UH!
UH!
UH!
GRAB HIM!
YOU JUST HAVE TO HANG ON-TO HIM!
UH!
" IT CAN'T BE MUCH LONGER NOW..."

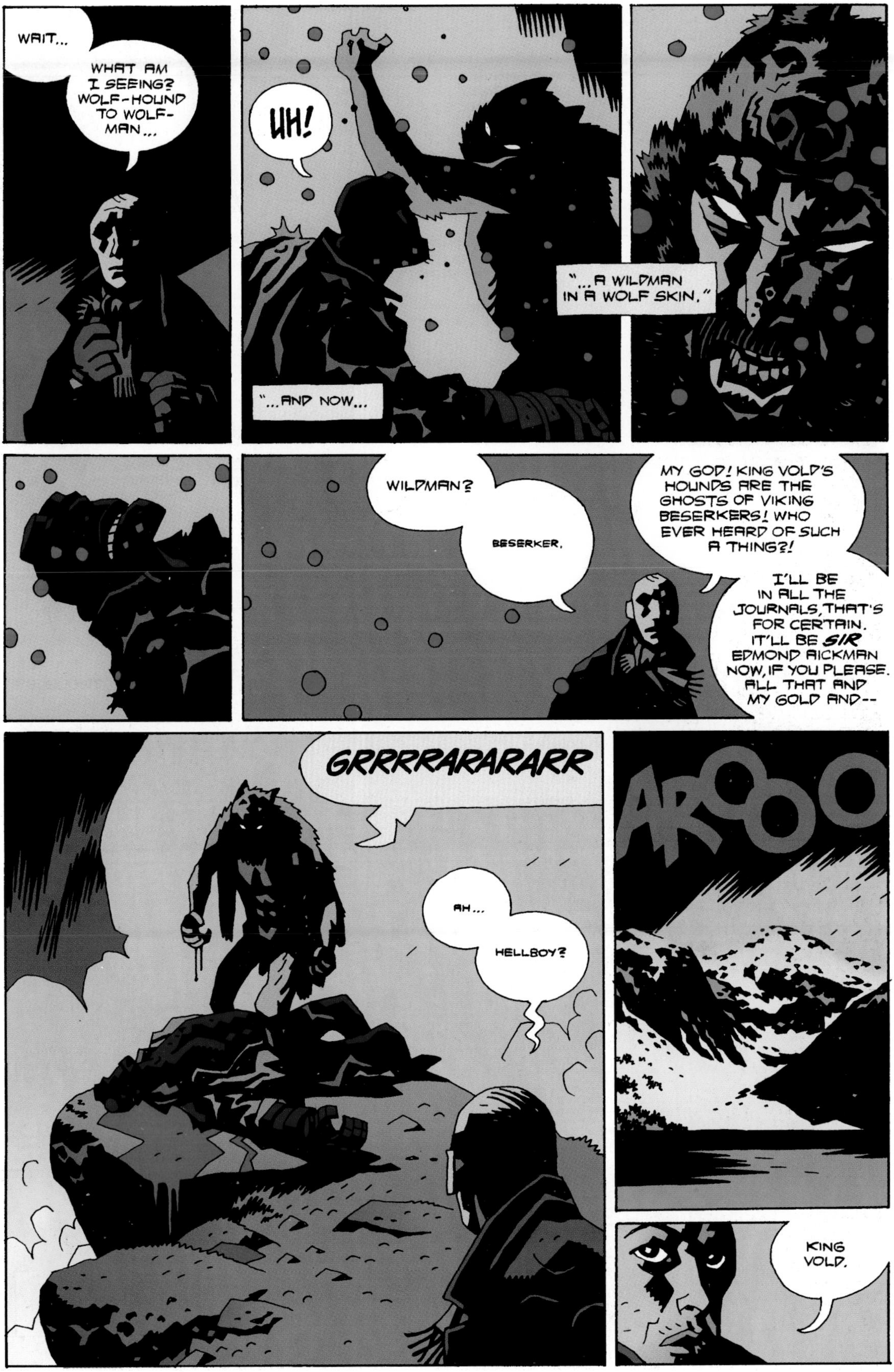

WAIT...
WHAT AM I SEEING? WOLF-HOUND TO WOLF-MAN...
UH!
"...AND NOW...
"...A WILDMAN IN A WOLF SKIN."
WILDMAN?
BESERKER.
MY GOD! KING VOLD'S HOUNDS ARE THE GHOSTS OF VIKING BESERKERS! WHO EVER HEARD OF SUCH A THING?!
I'LL BE IN ALL THE JOURNALS, THAT'S FOR CERTAIN. IT'LL BE SIR EDMOND AICKMAN NOW, IF YOU PLEASE. ALL THAT AND MY GOLD AND--
GRRRRARARARR
AH...
HELLBOY?
AROOOO
KING VOLD.

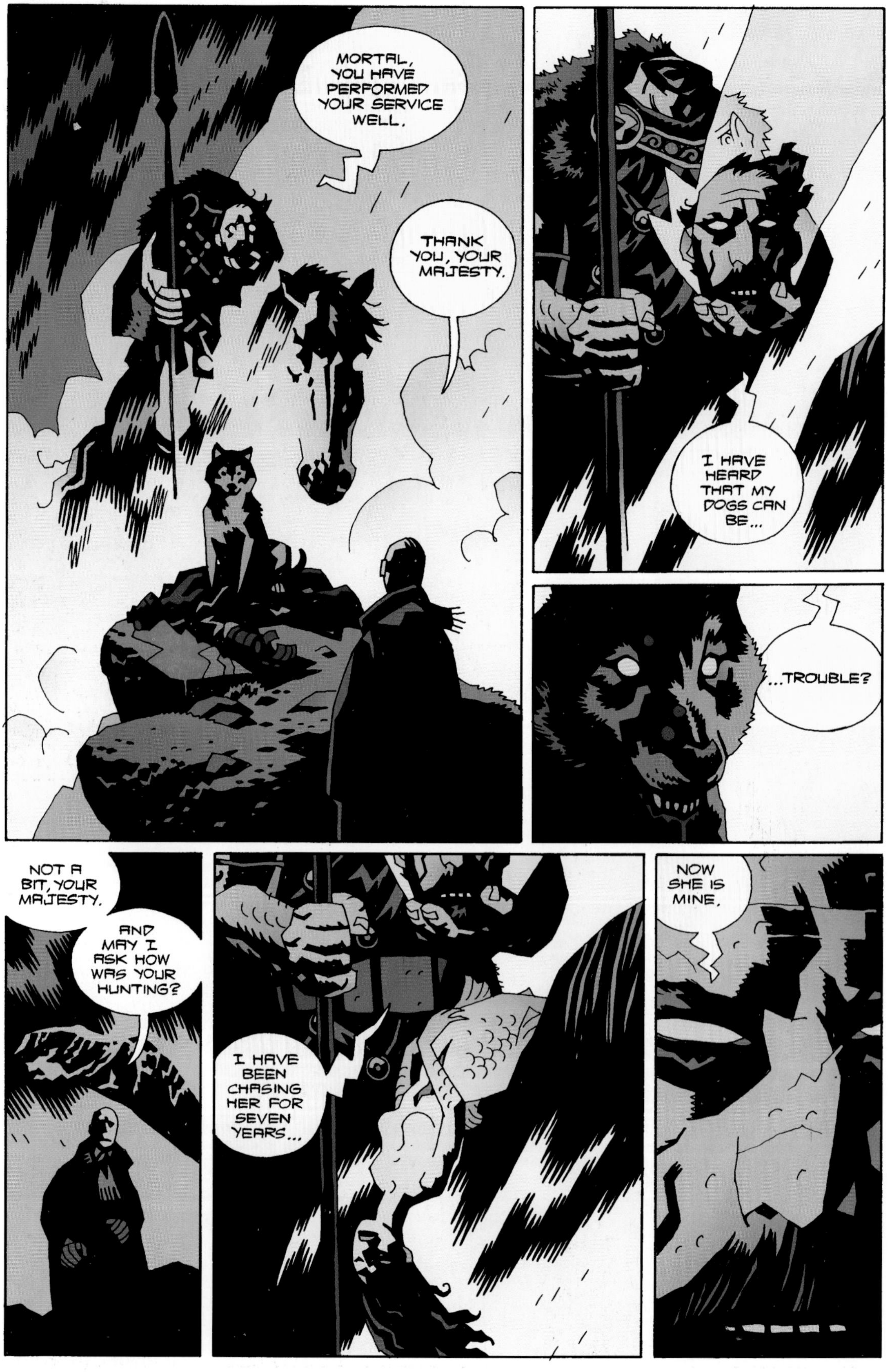
MORTAL, YOU HAVE PERFORMED YOUR SERVICE WELL.
THANK YOU, YOUR MAJESTY.
I HAVE HEARD THAT MY DOGS CAN BE...
...TROUBLE?
NOT A BIT, YOUR MAJESTY.
AND MAY I ASK HOW WAS YOUR HUNTING?
I HAVE BEEN CHASING HER FOR SEVEN YEARS...
NOW SHE IS MINE.

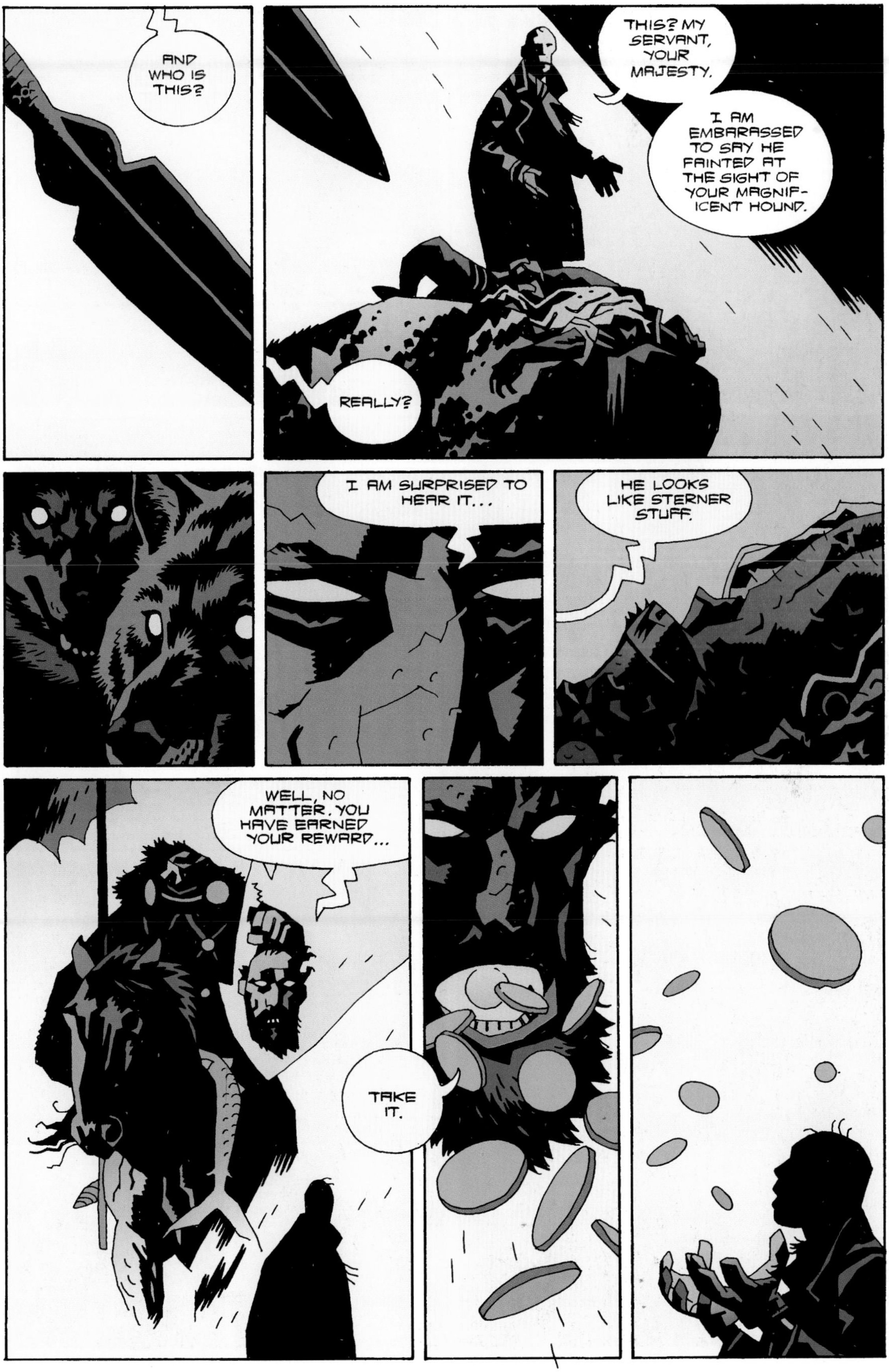
AND WHO IS THIS?
THIS? MY SERVANT, YOUR MAJESTY.
I AM EMBARASSED TO SAY HE FAINTED AT THE SIGHT OF YOUR MAGNIF-ICENT HOUND.
REALLY?
I AM SURPRISED TO HEAR IT...
HE LOOKS LIKE STERNER STUFF.
WELL, NO MATTER. YOU HAVE EARNED YOUR REWARD...
TAKE IT.

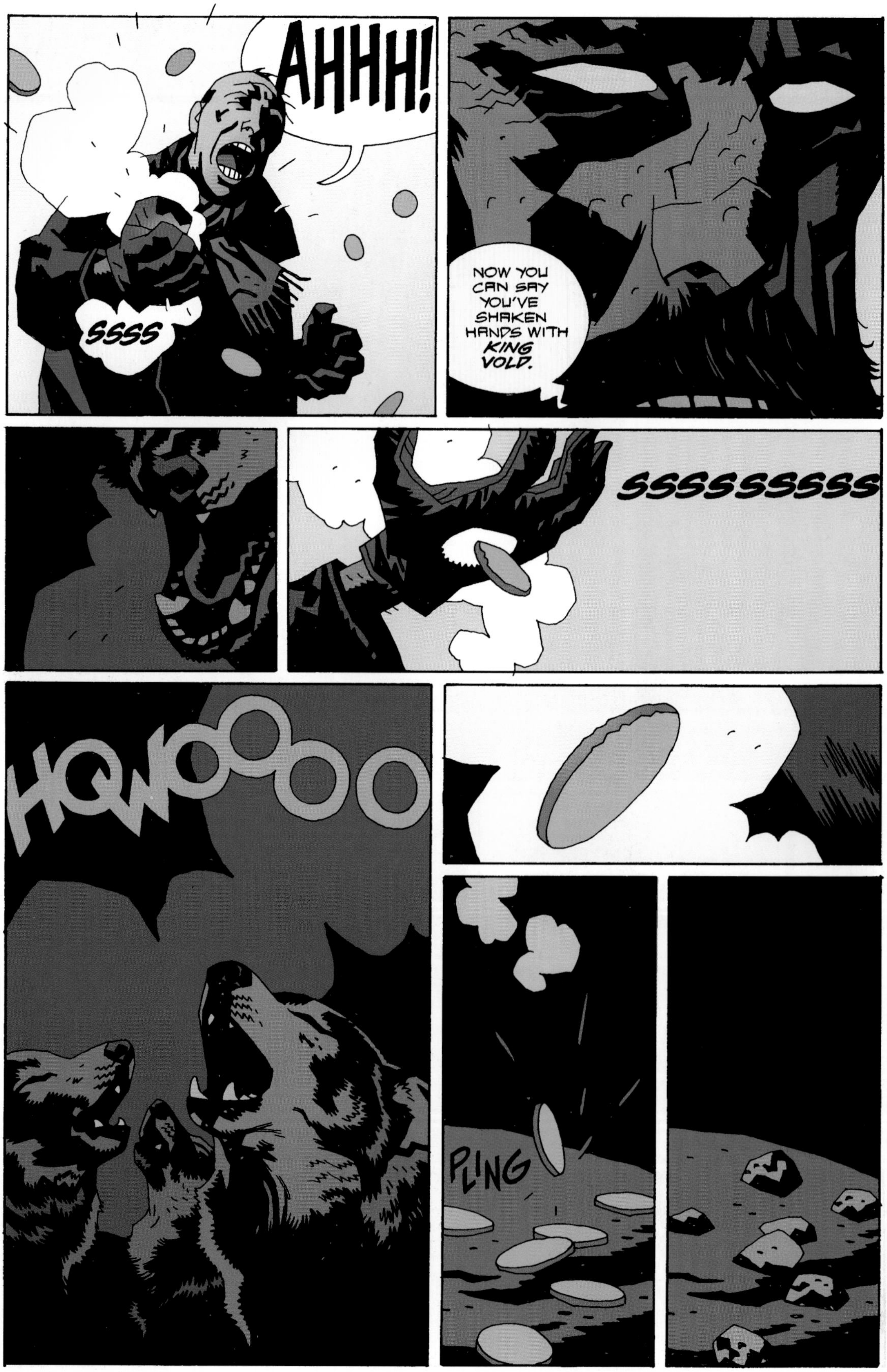
AHHH!
SSSS
NOW YOU CAN SAY YOU'VE SHAKEN HANDS WITH KING VOLD.
SSSSSSSSSS
HOWOOOOO
PLING

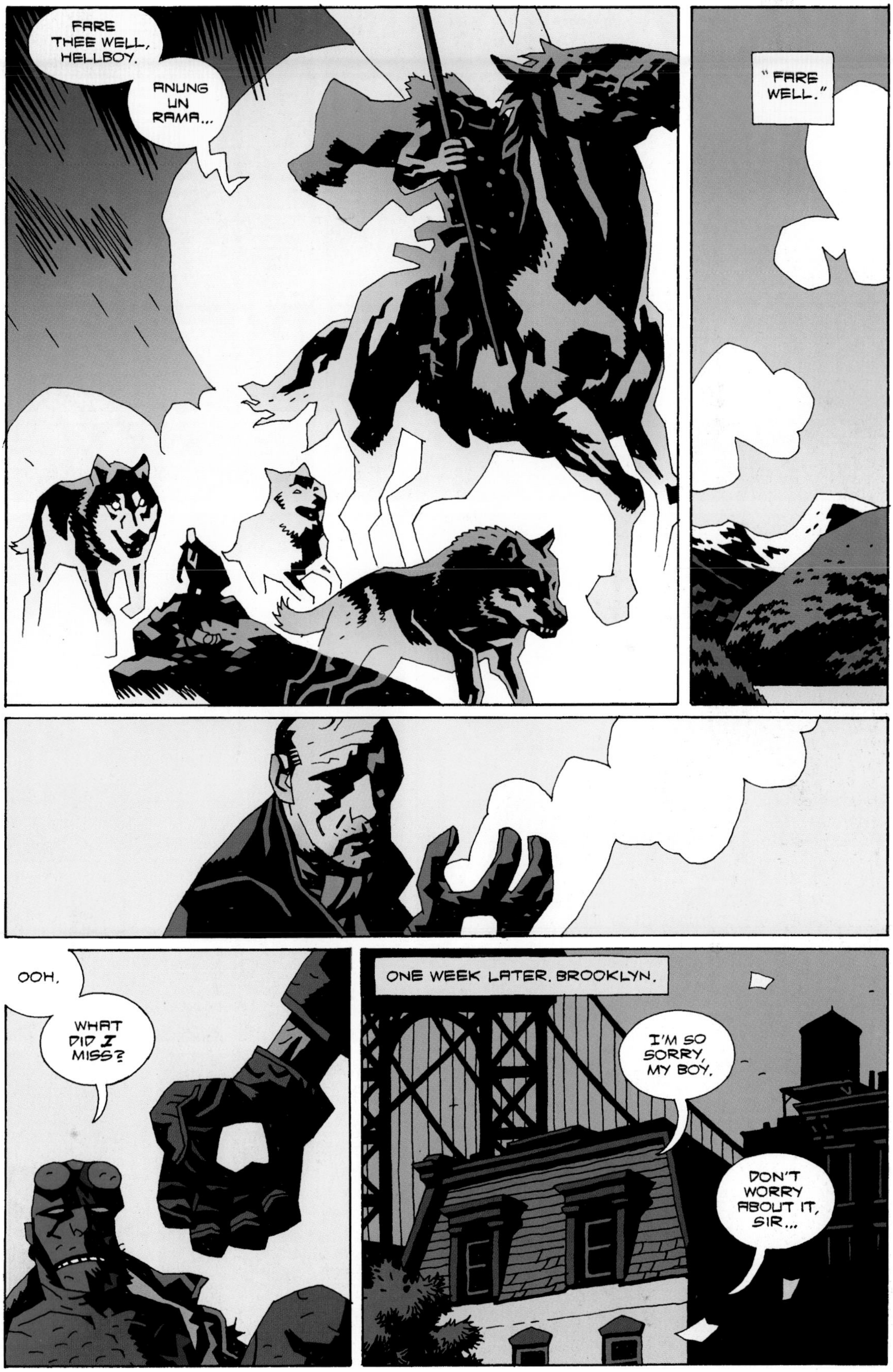
FARE THEE WELL, HELLBOY.
ANUNG UN RAMA...
"FARE WELL."
OOH,
WHAT DID I MISS?
ONE WEEK LATER. BROOKLYN.
I'M SO SORRY, MY BOY.
DON'T WORRY ABOUT IT, SIR...

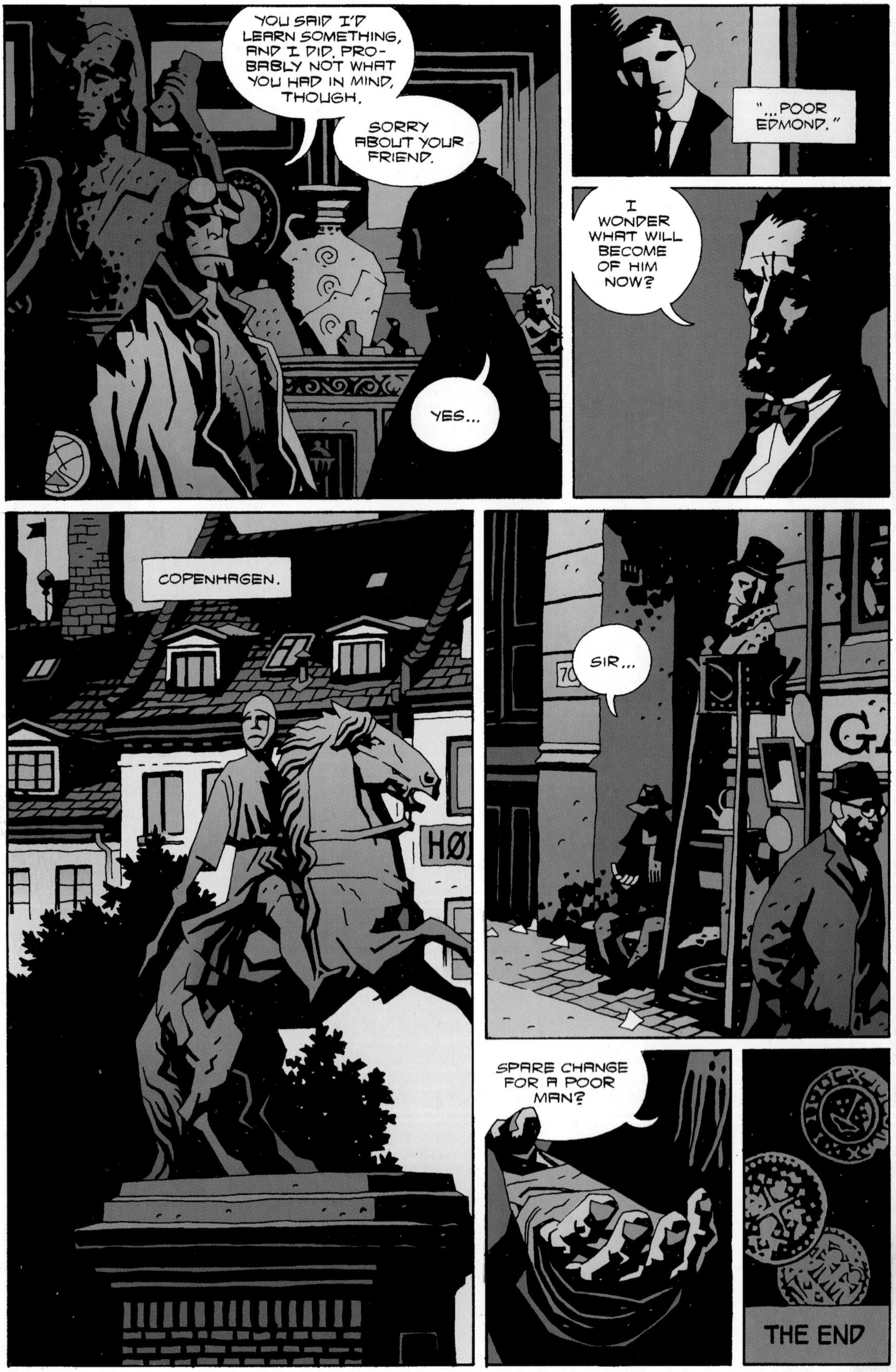

YOU SAID I'D LEARN SOMETHING, AND I DID. PROBABLY NOT WHAT YOU HAD IN MIND, THOUGH.
SORRY ABOUT YOUR FRIEND.
YES...
"...POOR EDMOND."
I WONDER WHAT WILL BECOME OF HIM NOW?
COPENHAGEN.
HØ
SIR...
70
GA
SPARE CHANGE FOR A POOR MAN?
THE END

PART TWO
THE MIDDLE YEARS

Heads

THIS IS ONE of my favorite Hellboy stories. It was also one of the most difficult, because I know nothing about Japan, but wanted the thing to have a very Japanese feel. It is a very close adaptation of a Japanese folktale, but I left out the part where the flying heads were eating bugs.

"Heads" originally appeared as a backup feature in the *Abe Sapien* one-shot, published in March 1998.

✠

Goodbye, Mister Tod

A FEW YEARS BACK I was fooling with an idea for a non-*Hellboy* mini-series. It didn't go anywhere, but I did like the opening sequence, and eventually it turned into this. The story not only shows my continuing fascination with H.P. Lovecraft monsters, but also with ectoplasm. In fact, back in 1993, when I first conceived *Hellboy* as a team book, one of the characters was going to be an ectoplasm guy. Anyway …

"Goodbye, Mister Tod" was originally published as a backup feature in *Gary Gianni's The MonsterMen* in August of 1999.

✠

The Vârcolac

THIS STORY WAS inspired by a single paragraph I read twenty years ago describing a type of Romanian vampire which "eats the sun and the moon and is able to cause eclipses." The hardest thing about this job was finding that one book again so I could get the name of the vampire.

"The Vârcolac" was done in six installments in Sunday-news-paper-strip format for *Dark Horse Extra*. For this collection, I have completely redrawn the thing, expanding it and putting it into regular comic-book-page format. There are things that I like better about the original, and there are things that I like better about this new version. That's the way it goes.

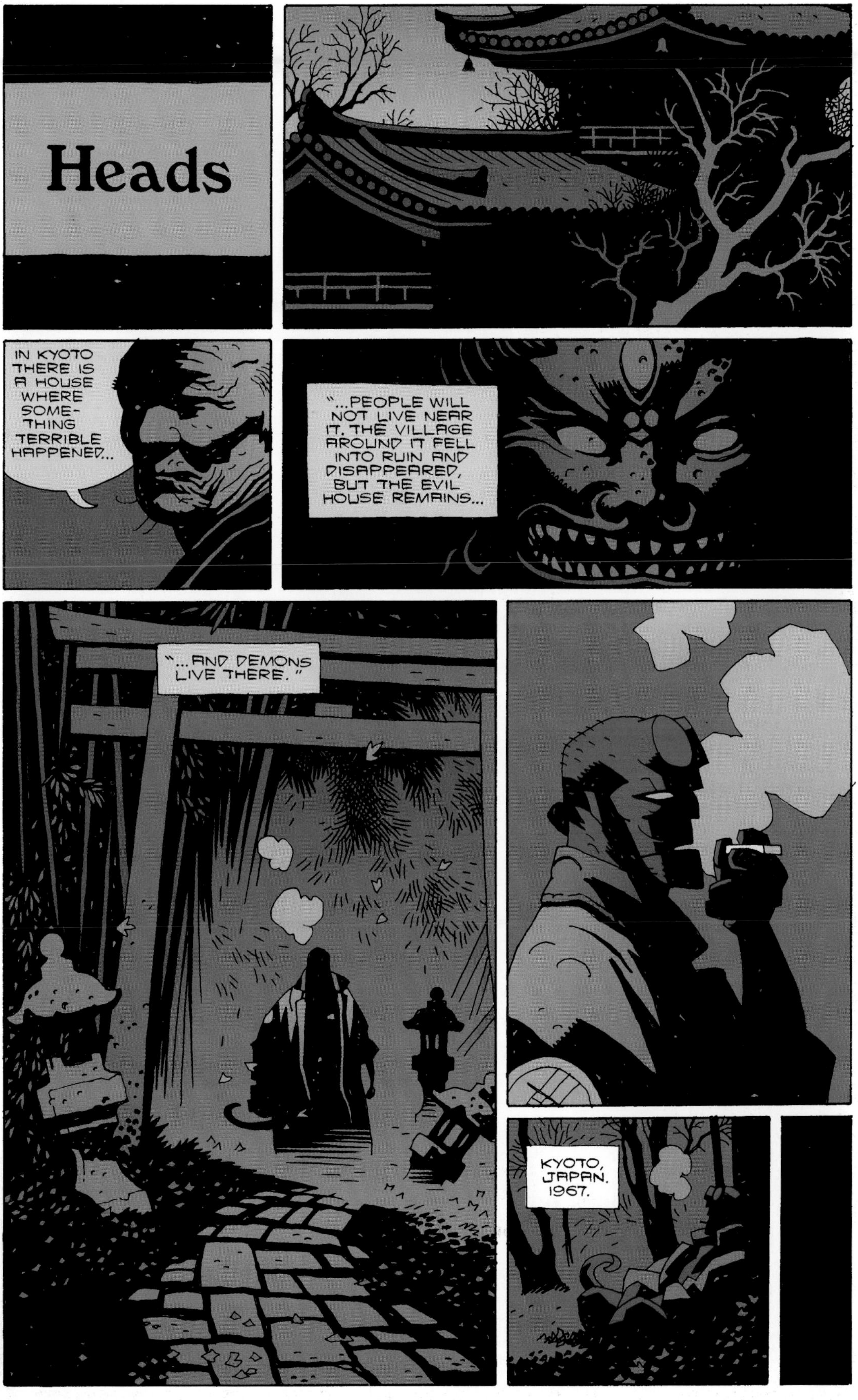
Heads
IN KYOTO THERE IS A HOUSE WHERE SOME-THING TERRIBLE HAPPENED...
"...PEOPLE WILL NOT LIVE NEAR IT. THE VILLAGE AROUND IT FELL INTO RUIN AND DISAPPEARED, BUT THE EVIL HOUSE REMAINS...
"...AND DEMONS LIVE THERE."
KYOTO, JAPAN. 1967.

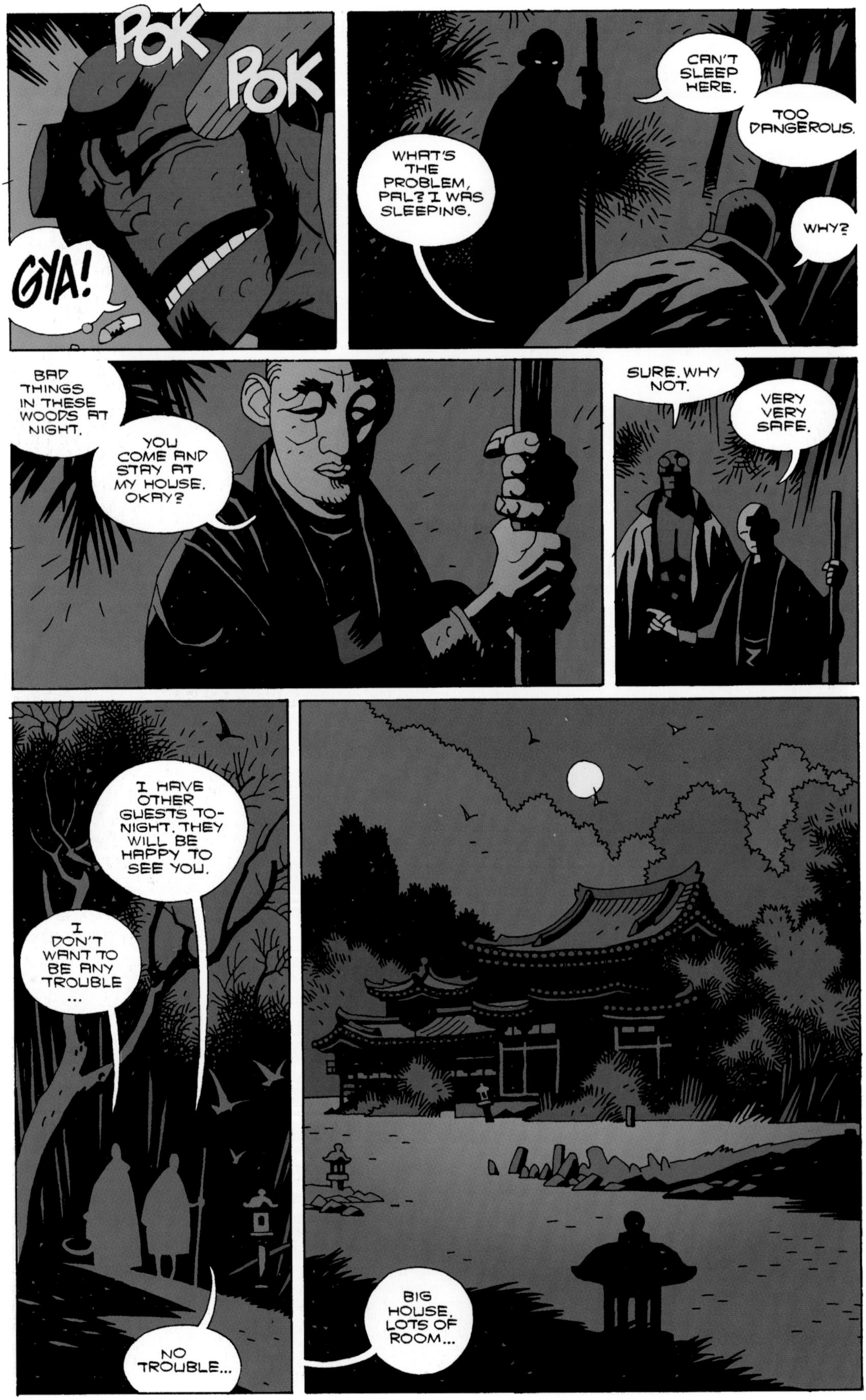

POK
POK
GYA!
WHAT'S THE PROBLEM, PAL? I WAS SLEEPING.
CAN'T SLEEP HERE.
TOO DANGEROUS.
WHY?
BAD THINGS IN THESE WOODS AT NIGHT.
YOU COME AND STAY AT MY HOUSE. OKAY?
SURE. WHY NOT.
VERY VERY SAFE.
I HAVE OTHER GUESTS TO-NIGHT. THEY WILL BE HAPPY TO SEE YOU.
I DON'T WANT TO BE ANY TROUBLE ...
NO TROUBLE...
BIG HOUSE. LOTS OF ROOM...

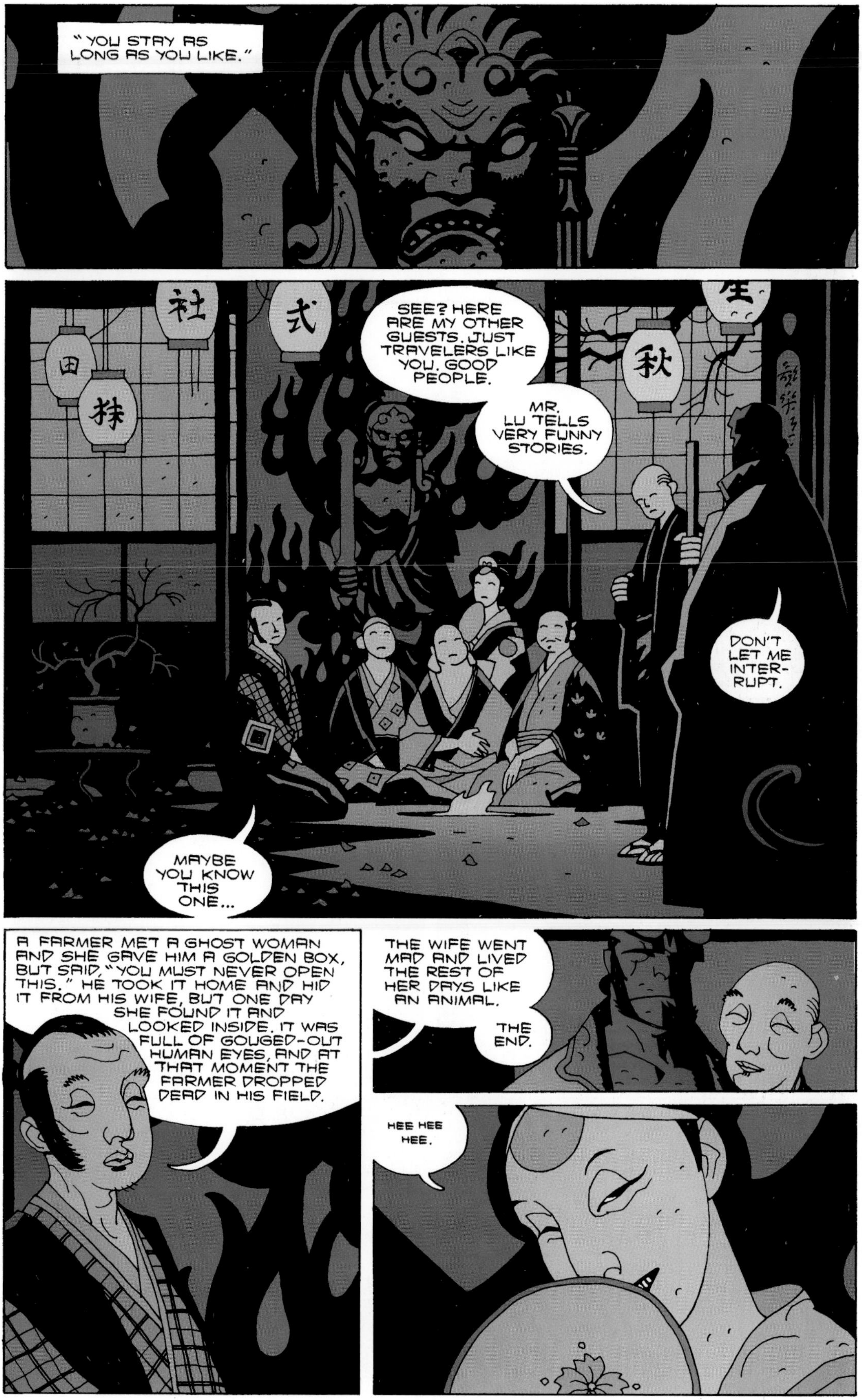
"YOU STAY AS LONG AS YOU LIKE."
SEE? HERE ARE MY OTHER GUESTS. JUST TRAVELERS LIKE YOU. GOOD PEOPLE.
MR. LU TELLS VERY FUNNY STORIES.
DON'T LET ME INTER-RUPT.
MAYBE YOU KNOW THIS ONE...
A FARMER MET A GHOST WOMAN AND SHE GAVE HIM A GOLDEN BOX, BUT SAID, "YOU MUST NEVER OPEN THIS." HE TOOK IT HOME AND HID IT FROM HIS WIFE, BUT ONE DAY SHE FOUND IT AND LOOKED INSIDE. IT WAS FULL OF GOUGED-OUT HUMAN EYES, AND AT THAT MOMENT THE FARMER DROPPED DEAD IN HIS FIELD.
THE WIFE WENT MAD AND LIVED THE REST OF HER DAYS LIKE AN ANIMAL.
THE END.
HEE HEE HEE.

WOW... THAT *IS* A FUNNY STORY.

YOU KNOW, I JUST REALIZED I'M AWFULLY TIRED...

THIS WAY.

HERE IS A SPECIAL ROOM FOR YOU. GOOD AND SAFE. VERY COMFORTABLE.

IT'S GREAT, THANKS.

SLEEP WELL.

VERY SAFE.

YEAH, I BET.

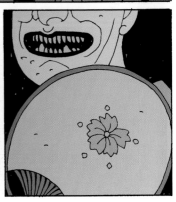

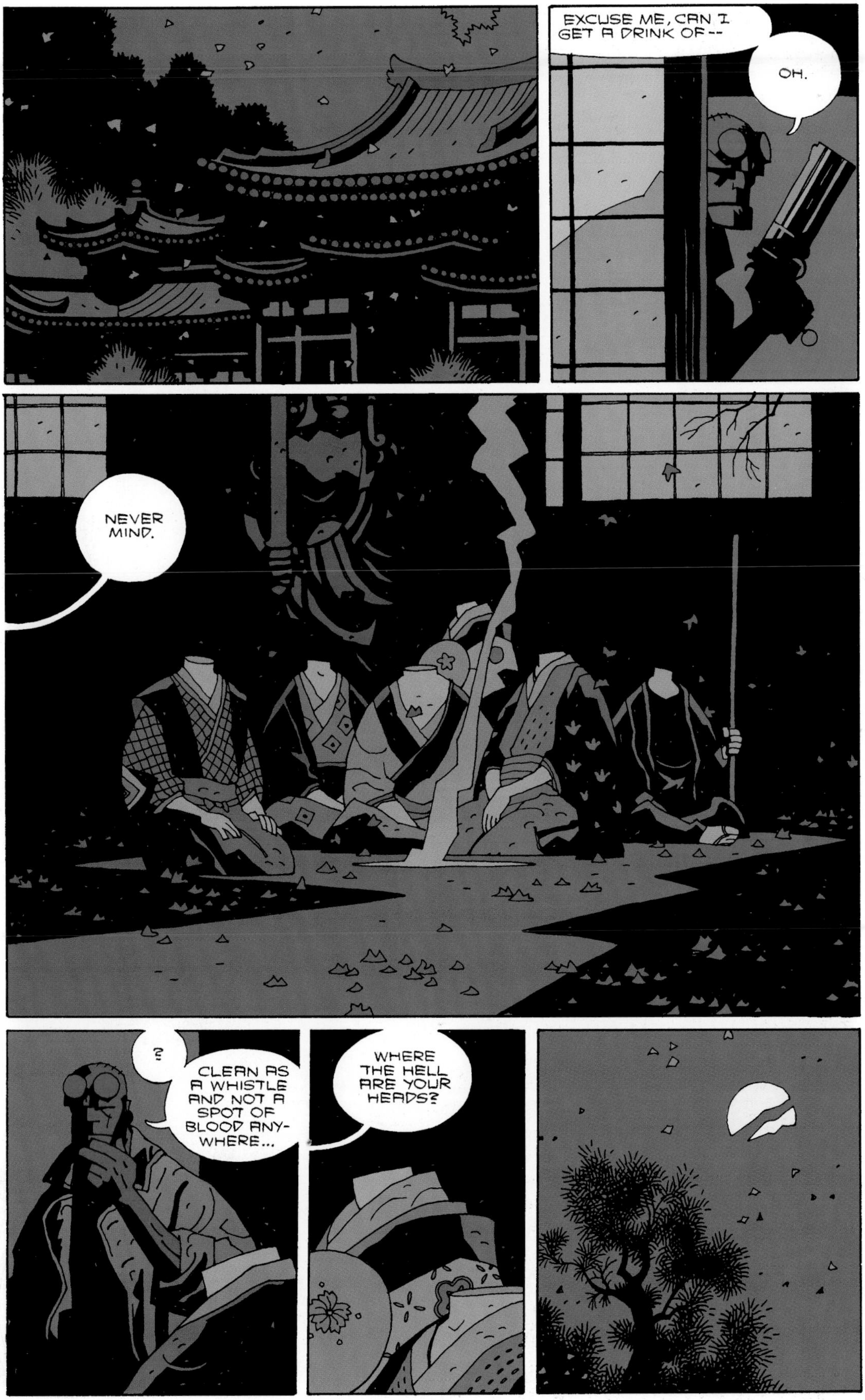
EXCUSE ME, CAN I GET A DRINK OF --
OH.
NEVER MIND.
?
CLEAN AS A WHISTLE AND NOT A SPOT OF BLOOD ANY-WHERE...
WHERE THE HELL ARE YOUR HEADS?

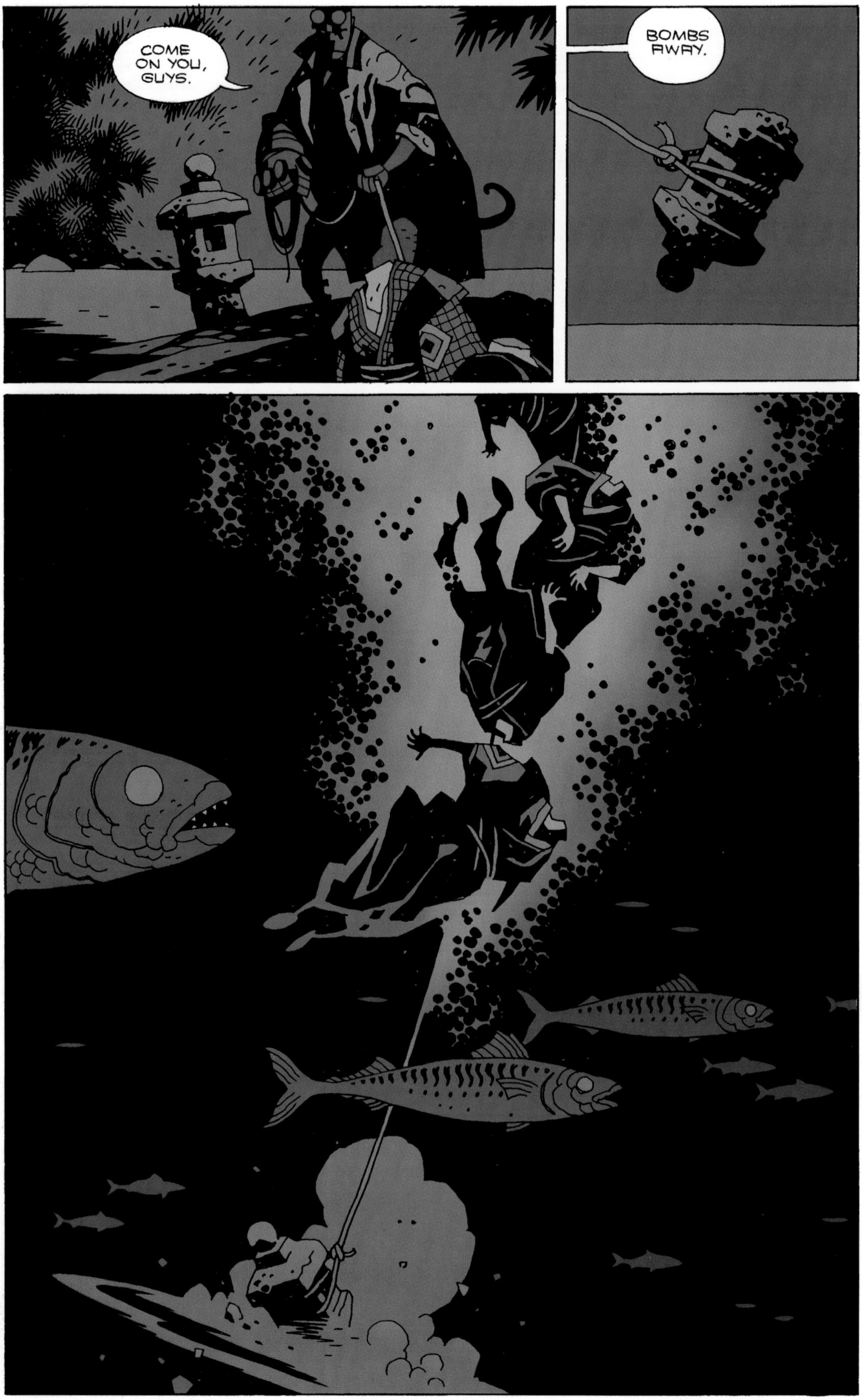
COME ON YOU, GUYS.
BOMBS AWAY.

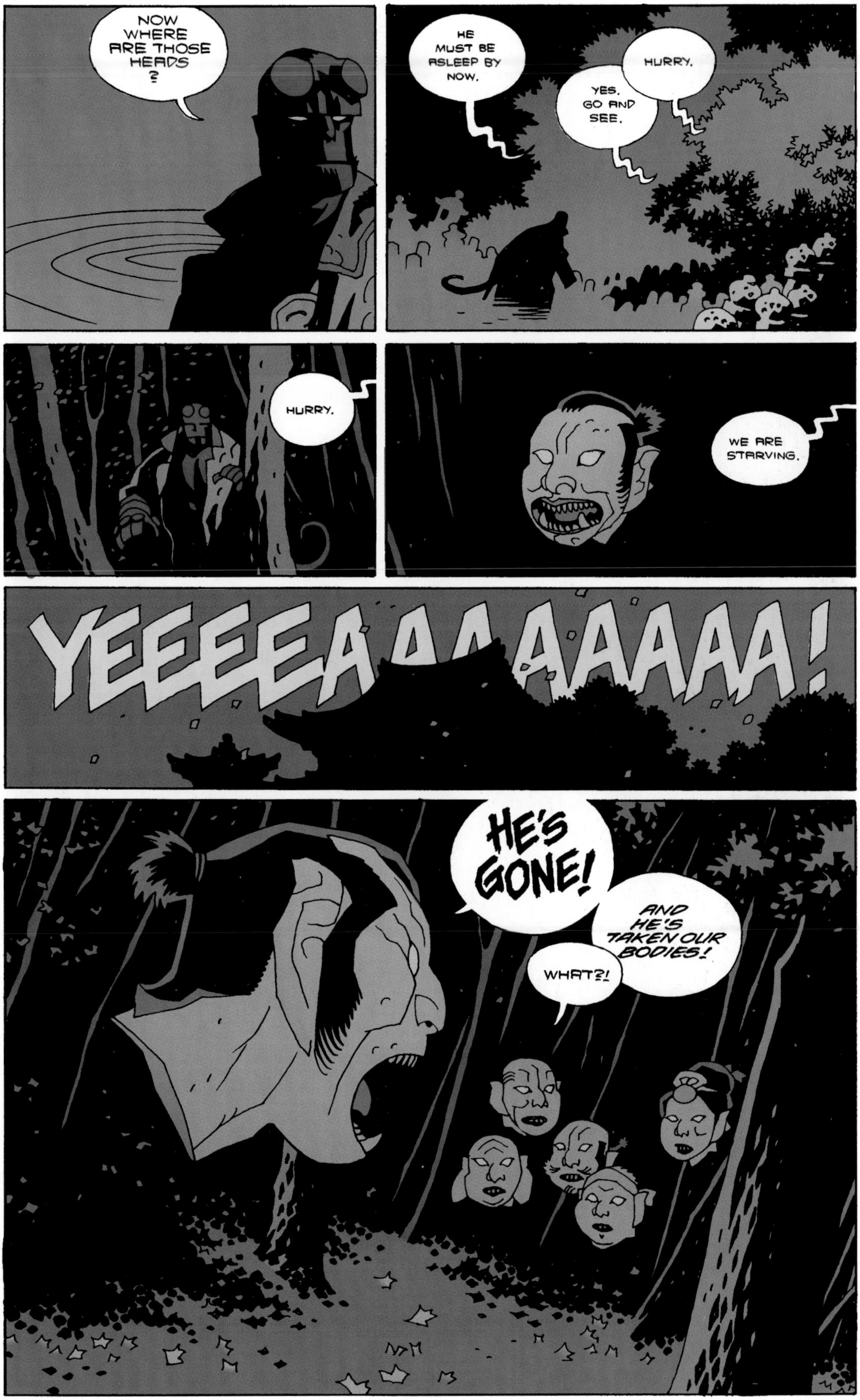

NOW WHERE ARE THOSE HEADS ?
HE MUST BE ASLEEP BY NOW.
YES, GO AND SEE.
HURRY.
HURRY.
WE ARE STARVING.
YEEEEAAAAAAAA!
HE'S GONE!
WHAT?!
AND HE'S TAKEN OUR BODIES!

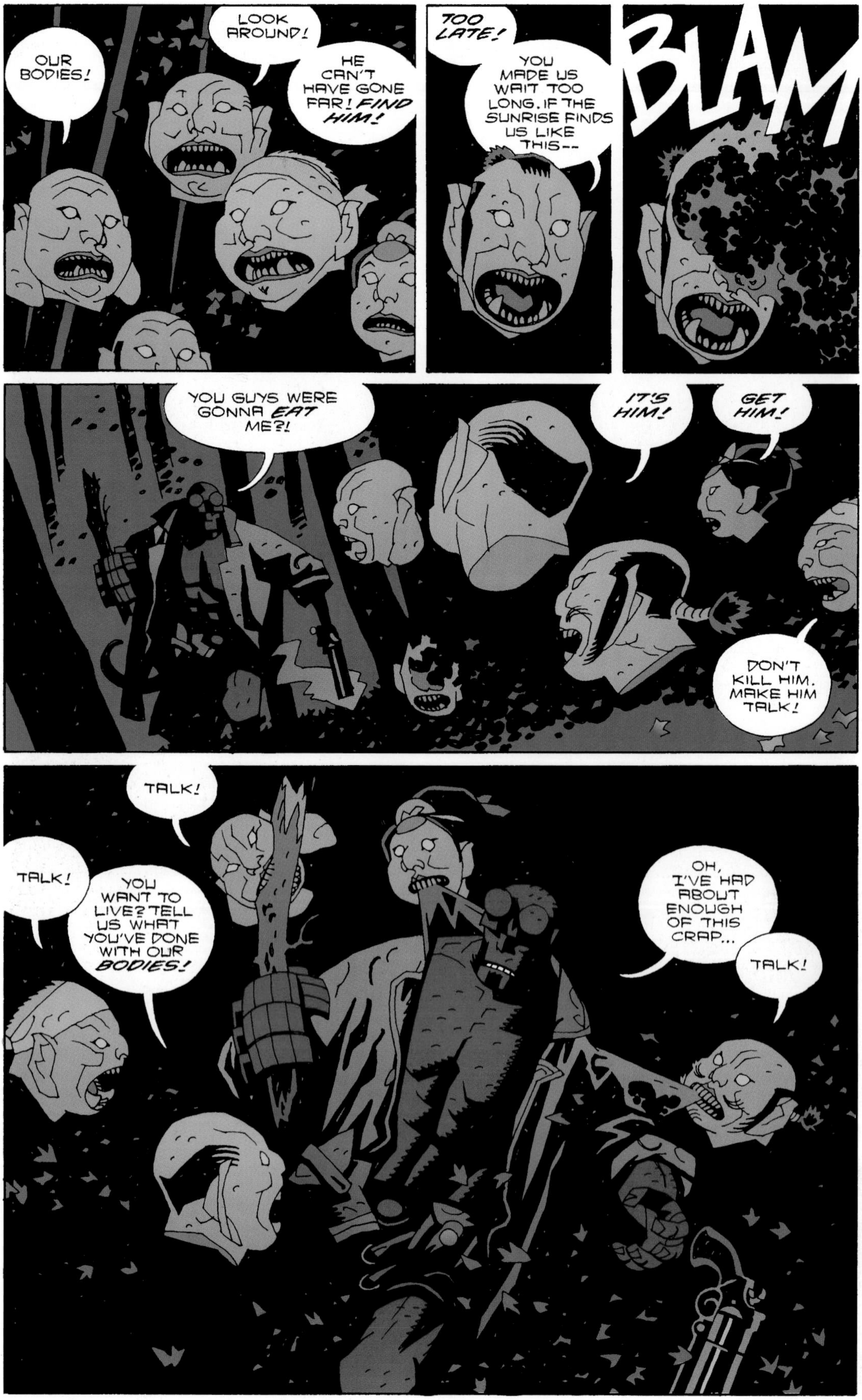
OUR BODIES!
LOOK AROUND!
HE CAN'T HAVE GONE FAR! FIND HIM!
TOO LATE!
YOU MADE US WAIT TOO LONG. IF THE SUNRISE FINDS US LIKE THIS--
BLAM
YOU GUYS WERE GONNA EAT ME?!
IT'S HIM!
GET HIM!
DON'T KILL HIM. MAKE HIM TALK!
TALK!
TALK!
YOU WANT TO LIVE? TELL US WHAT YOU'VE DONE WITH OUR BODIES!
OH, I'VE HAD ABOUT ENOUGH OF THIS CRAP...
TALK!

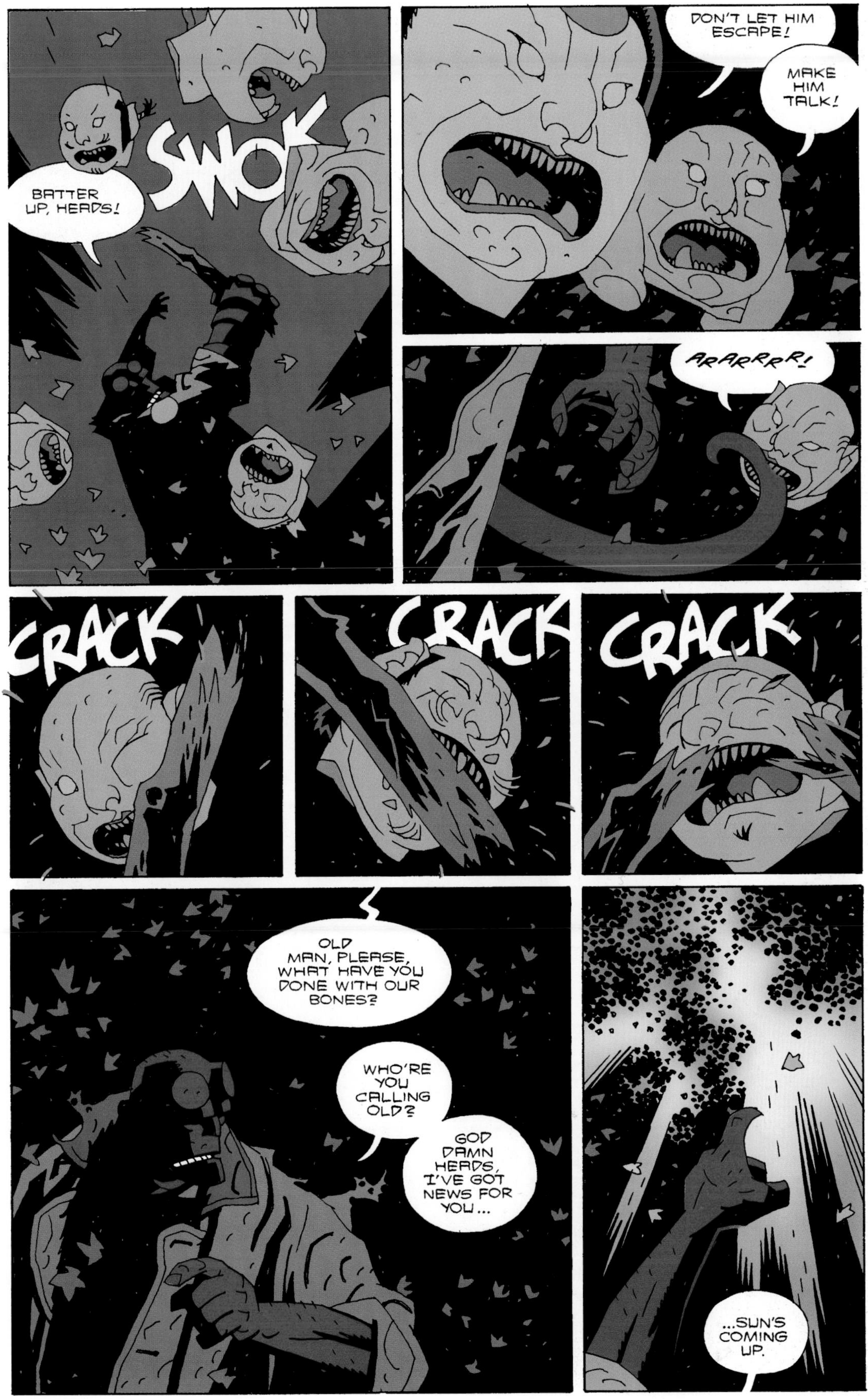
SWOK
BATTER UP, HEADS!
DON'T LET HIM ESCAPE!
MAKE HIM TALK!
ARARRRR!
CRACK
CRACK
CRACK
OLD MAN, PLEASE, WHAT HAVE YOU DONE WITH OUR BONES?
WHO'RE YOU CALLING OLD?
GOD DAMN HEADS, I'VE GOT NEWS FOR YOU...
...SUN'S COMING UP.

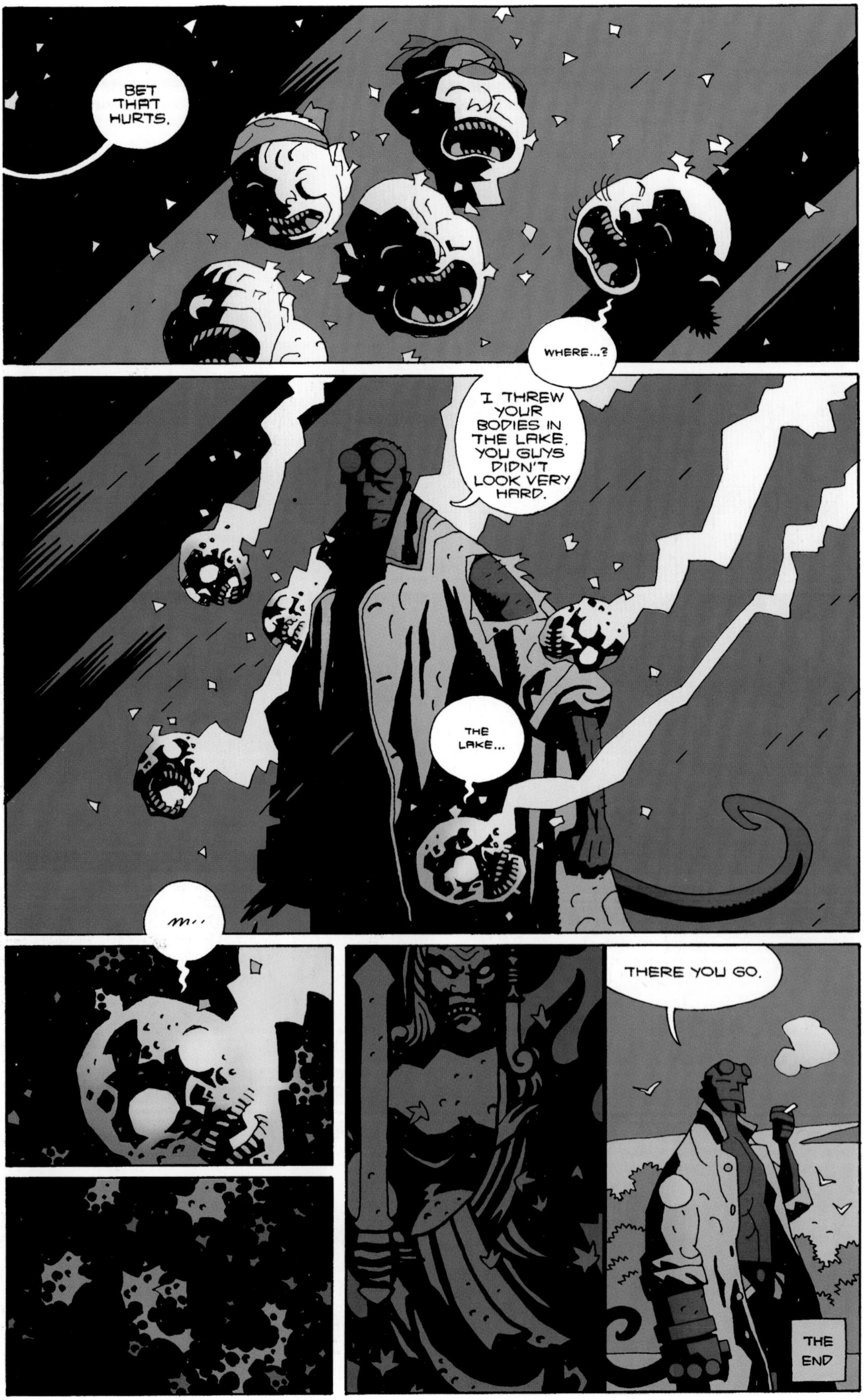
BET THAT HURTS.
WHERE...?
I THREW YOUR BODIES IN THE LAKE. YOU GUYS DIDN'T LOOK VERY HARD.
THE LAKE...
THERE YOU GO.
THE END

Goodbye
Mister Tod

PORTLAND, OREGON. 1979.

WOW, WHAT AN AWFUL PLACE.

FOR SALE

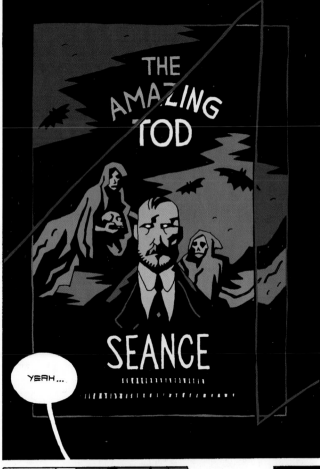

THE AMAZING TOD

SEANCE

YEAH...

SOME-THING TELLS ME THIS ISN'T GOING TO BE TOO GOOD.

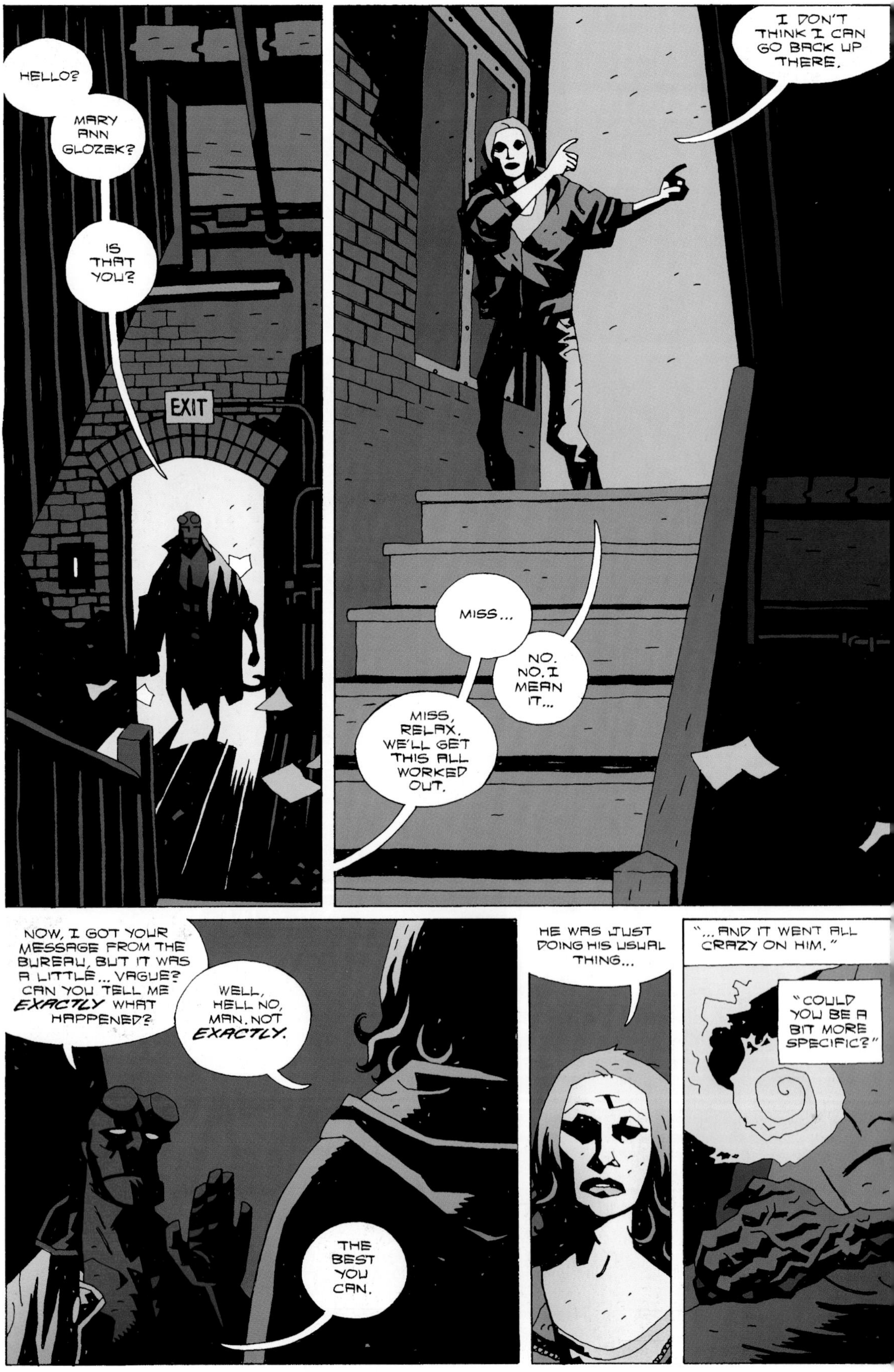
HELLO?
MARY ANN GLOZEK?
IS THAT YOU?
EXIT
I DON'T THINK I CAN GO BACK UP THERE.
MISS...
NO. NO, I MEAN IT...
MISS, RELAX. WE'LL GET THIS ALL WORKED OUT.
NOW, I GOT YOUR MESSAGE FROM THE BUREAU, BUT IT WAS A LITTLE... VAGUE? CAN YOU TELL ME *EXACTLY* WHAT HAPPENED?
WELL, HELL NO, MAN, NOT *EXACTLY*.
THE BEST YOU CAN.
HE WAS JUST DOING HIS USUAL THING...
"...AND IT WENT ALL CRAZY ON HIM."
"COULD YOU BE A BIT MORE SPECIFIC?"

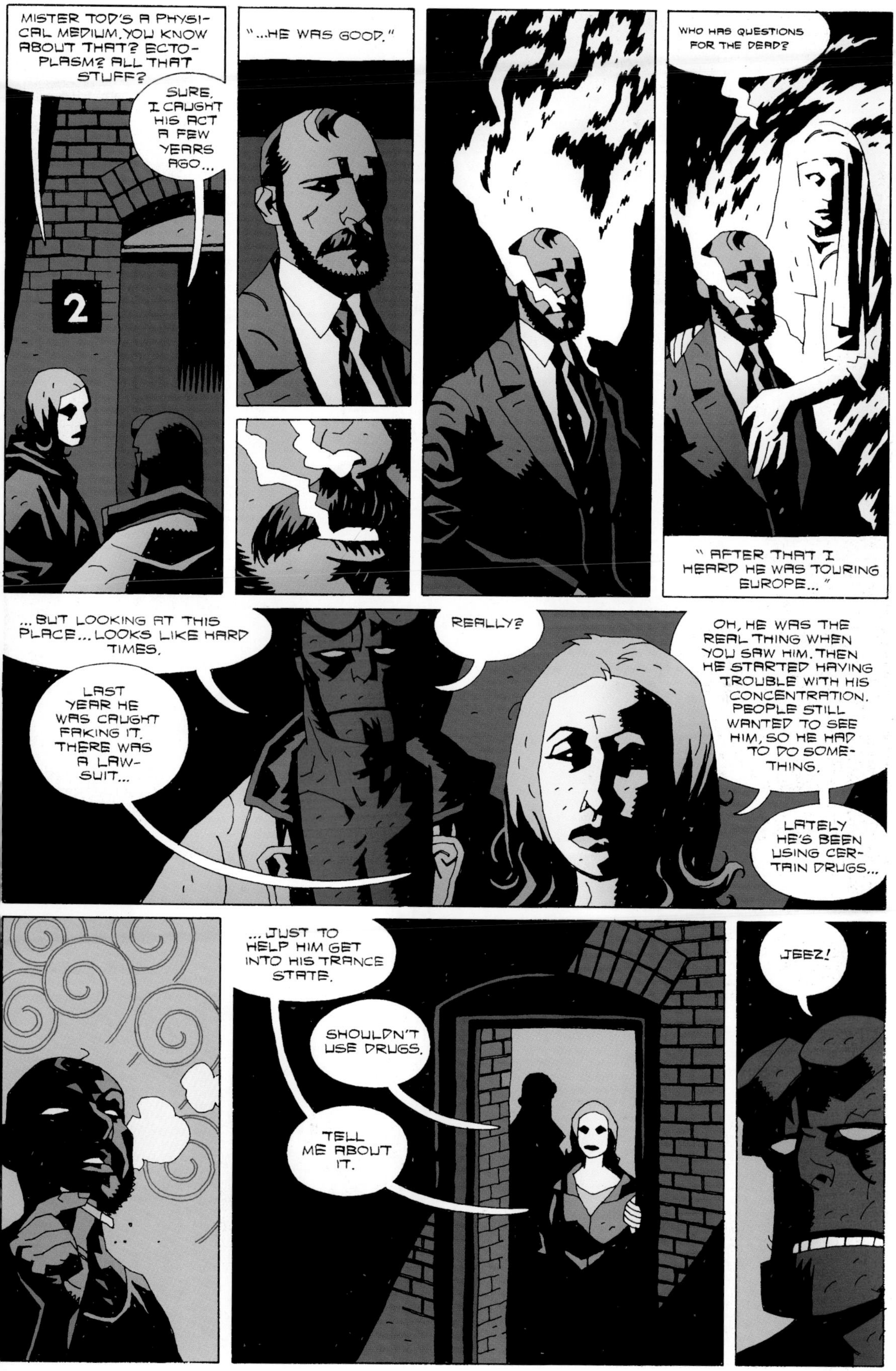
MISTER TOD'S A PHYSICAL MEDIUM. YOU KNOW ABOUT THAT? ECTOPLASM? ALL THAT STUFF?
SURE. I CAUGHT HIS ACT A FEW YEARS AGO...
"...HE WAS GOOD."
WHO HAS QUESTIONS FOR THE DEAD?
" AFTER THAT I HEARD HE WAS TOURING EUROPE..."
...BUT LOOKING AT THIS PLACE... LOOKS LIKE HARD TIMES.
LAST YEAR HE WAS CAUGHT FAKING IT. THERE WAS A LAWSUIT...
REALLY?
OH, HE WAS THE REAL THING WHEN YOU SAW HIM. THEN HE STARTED HAVING TROUBLE WITH HIS CONCENTRATION. PEOPLE STILL WANTED TO SEE HIM, SO HE HAD TO DO SOMETHING.
LATELY HE'S BEEN USING CERTAIN DRUGS...
...JUST TO HELP HIM GET INTO HIS TRANCE STATE.
SHOULDN'T USE DRUGS.
TELL ME ABOUT IT.
JEEZ!

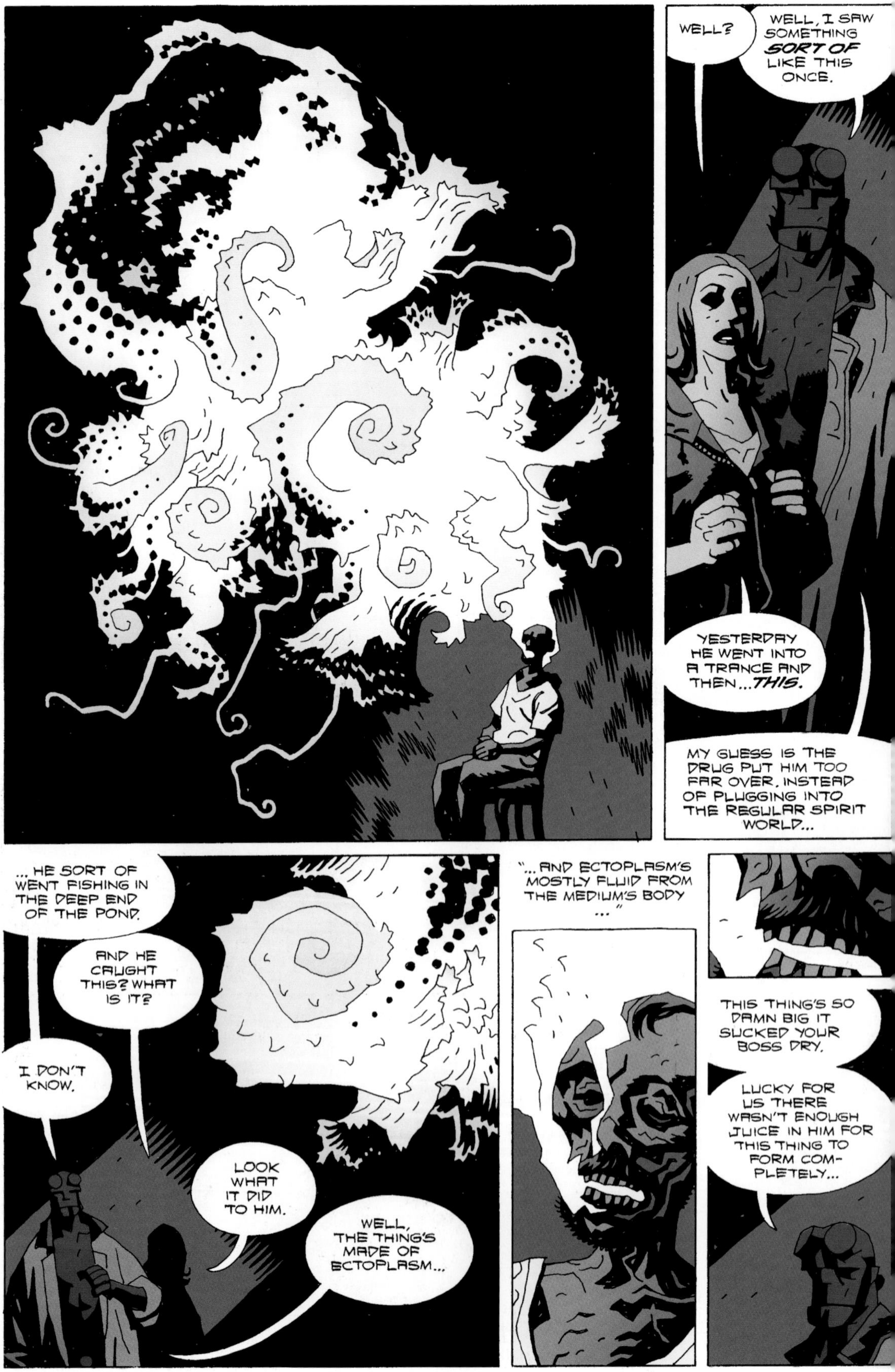
WELL?
WELL, I SAW SOMETHING SORT OF LIKE THIS ONCE.
YESTERDAY HE WENT INTO A TRANCE AND THEN... THIS.
MY GUESS IS THE DRUG PUT HIM TOO FAR OVER. INSTEAD OF PLUGGING INTO THE REGULAR SPIRIT WORLD...
... HE SORT OF WENT FISHING IN THE DEEP END OF THE POND.
AND HE CAUGHT THIS? WHAT IS IT?
I DON'T KNOW.
LOOK WHAT IT DID TO HIM.
WELL, THE THING'S MADE OF ECTOPLASM...
"... AND ECTOPLASM'S MOSTLY FLUID FROM THE MEDIUM'S BODY ..."
THIS THING'S SO DAMN BIG IT SUCKED YOUR BOSS DRY.
LUCKY FOR US THERE WASN'T ENOUGH JUICE IN HIM FOR THIS THING TO FORM COM-PLETELY...

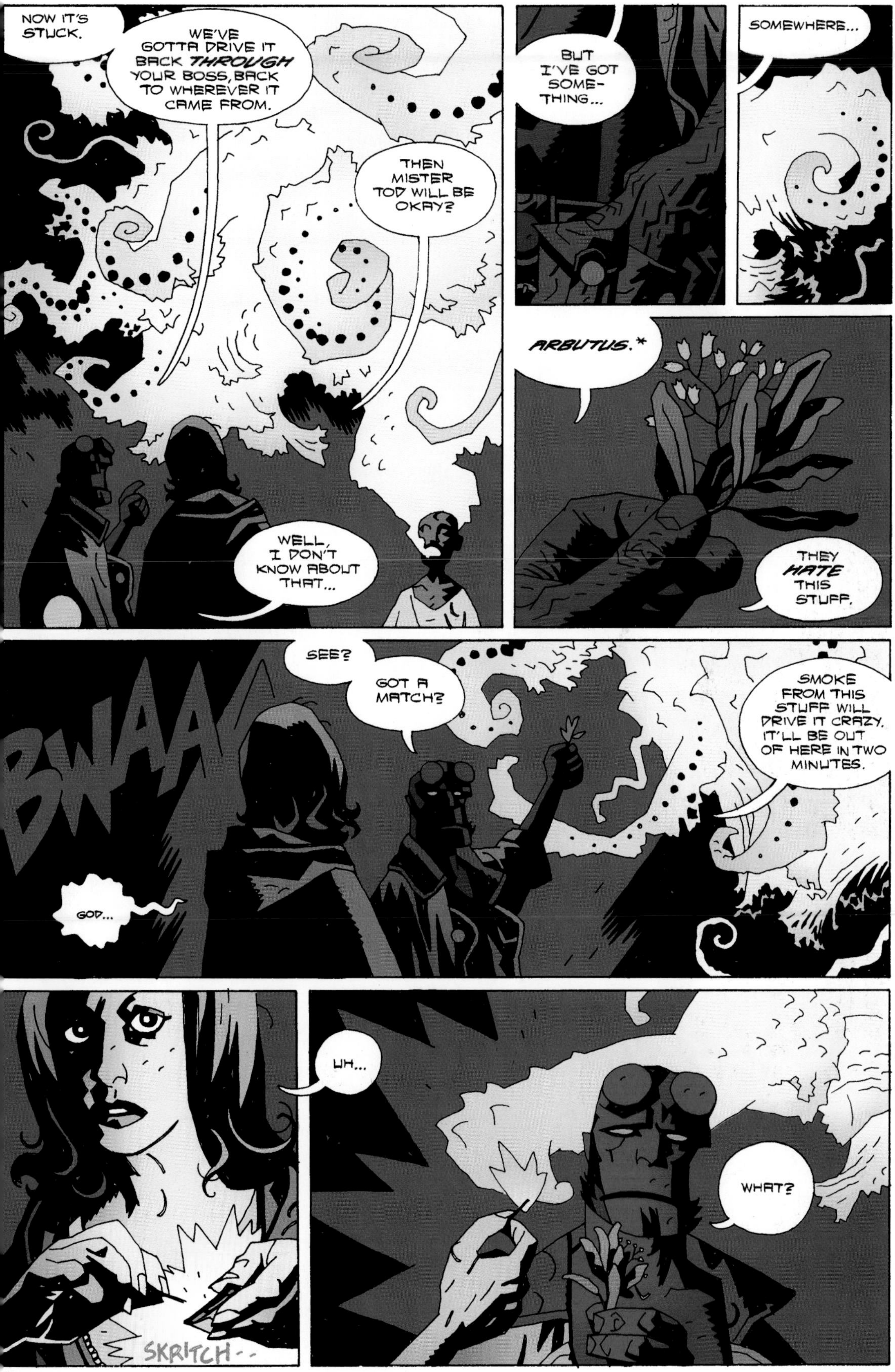
NOW IT'S STUCK.
WE'VE GOTTA DRIVE IT BACK THROUGH YOUR BOSS, BACK TO WHEREVER IT CAME FROM.
THEN MISTER TOD WILL BE OKAY?
WELL, I DON'T KNOW ABOUT THAT...
BUT I'VE GOT SOME-THING...
SOMEWHERE...
ARBUTUS.*
THEY HATE THIS STUFF.
BWAA
SEE?
GOT A MATCH?
SMOKE FROM THIS STUFF WILL DRIVE IT CRAZY. IT'LL BE OUT OF HERE IN TWO MINUTES.
GOD...
UH...
WHAT?
SKRITCH--

*Arbutus Unede: USED BY ANCIENT GREEKS AND ROMANS TO CHASE AWAY EVIL AND PROTECT SMALL CHILDREN.

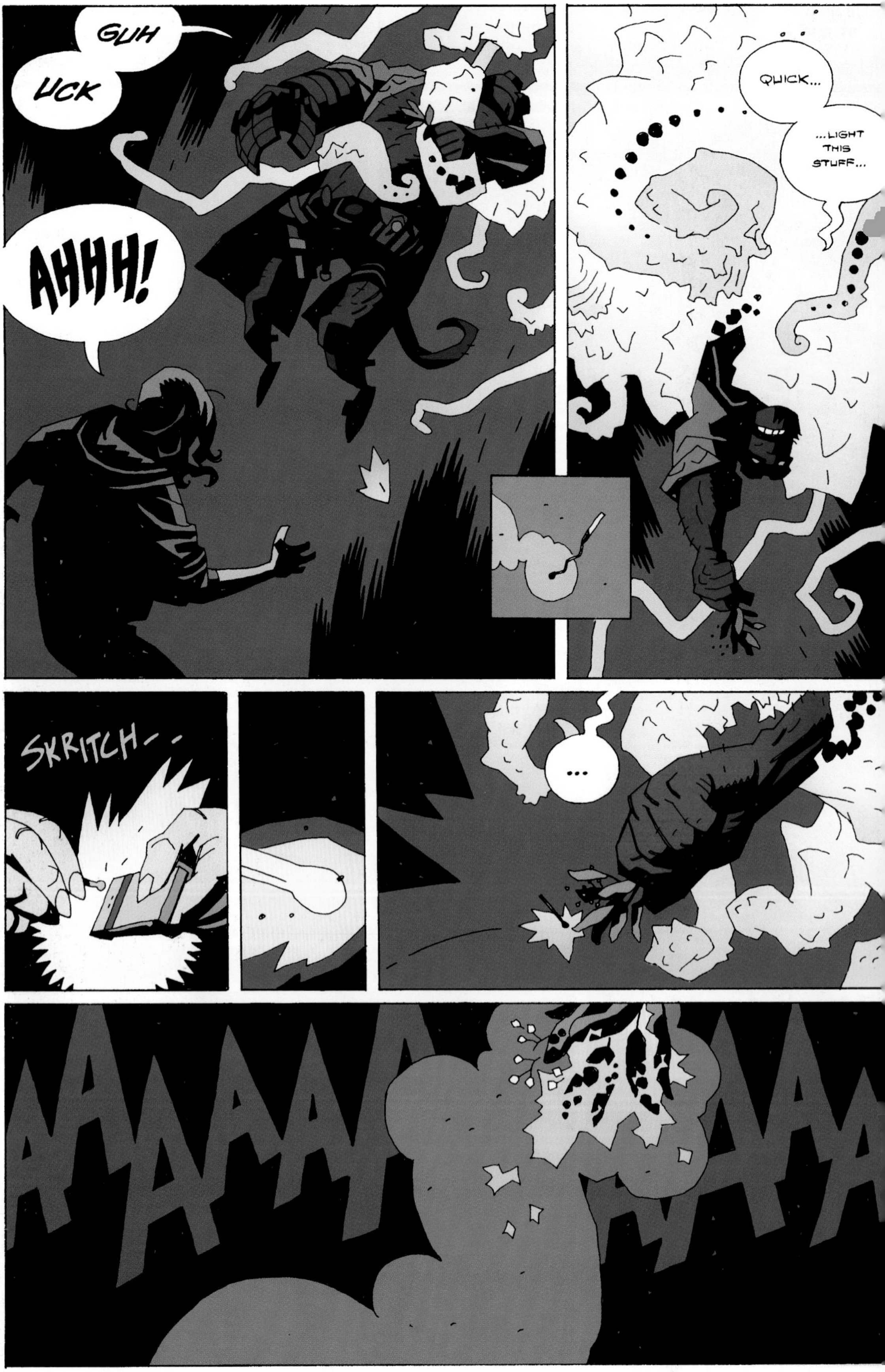
GUH
UCK
AHHH!
QUICK...
...LIGHT THIS STUFF...
SKRITCH
...
AAAAAAAAAAAA

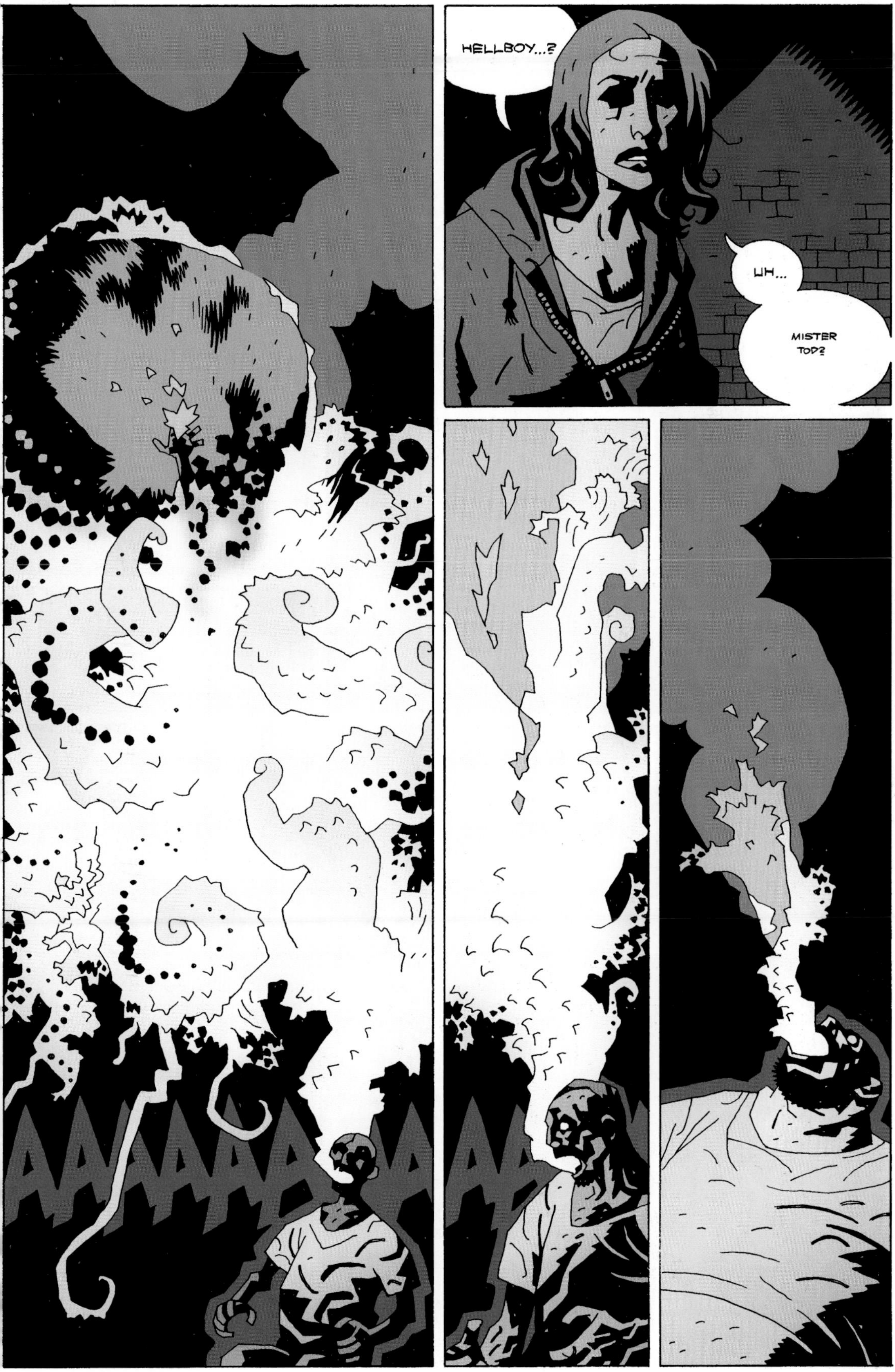
HELLBOY...?
UH...
MISTER TOD?
AAAAAAAA

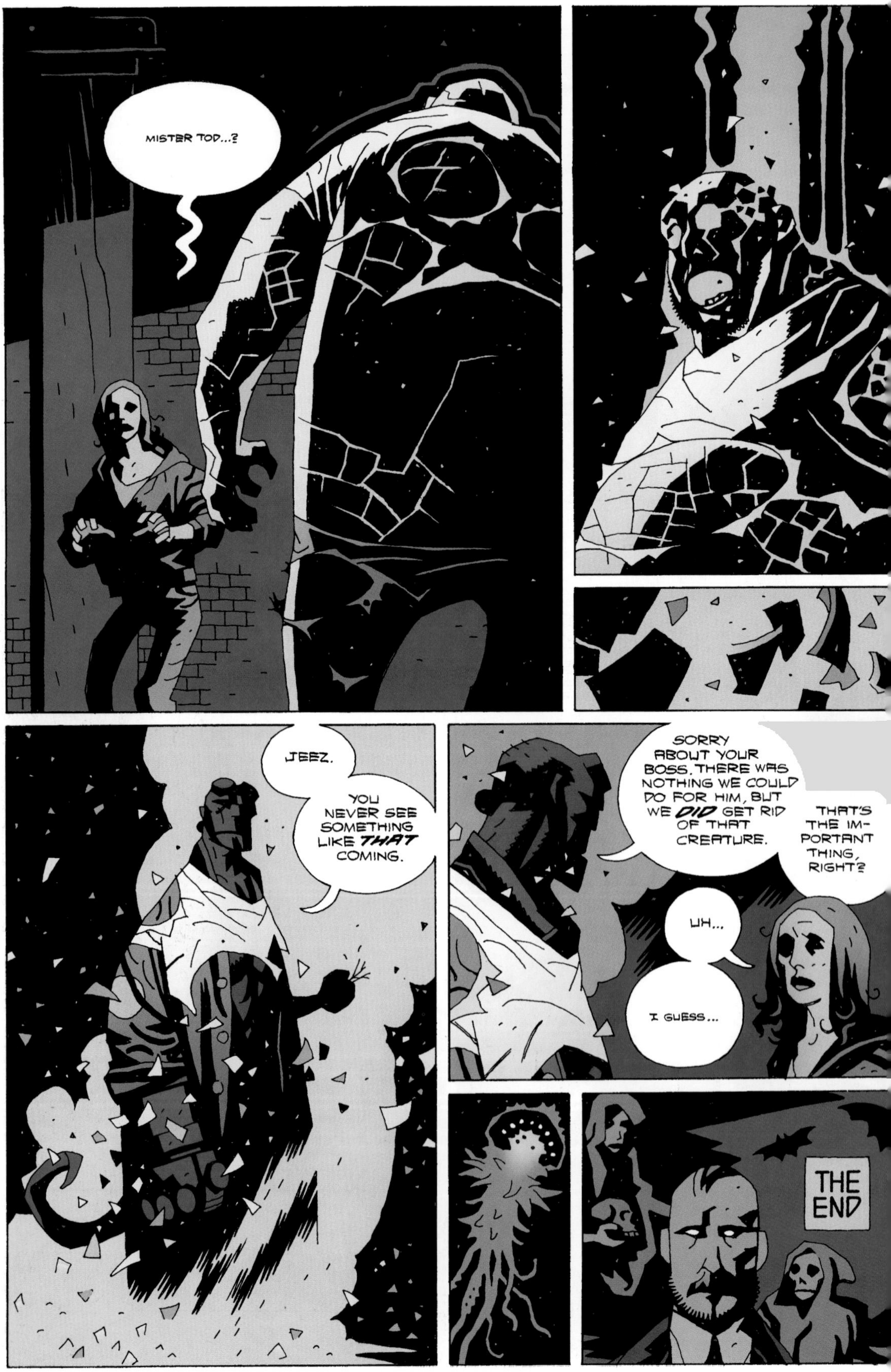
MISTER TOD...?
JEEZ.
YOU NEVER SEE SOMETHING LIKE THAT COMING.
SORRY ABOUT YOUR BOSS. THERE WAS NOTHING WE COULD DO FOR HIM, BUT WE DID GET RID OF THAT CREATURE.
THAT'S THE IMPORTANT THING, RIGHT?
UH...
I GUESS...
THE END

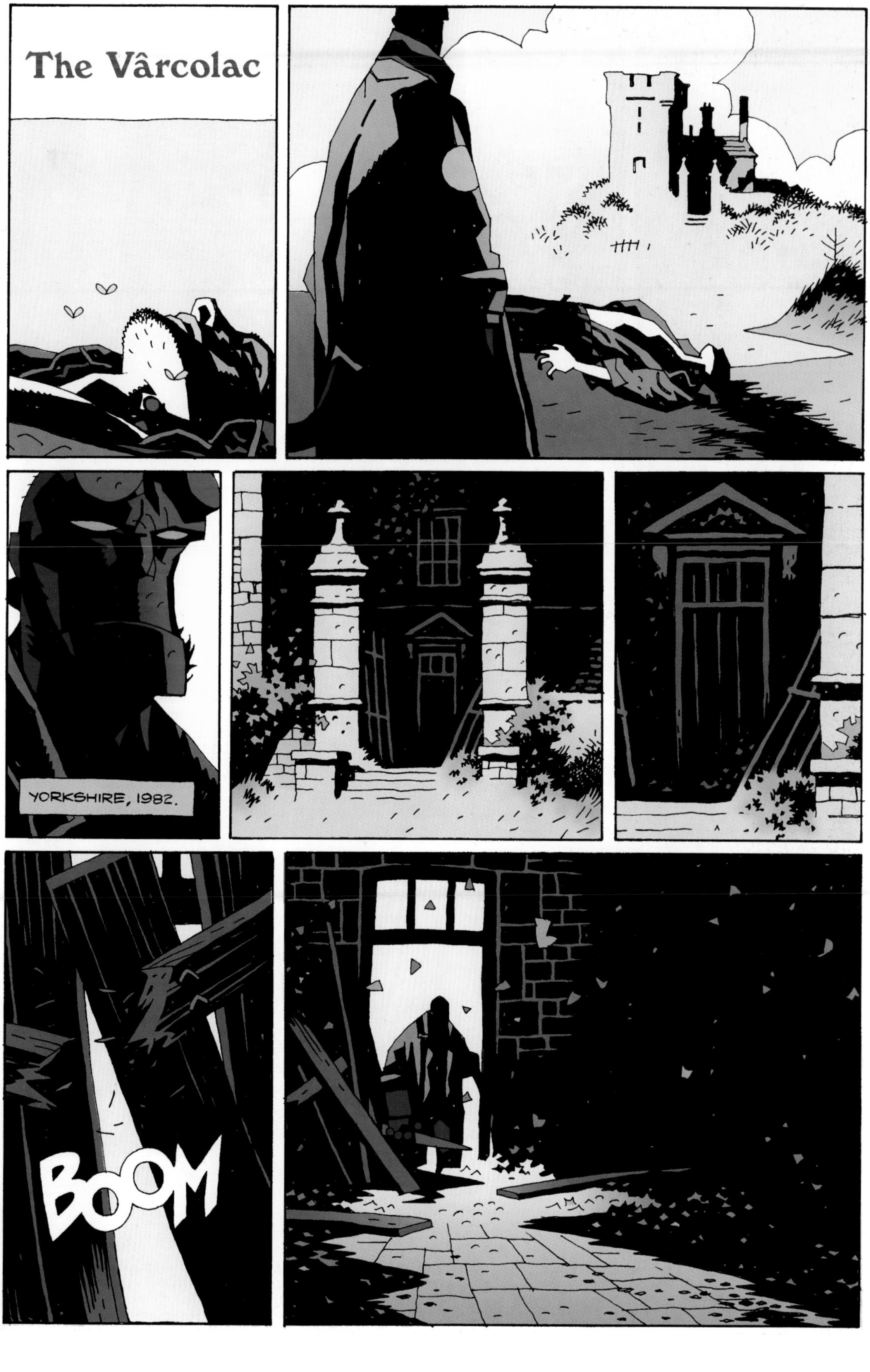
The Vârcolac
YORKSHIRE, 1982.
BOOM

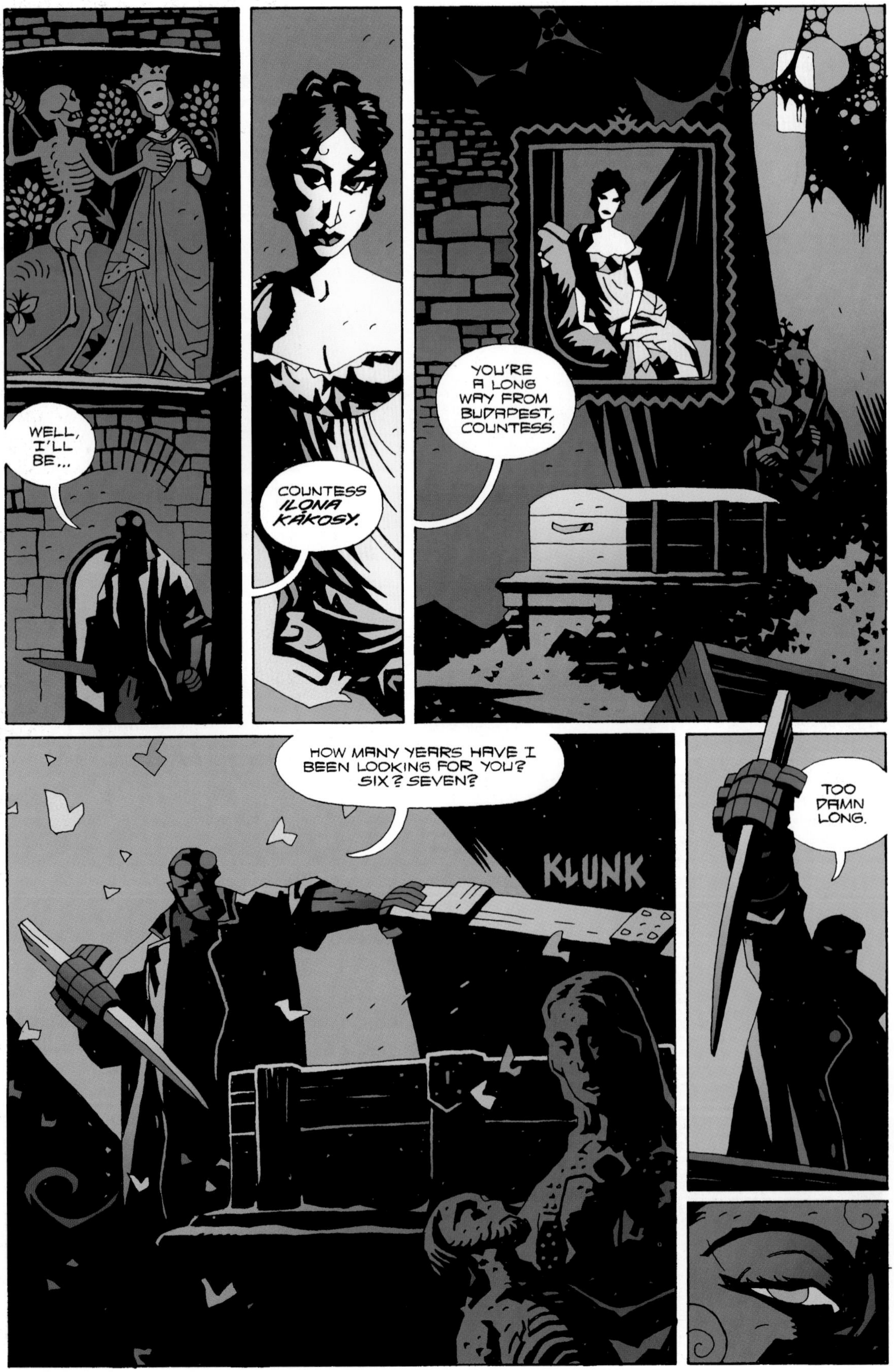
WELL, I'LL BE...
COUNTESS ILONA KÁKOSY.
YOU'RE A LONG WAY FROM BUDAPEST, COUNTESS.
HOW MANY YEARS HAVE I BEEN LOOKING FOR YOU? SIX? SEVEN?
KLUNK
TOO DAMN LONG.

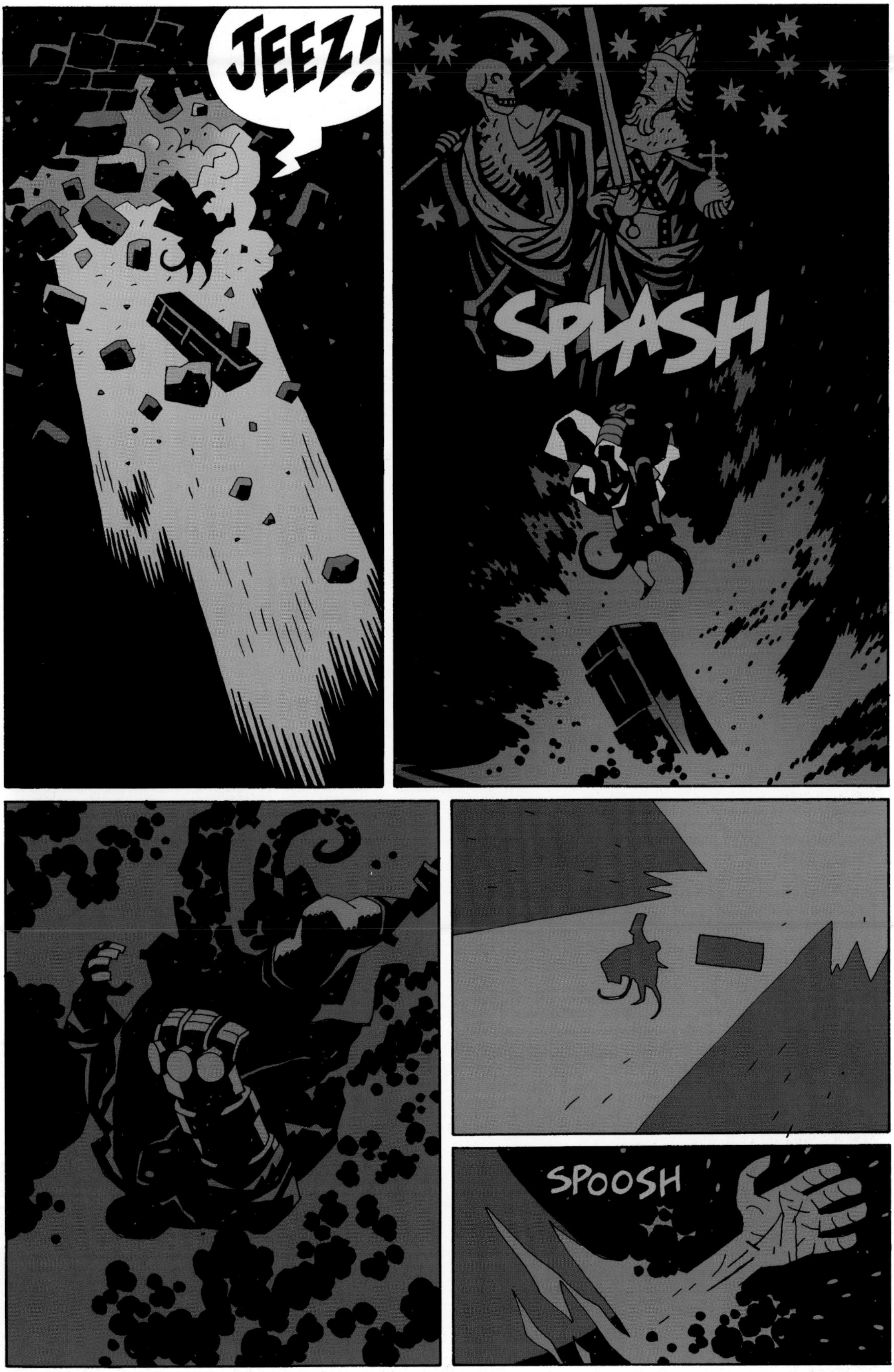

JEEZ!
SPLASH
SPOOSH

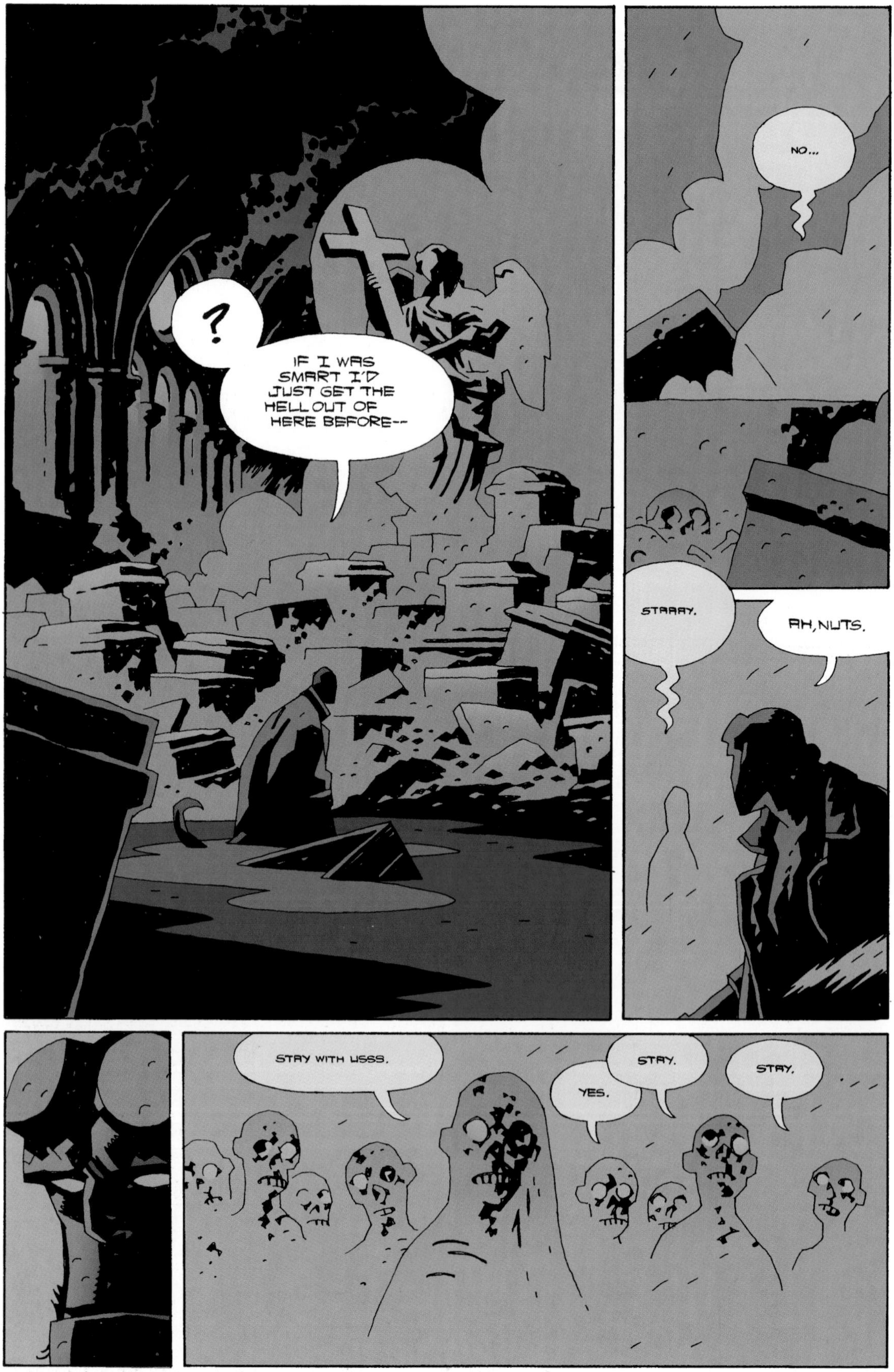
?
IF I WAS SMART I'D JUST GET THE HELL OUT OF HERE BEFORE--
NO...
STAAAY.
AH, NUTS.
STAY WITH USSS.
YES.
STAY.
STAY.

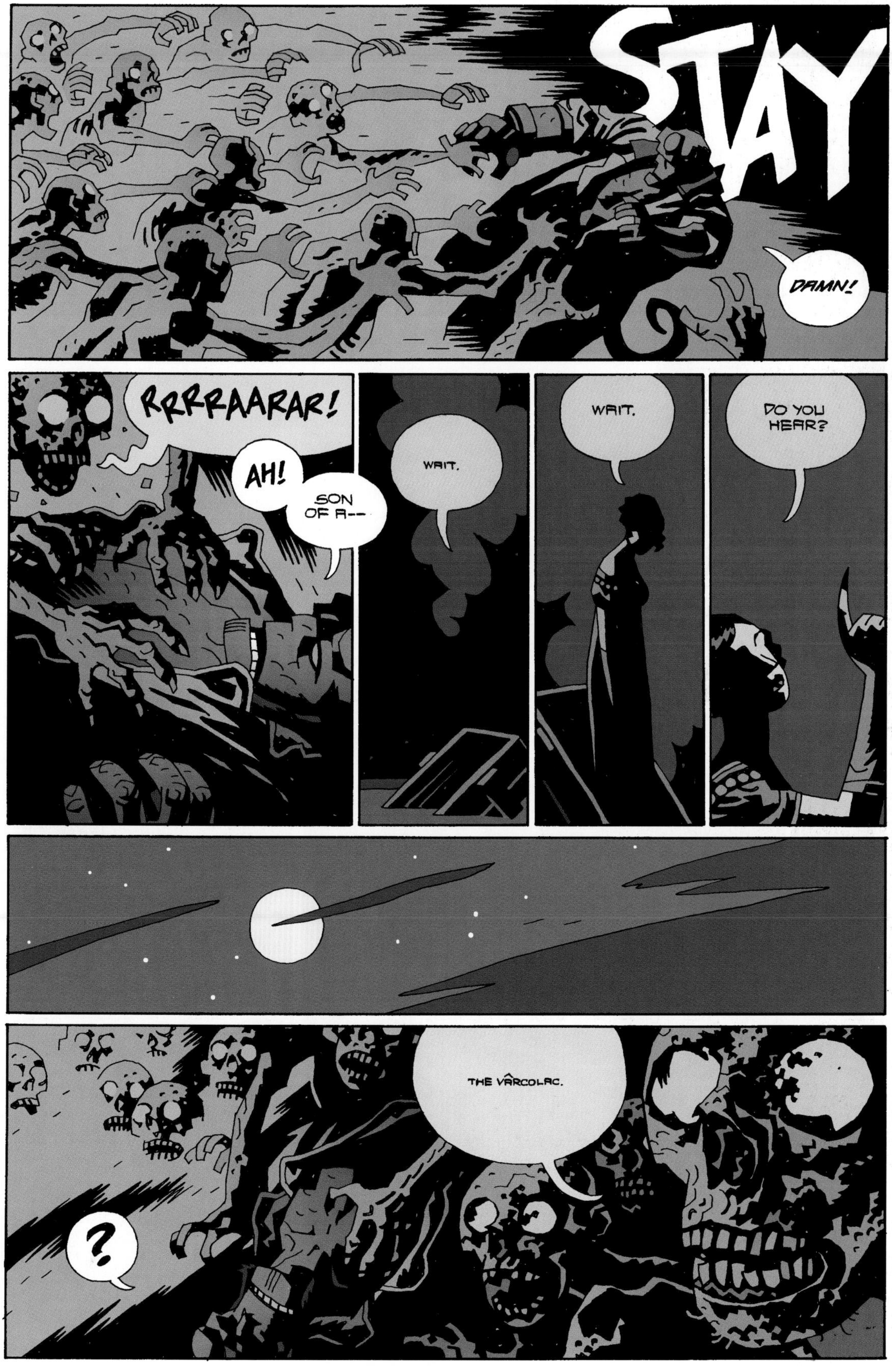
STAY
DAMN!
RRRRAARAR!
AH!
SON OF A--
WAIT.
WAIT.
DO YOU HEAR?
?
THE VÂRCOLAC.

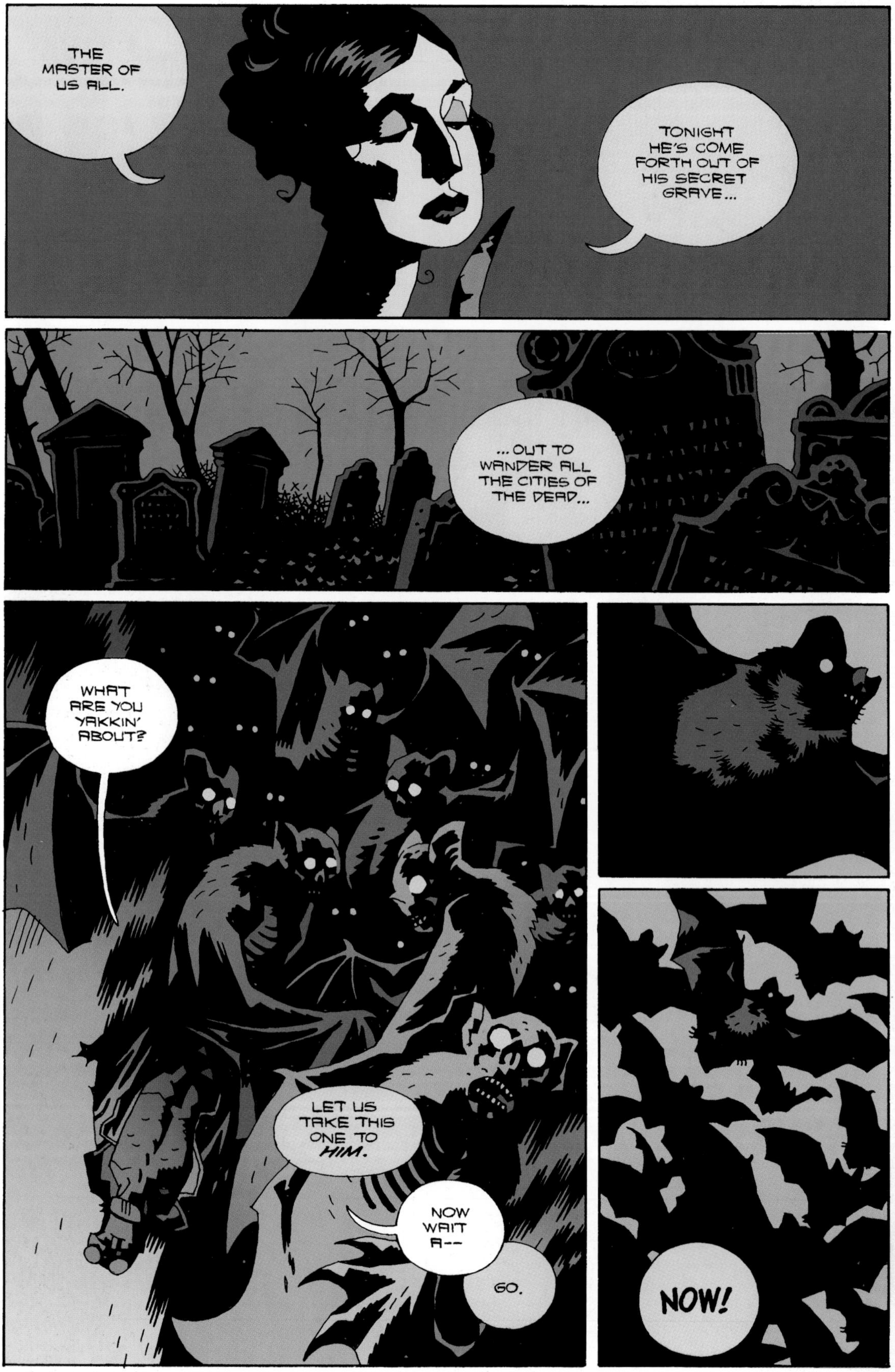
THE MASTER OF US ALL.
TONIGHT HE'S COME FORTH OUT OF HIS SECRET GRAVE...
...OUT TO WANDER ALL THE CITIES OF THE DEAD...
WHAT ARE YOU YAKKIN' ABOUT?
LET US TAKE THIS ONE TO *HIM*.
NOW WAIT A--
GO.
NOW!

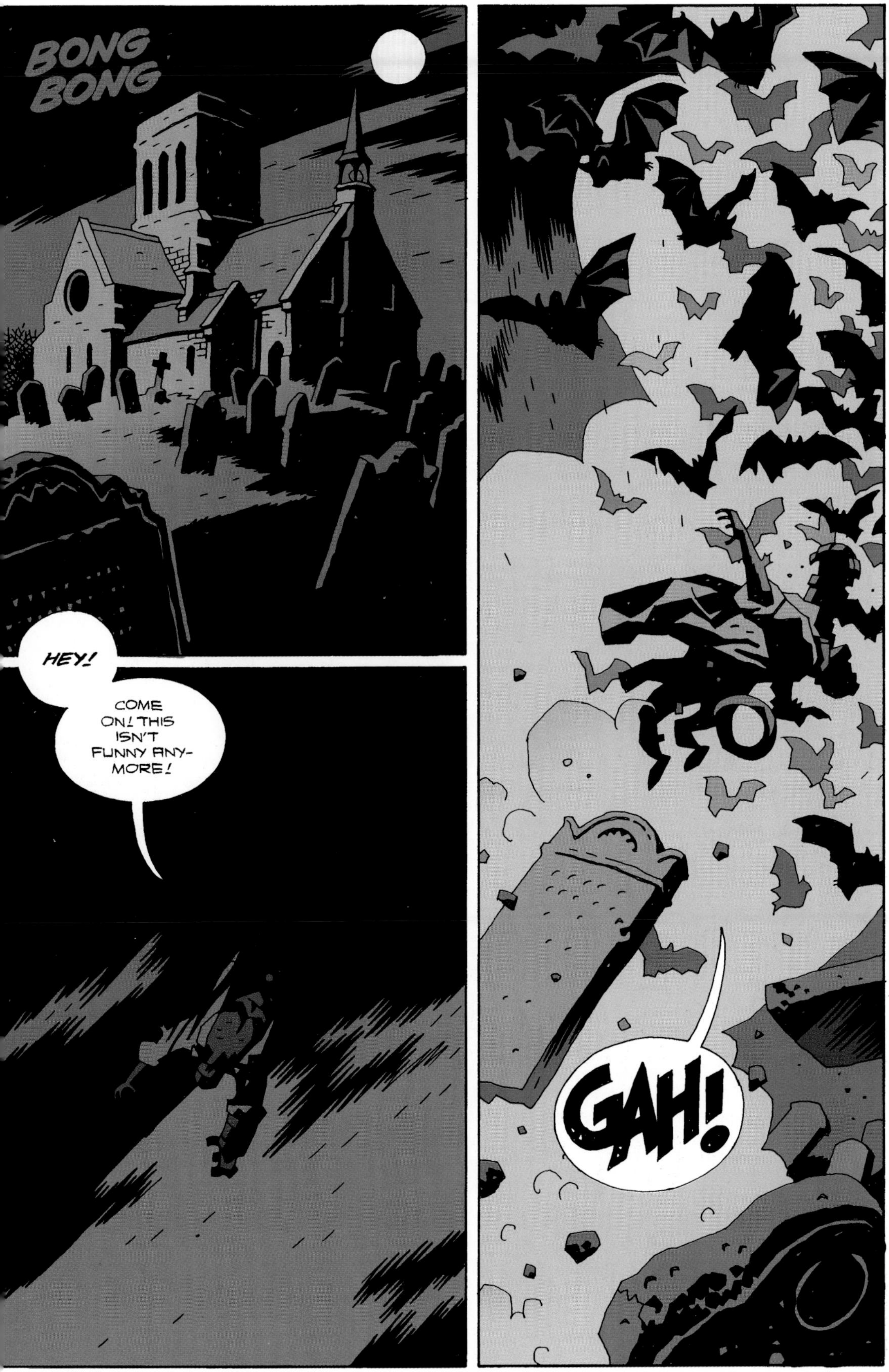
BONG
BONG
HEY!
COME ON! THIS ISN'T FUNNY ANY-MORE!
GAH!

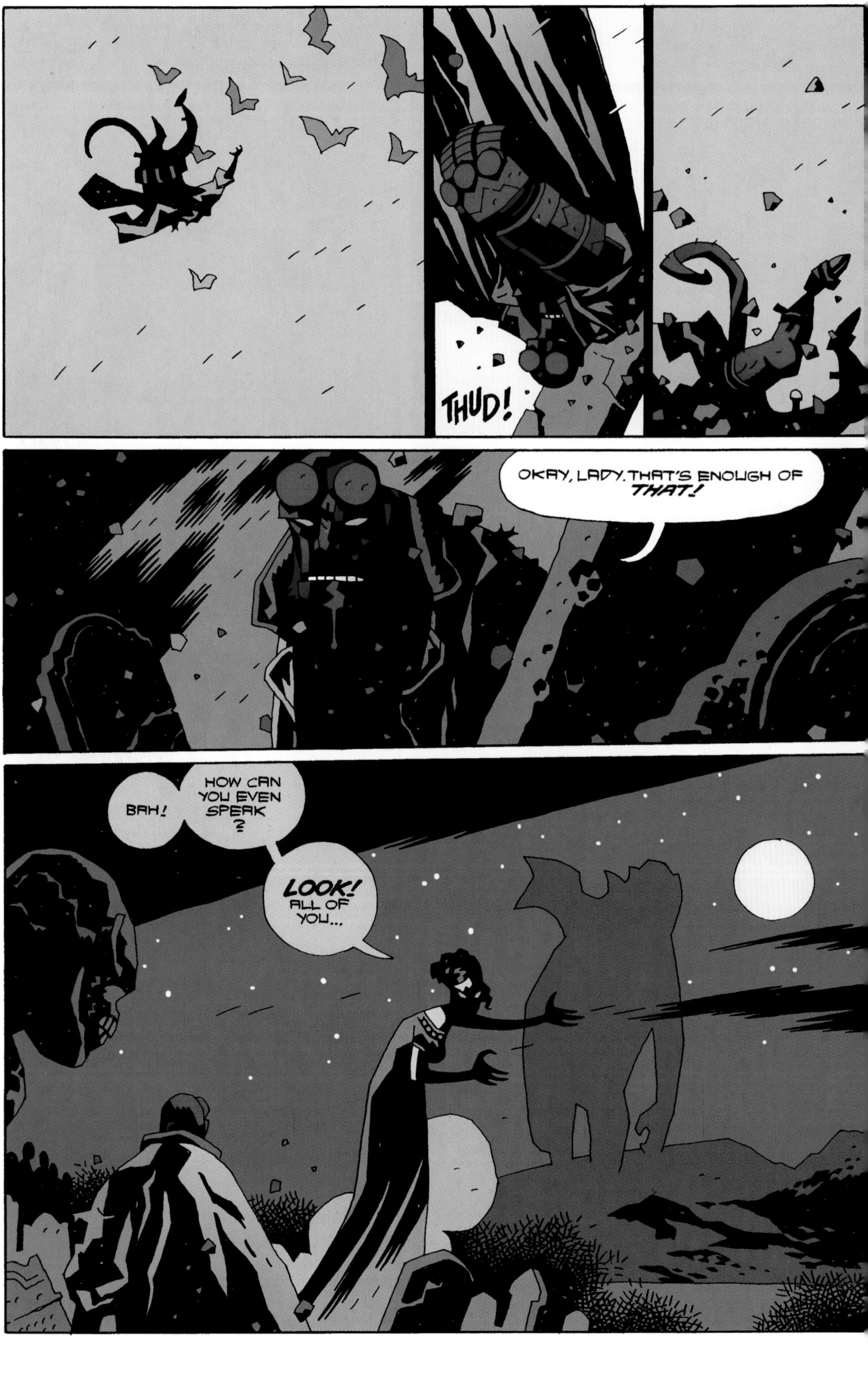

THUD!
OKAY, LADY. THAT'S ENOUGH OF THAT!
BAH!
HOW CAN YOU EVEN SPEAK?
LOOK! ALL OF YOU...

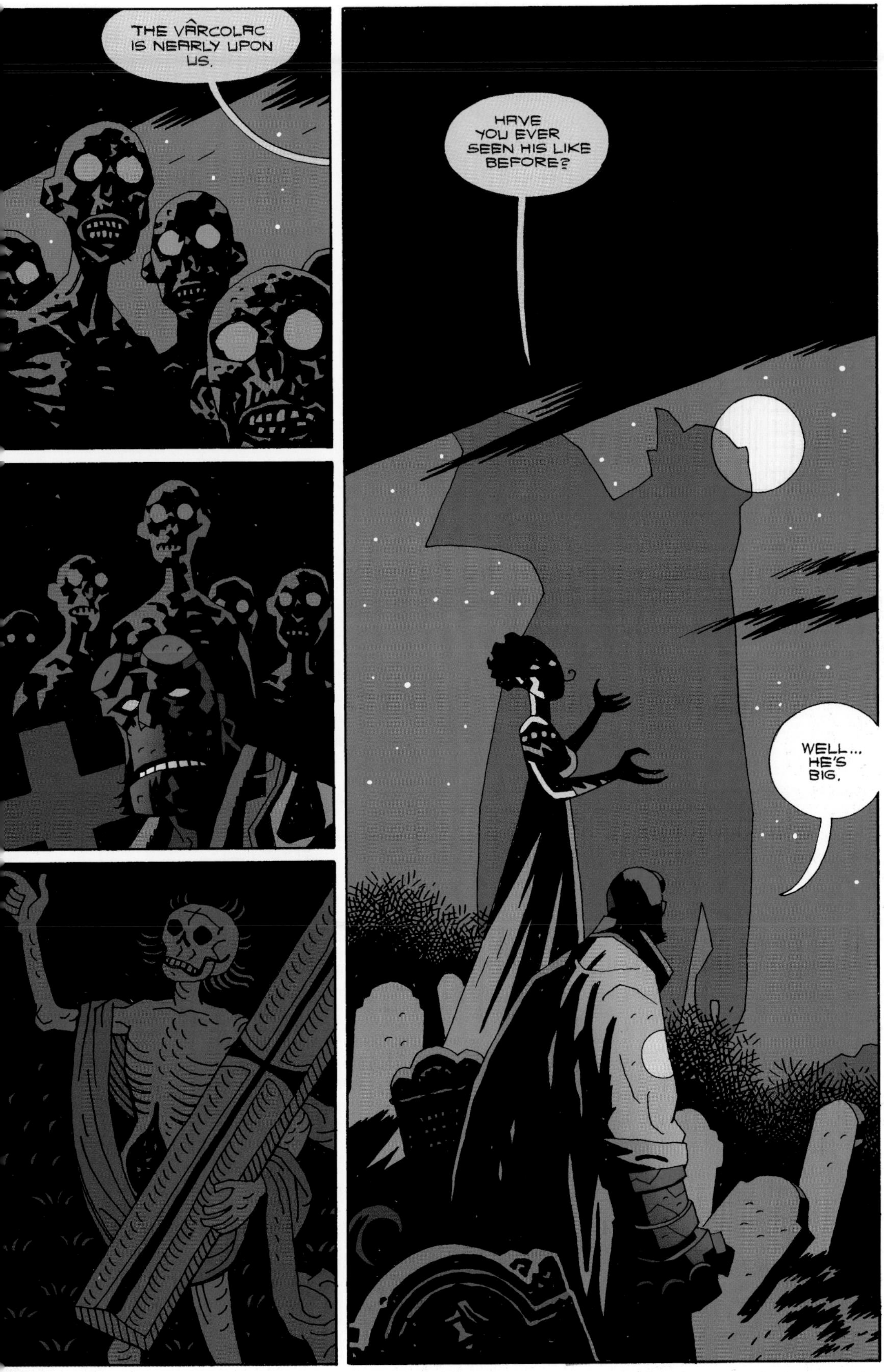
THE VÂRCOLAC IS NEARLY UPON US.
HAVE YOU EVER SEEN HIS LIKE BEFORE?
WELL... HE'S BIG.

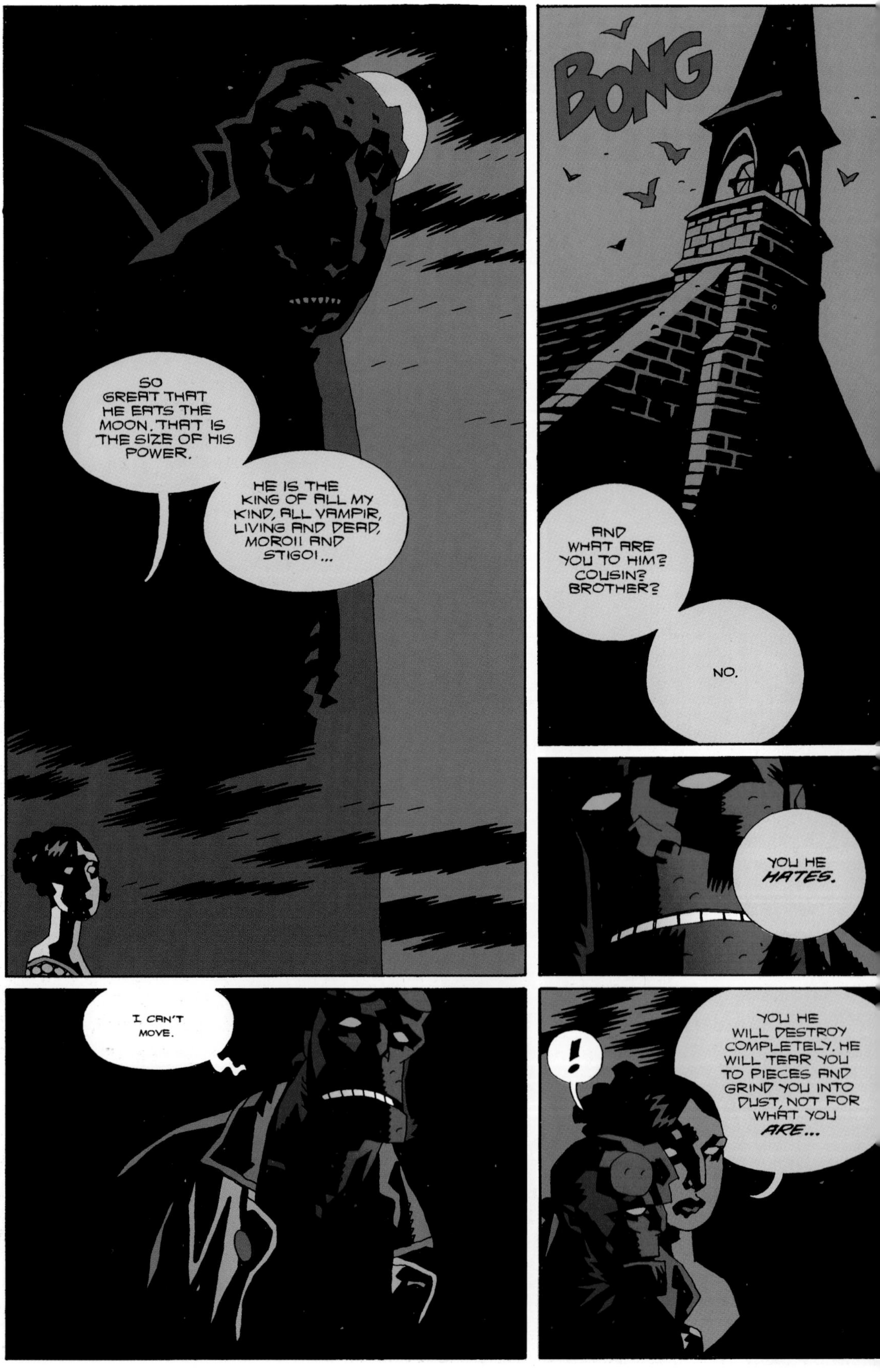
SO GREAT THAT HE EATS THE MOON. THAT IS THE SIZE OF HIS POWER.
HE IS THE KING OF ALL MY KIND, ALL VAMPIR, LIVING AND DEAD, MOROII AND STIGOI...
BONG
AND WHAT ARE YOU TO HIM? COUSIN? BROTHER?
NO.
YOU HE HATES.
I CAN'T MOVE.
!
YOU HE WILL DESTROY COMPLETELY. HE WILL TEAR YOU TO PIECES AND GRIND YOU INTO DUST, NOT FOR WHAT YOU ARE...

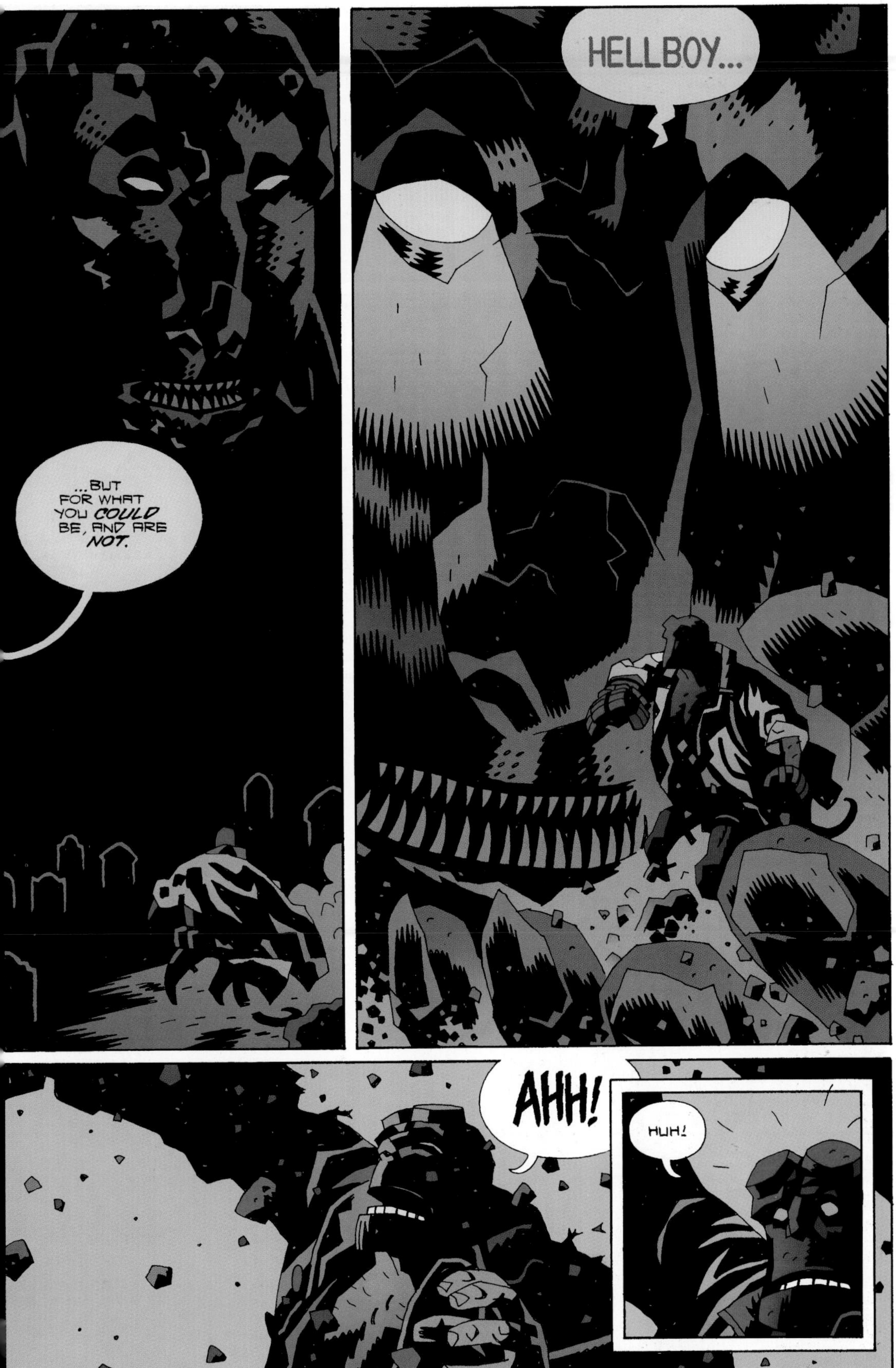
...BUT FOR WHAT YOU COULD BE, AND ARE NOT.
HELLBOY...
AHH!
HUH!

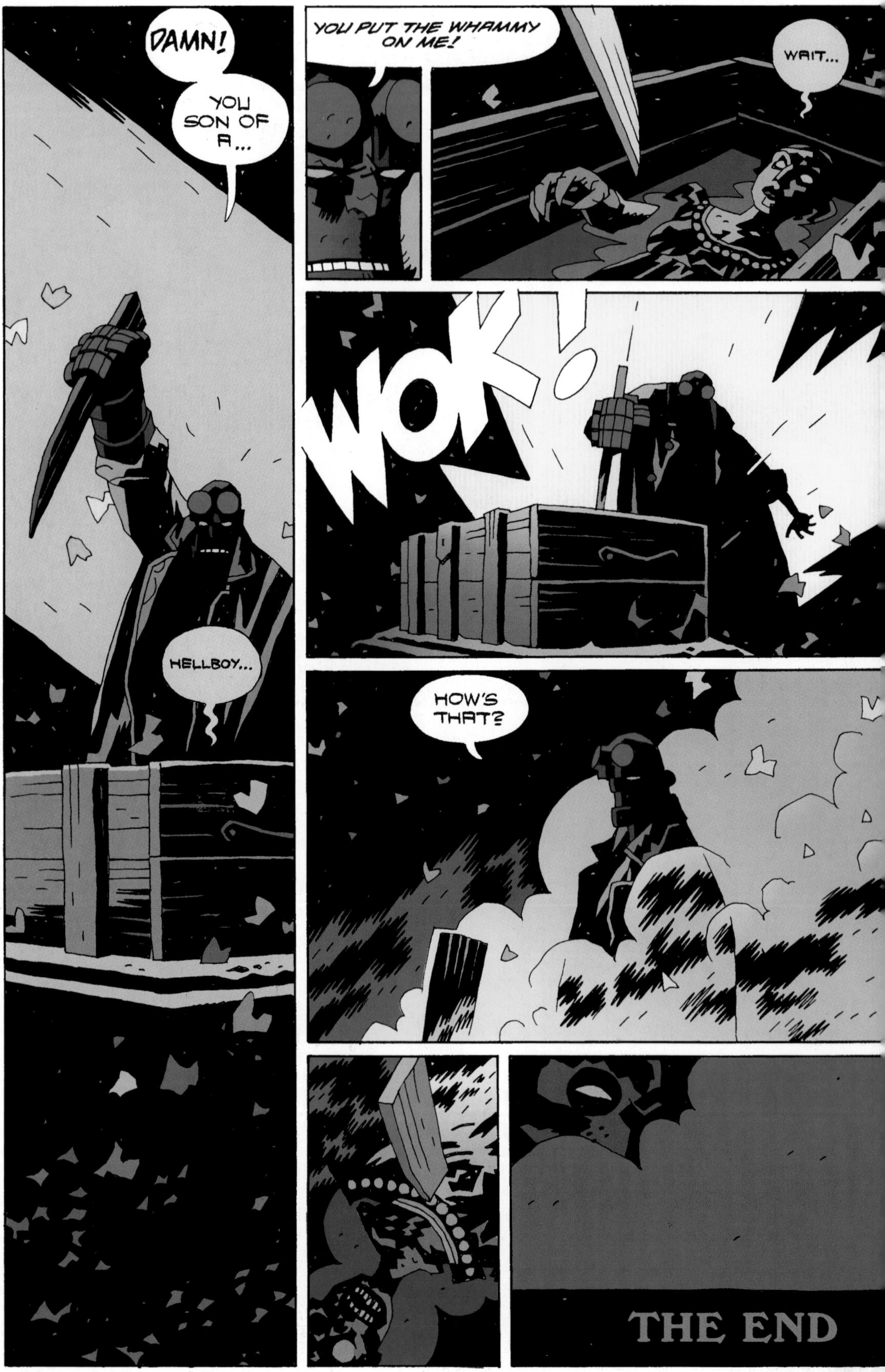
DAMN!
YOU SON OF A...
HELLBOY...
YOU PUT THE WHAMMY ON ME!
WAIT...
WOK!
HOW'S THAT?
THE END

PART THREE
THE RIGHT HAND OF DOOM

The Right Hand of Doom

AFTER I'D BEEN doing *Hellboy* for five years, very few people were asking what the deal was with the big stone hand. I decided to direct attention to it with this story. Of course I wasn't going to tell what the hand was, but at least now readers would know it was something.

"The Right Hand of Doom" was published in the 1998 *Dark Horse Presents Annual.* This is its first appearance in color.

✠

Box Full of Evil

FOLLOWING UP "The Right Hand of Doom," I wanted to say a little bit more about Hellboy and his big hand, and I wanted to resolve the whole Beast of the Apocalypse business once and for all. I think I did, but you can never be sure about something like that.

The stuff Igor Bromhead says to control and command demons is mostly taken from old occult ritual. The hand of glory is a real thing. The Saint Dunstan legend is a real legend, but I made up the part about the box. *Box Full of Evil* was published as a two-issue miniseries in 1999. For this collection I've added a four-page epilogue to give Hellboy a chance to reflect on events, and to get rid of that scrap of paper from "The Right Hand of Doom."

That's it.

Mike Mignola

Mike Mignola
Portland, Oregon

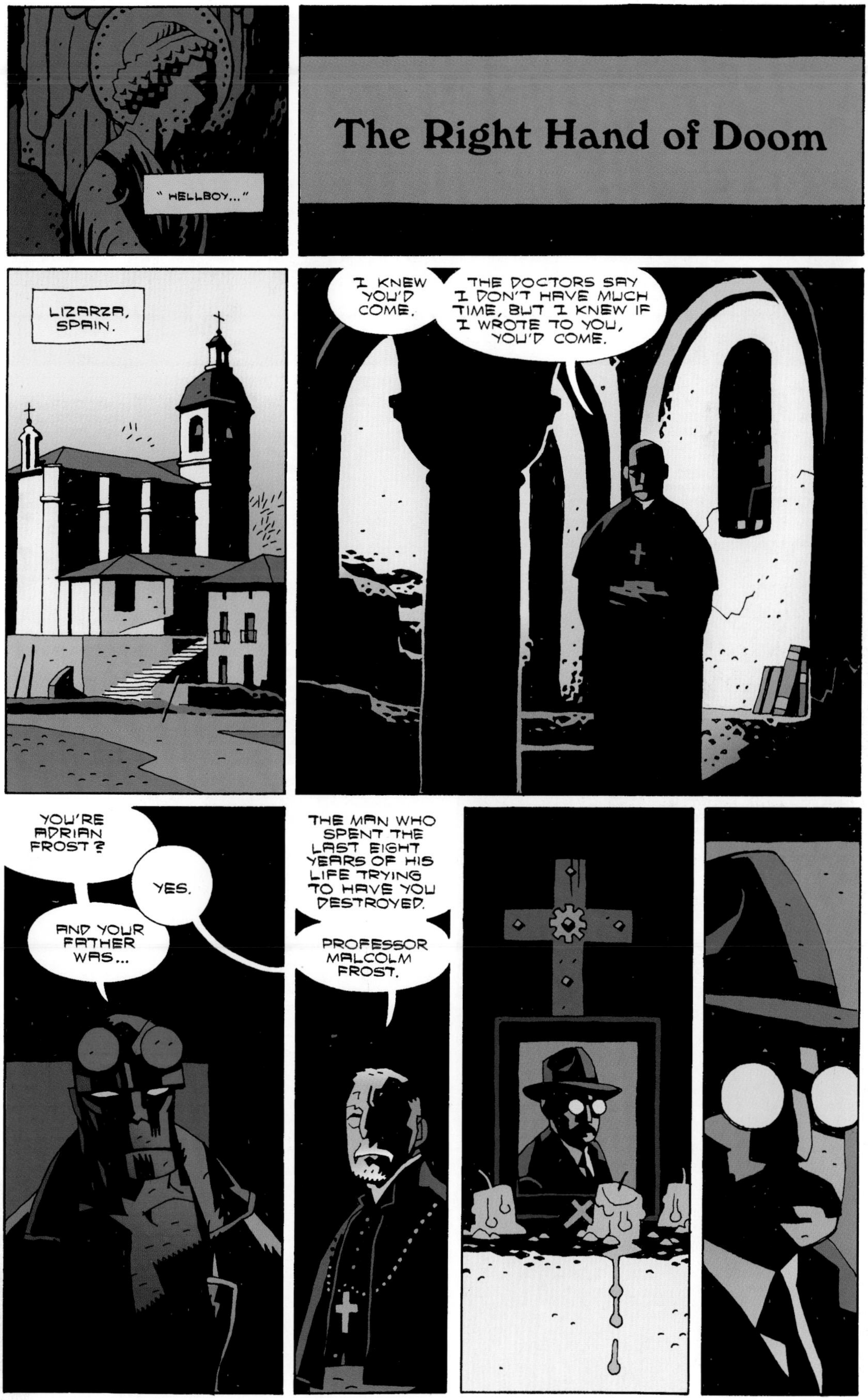
"HELLBOY..."
The Right Hand of Doom
LIZARZA, SPAIN.
I KNEW YOU'D COME.
THE DOCTORS SAY I DON'T HAVE MUCH TIME, BUT I KNEW IF I WROTE TO YOU, YOU'D COME.
YOU'RE ADRIAN FROST?
YES.
AND YOUR FATHER WAS...
THE MAN WHO SPENT THE LAST EIGHT YEARS OF HIS LIFE TRYING TO HAVE YOU DESTROYED.
PROFESSOR MALCOLM FROST.

YEAH...

KILL IT!

IT'S A DEMON COME FROM HELL TO DESTROY US ALL!

IT LOOKS MORE LIKE A LITTLE BOY...

"HELLBOY..."

DEC. 23, 1944.

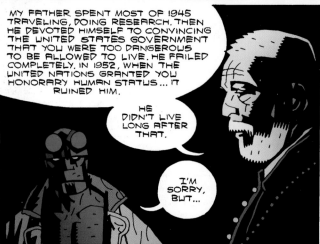

MY FATHER SPENT MOST OF 1945 TRAVELING, DOING RESEARCH. THEN HE DEVOTED HIMSELF TO CONVINCING THE UNITED STATES GOVERNMENT THAT YOU WERE TOO DANGEROUS TO BE ALLOWED TO LIVE. HE FAILED COMPLETELY. IN 1952, WHEN THE UNITED NATIONS GRANTED YOU HONORARY HUMAN STATUS... IT RUINED HIM.

HE DIDN'T LIVE LONG AFTER THAT.

I'M SORRY, BUT...

IT'S IMPORTANT THAT YOU UNDER-STAND SOMETHING. HE *WASN'T* AN EVIL MAN. HE WAS JUST AFRAID.

DID HE HAVE A REASON TO BE?

HE BURNED MOST OF HIS PAPERS BEFORE HE DIED, BUT I FOUND THIS TUCKED AWAY IN HIS BIBLE. BOOK OF REVELATIONS.

I'VE NEVER SEEN WRITING LIKE THIS ANY-WHERE.

IT'S OLD LEMURIAN.

TREVOR BRUTTENHOLM TAUGHT ME TO READ IT WHEN I WAS A KID. IT WAS SORT OF OUR SECRET LANGUAGE...

THIS SAYS: "BEHOLD THE RIGHT HAND OF DOOM."

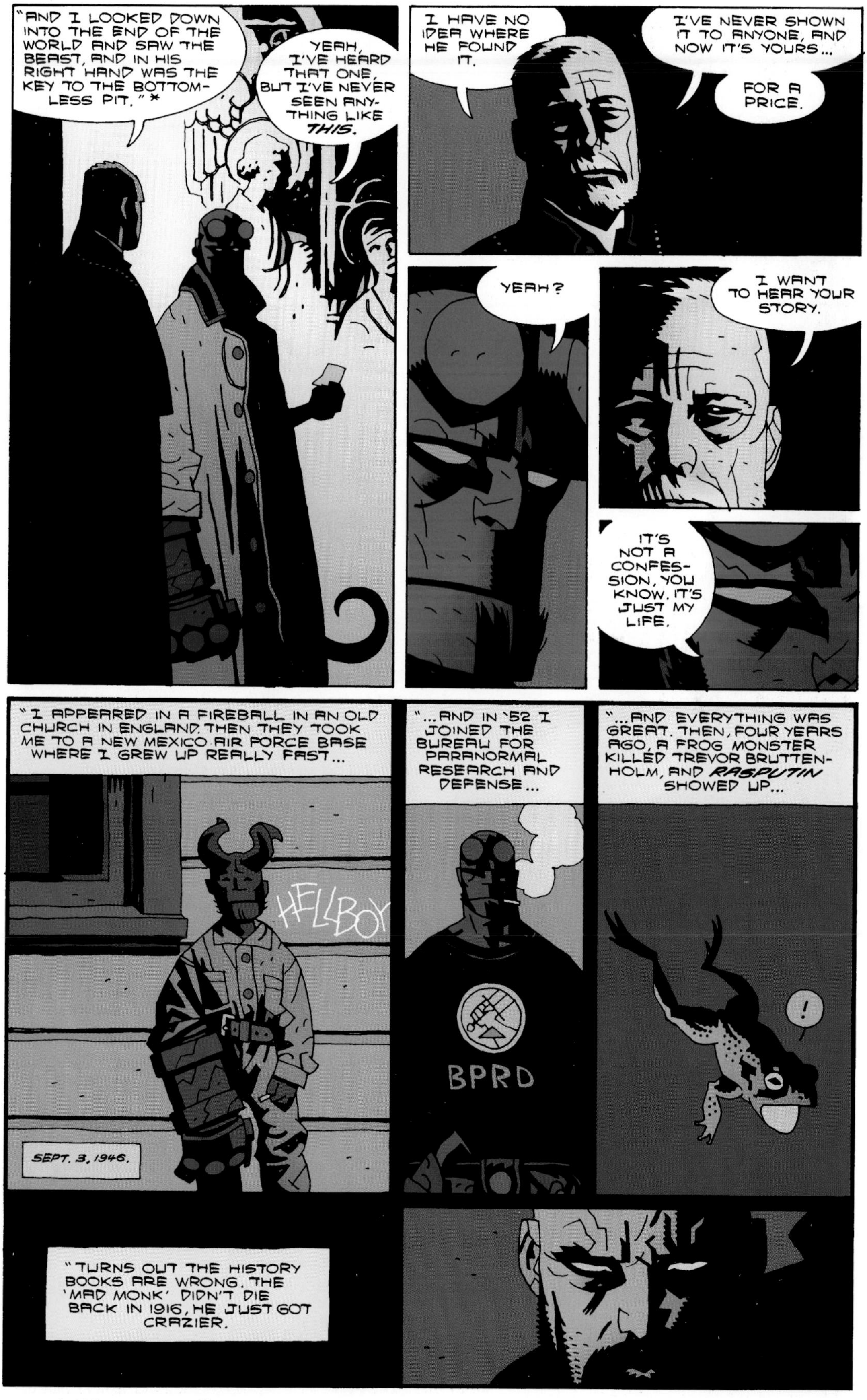
"AND I LOOKED DOWN INTO THE END OF THE WORLD AND SAW THE BEAST, AND IN HIS RIGHT HAND WAS THE KEY TO THE BOTTOMLESS PIT." *
YEAH, I'VE HEARD THAT ONE, BUT I'VE NEVER SEEN ANYTHING LIKE *THIS*.
I HAVE NO IDEA WHERE HE FOUND IT.
I'VE NEVER SHOWN IT TO ANYONE, AND NOW IT'S YOURS...
FOR A PRICE.
YEAH?
I WANT TO HEAR YOUR STORY.
IT'S NOT A CONFESSION, YOU KNOW. IT'S JUST MY LIFE.
"I APPEARED IN A FIREBALL IN AN OLD CHURCH IN ENGLAND. THEN THEY TOOK ME TO A NEW MEXICO AIR FORCE BASE WHERE I GREW UP REALLY FAST...
HELLBOY
SEPT. 3, 1946.
"...AND IN '52 I JOINED THE BUREAU FOR PARANORMAL RESEARCH AND DEFENSE...
BPRD
"...AND EVERYTHING WAS GREAT. THEN, FOUR YEARS AGO, A FROG MONSTER KILLED TREVOR BRUTTENHOLM, AND *RASPUTIN* SHOWED UP...
!
"TURNS OUT THE HISTORY BOOKS ARE WRONG. THE 'MAD MONK' DIDN'T DIE BACK IN 1916, HE JUST GOT CRAZIER.

* *POPE SYLVESTER II, A.D. 999.*

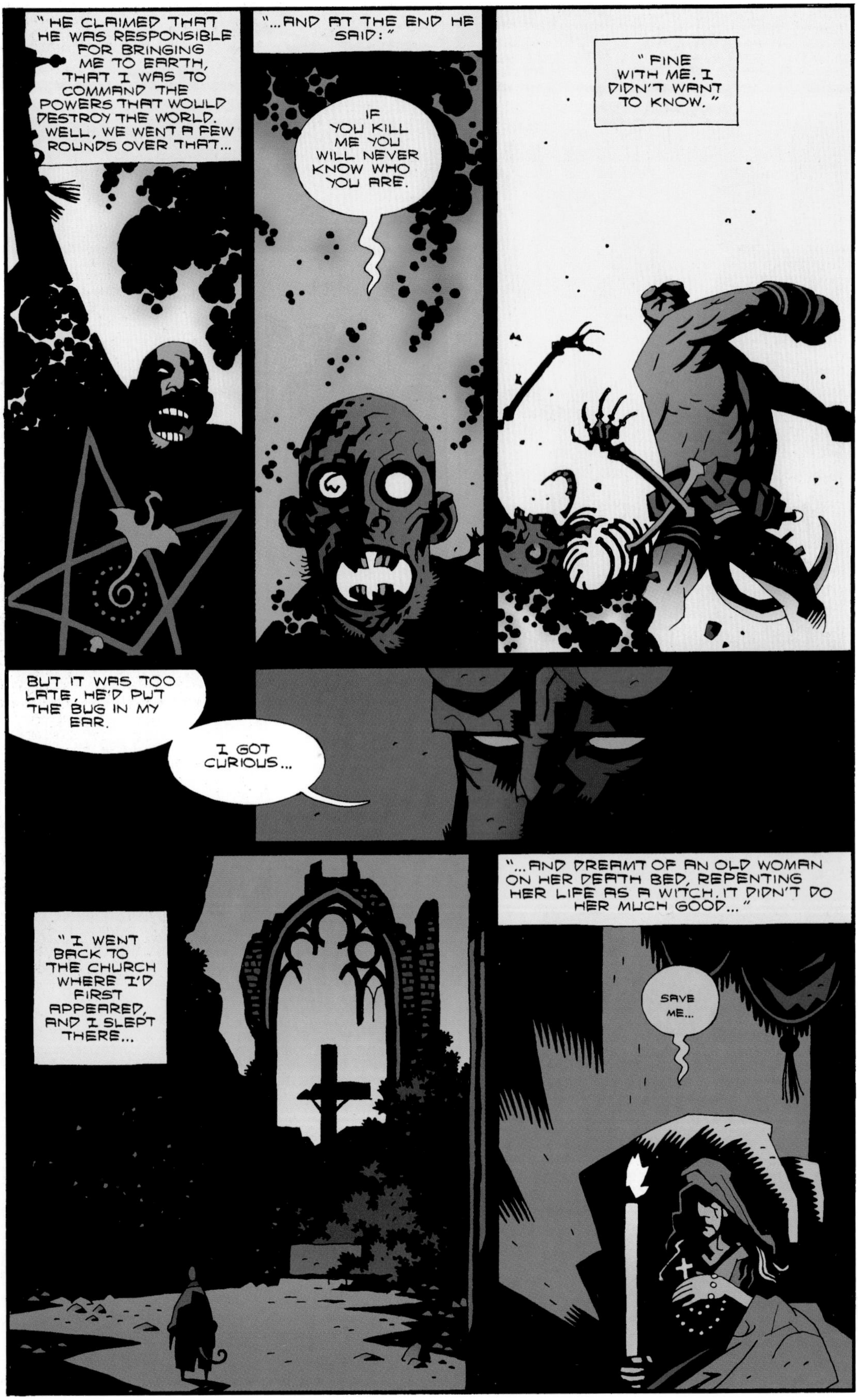
"HE CLAIMED THAT HE WAS RESPONSIBLE FOR BRINGING ME TO EARTH, THAT I WAS TO COMMAND THE POWERS THAT WOULD DESTROY THE WORLD. WELL, WE WENT A FEW ROUNDS OVER THAT...
"...AND AT THE END HE SAID:"
IF YOU KILL ME YOU WILL NEVER KNOW WHO YOU ARE.
"FINE WITH ME. I DIDN'T WANT TO KNOW."
BUT IT WAS TOO LATE, HE'D PUT THE BUG IN MY EAR.
I GOT CURIOUS...
"I WENT BACK TO THE CHURCH WHERE I'D FIRST APPEARED, AND I SLEPT THERE...
"...AND DREAMT OF AN OLD WOMAN ON HER DEATH BED, REPENTING HER LIFE AS A WITCH. IT DIDN'T DO HER MUCH GOOD..."
SAVE ME...

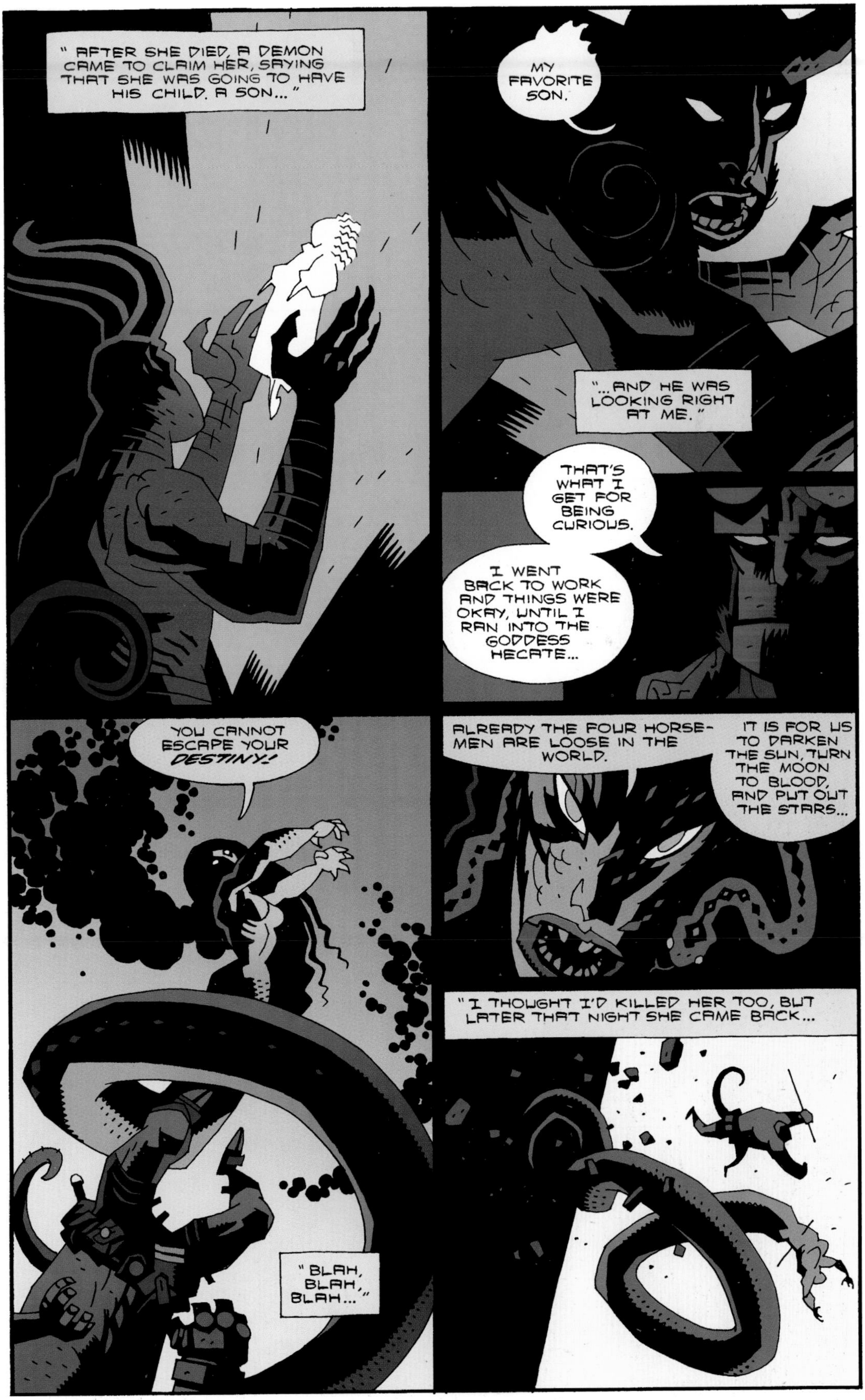
" AFTER SHE DIED, A DEMON CAME TO CLAIM HER, SAYING THAT SHE WAS GOING TO HAVE HIS CHILD. A SON... "
MY FAVORITE SON.
"...AND HE WAS LOOKING RIGHT AT ME."
THAT'S WHAT I GET FOR BEING CURIOUS.
I WENT BACK TO WORK AND THINGS WERE OKAY, UNTIL I RAN INTO THE GODDESS HECATE...
YOU CANNOT ESCAPE YOUR DESTINY!
"BLAH, BLAH, BLAH..."
ALREADY THE FOUR HORSE-MEN ARE LOOSE IN THE WORLD.
IT IS FOR US TO DARKEN THE SUN, TURN THE MOON TO BLOOD, AND PUT OUT THE STARS...
"I THOUGHT I'D KILLED HER TOO, BUT LATER THAT NIGHT SHE CAME BACK...

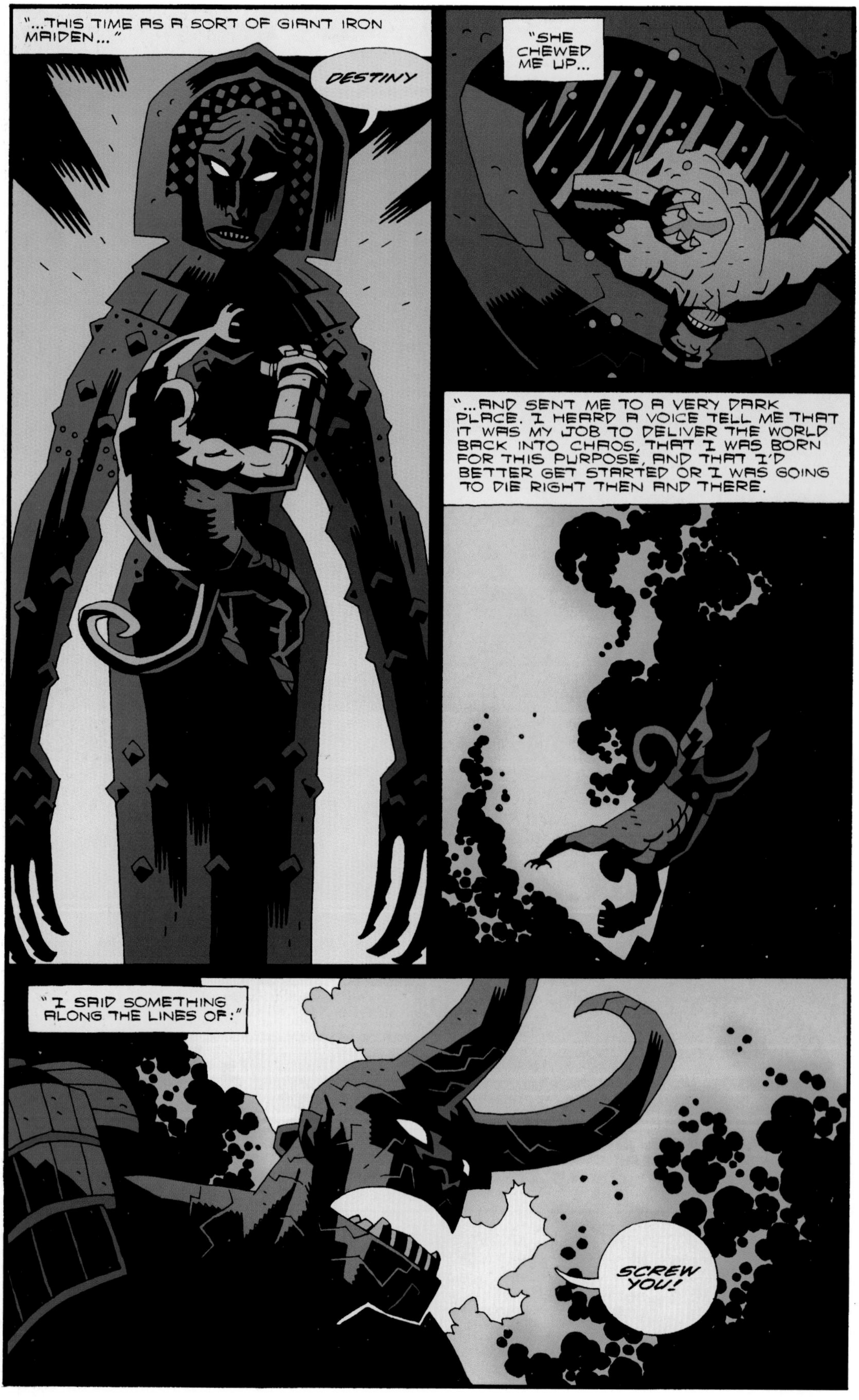
"...THIS TIME AS A SORT OF GIANT IRON MAIDEN..."
DESTINY
"SHE CHEWED ME UP...
"...AND SENT ME TO A VERY DARK PLACE. I HEARD A VOICE TELL ME THAT IT WAS MY JOB TO DELIVER THE WORLD BACK INTO CHAOS, THAT I WAS BORN FOR THIS PURPOSE, AND THAT I'D BETTER GET STARTED OR I WAS GOING TO DIE RIGHT THEN AND THERE.
"I SAID SOMETHING ALONG THE LINES OF:"
SCREW YOU!

IT'S *MY* GODDAMN LIFE, I'LL DO WHAT I WANT!

YOU DON'T LIKE THAT, KILL ME IF YOU CAN!

"AND I DIDN'T BLOW UP THE WORLD...

"...AND I DIDN'T DIE."

AND NOW YOU THINK MAYBE YOU'RE OFF THE HOOK.

WELL...

HOW CAN YOU BE?

WHAT ABOUT THE HAND?

WHAT IF I CUT IT OFF?

AND WHAT WOULD YOU DO WITH IT?

WHERE WOULD IT EVER BE SAFE?

WHAT IF IT WERE USED?

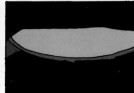

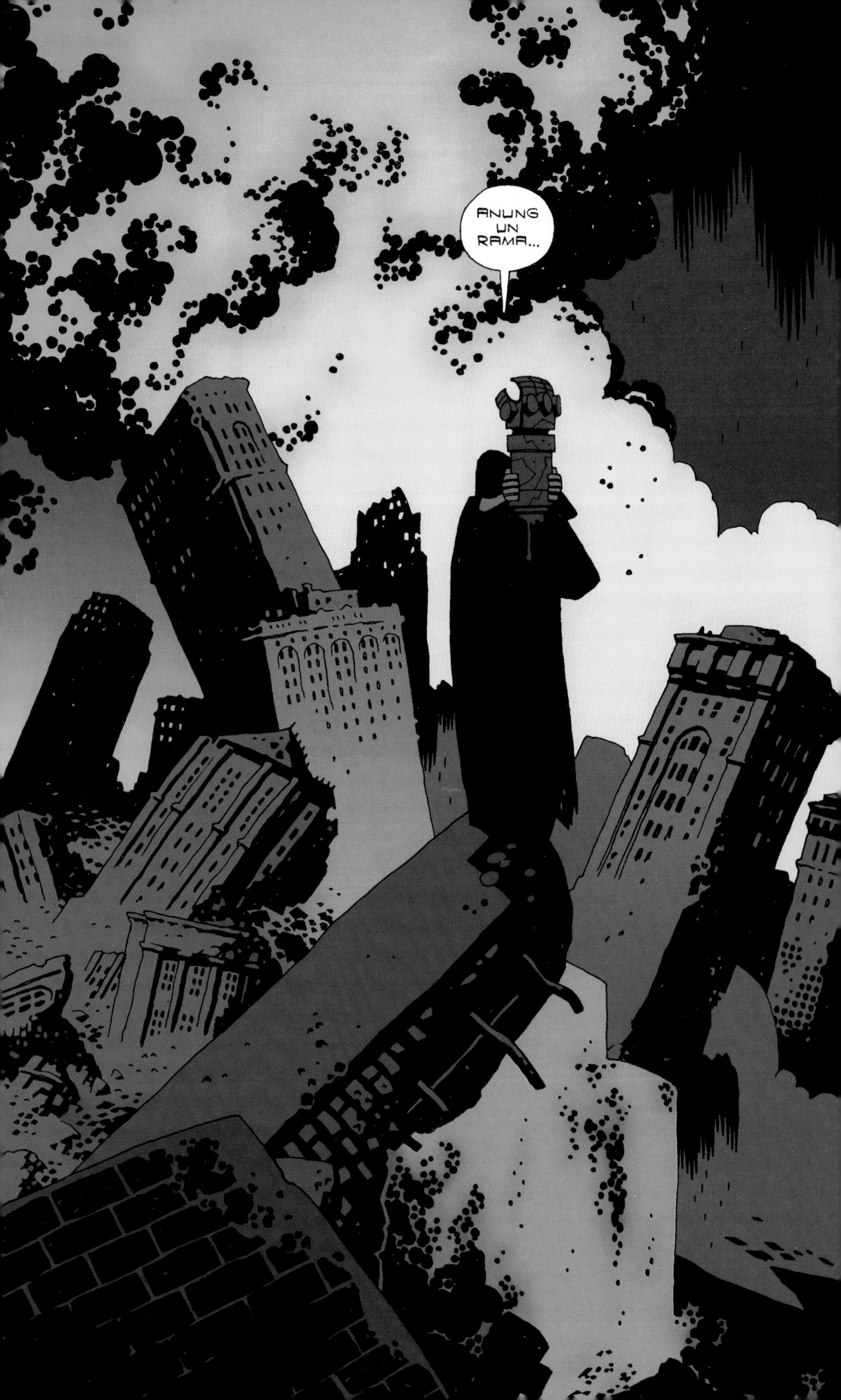
ANUNG UN RAMA...

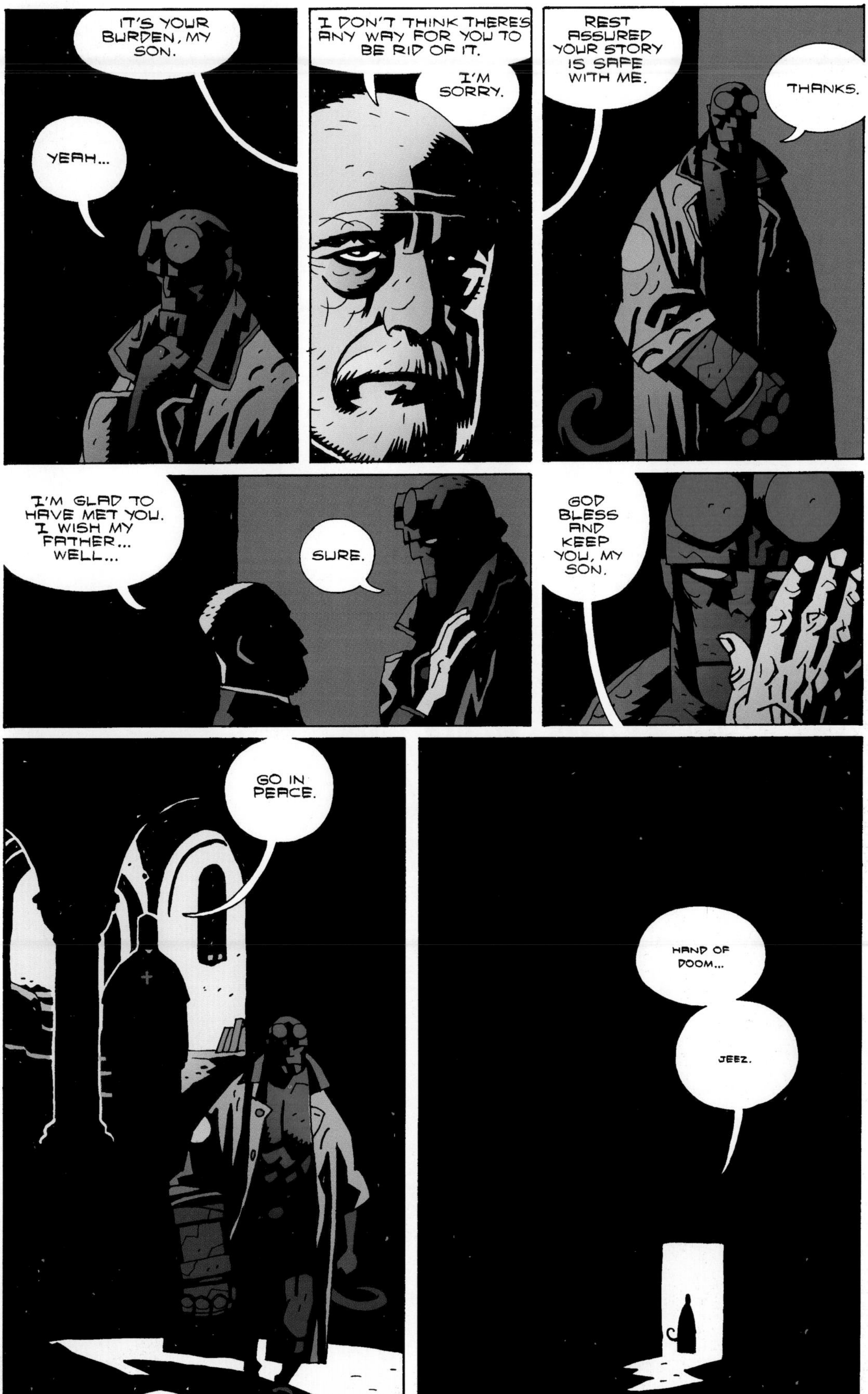
IT'S YOUR BURDEN, MY SON.
YEAH...
I DON'T THINK THERE'S ANY WAY FOR YOU TO BE RID OF IT.
I'M SORRY.
REST ASSURED YOUR STORY IS SAFE WITH ME.
THANKS.
I'M GLAD TO HAVE MET YOU. I WISH MY FATHER... WELL...
SURE.
GOD BLESS AND KEEP YOU, MY SON.
GO IN PEACE.
HAND OF DOOM...
JEEZ.

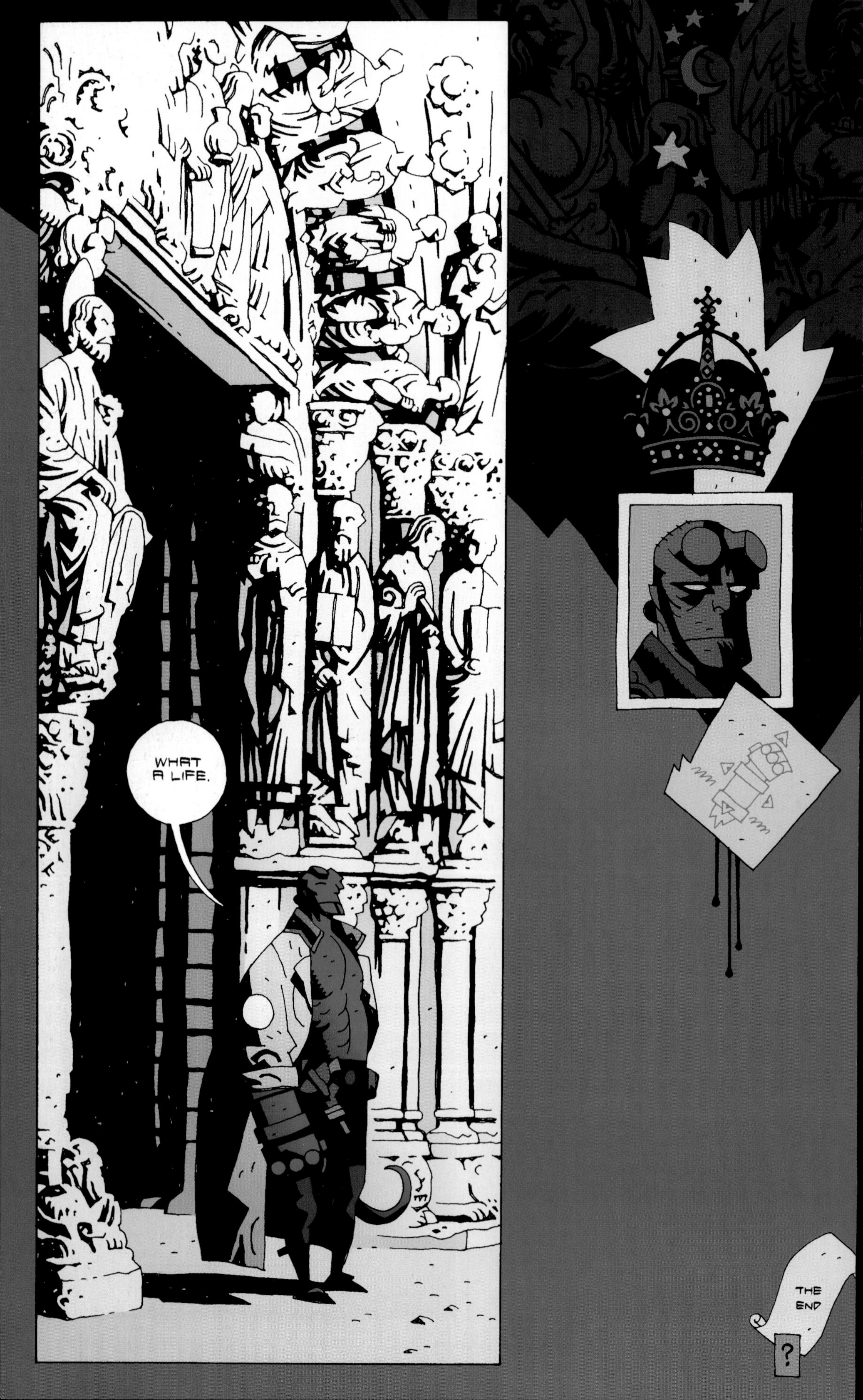
WHAT A LIFE.
THE END
?

Box Full *of* Evil

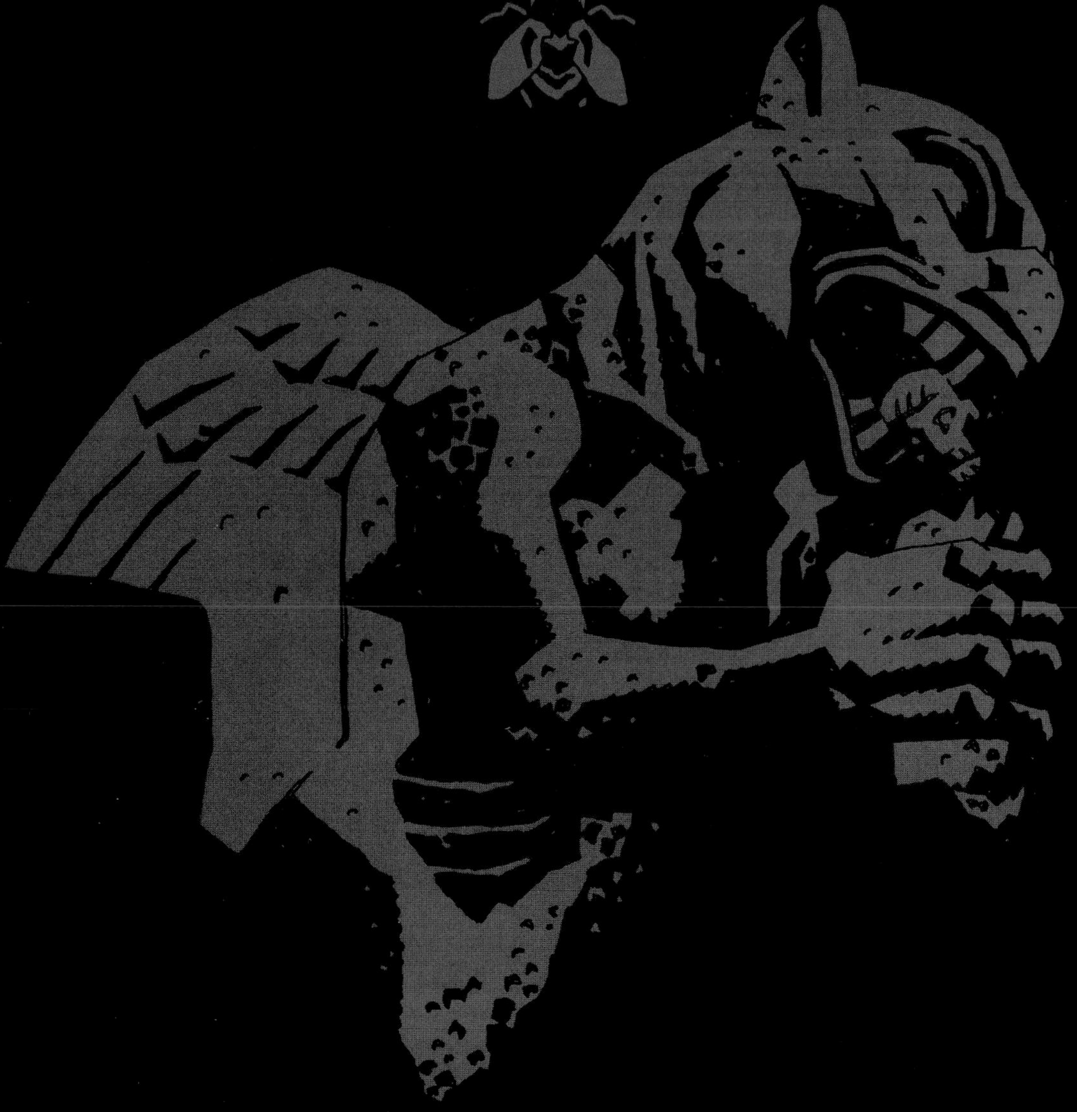

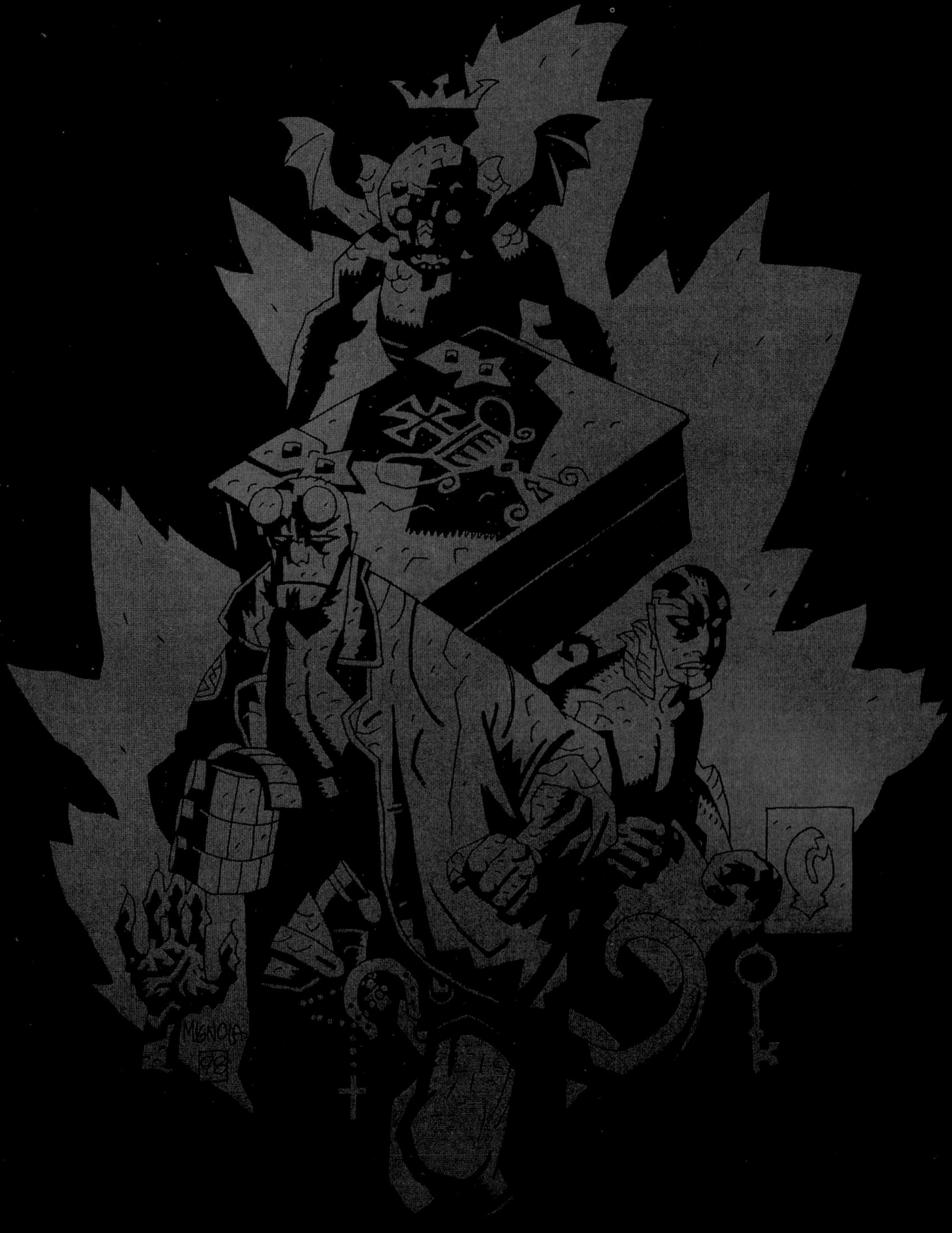
MIGNOLA
98

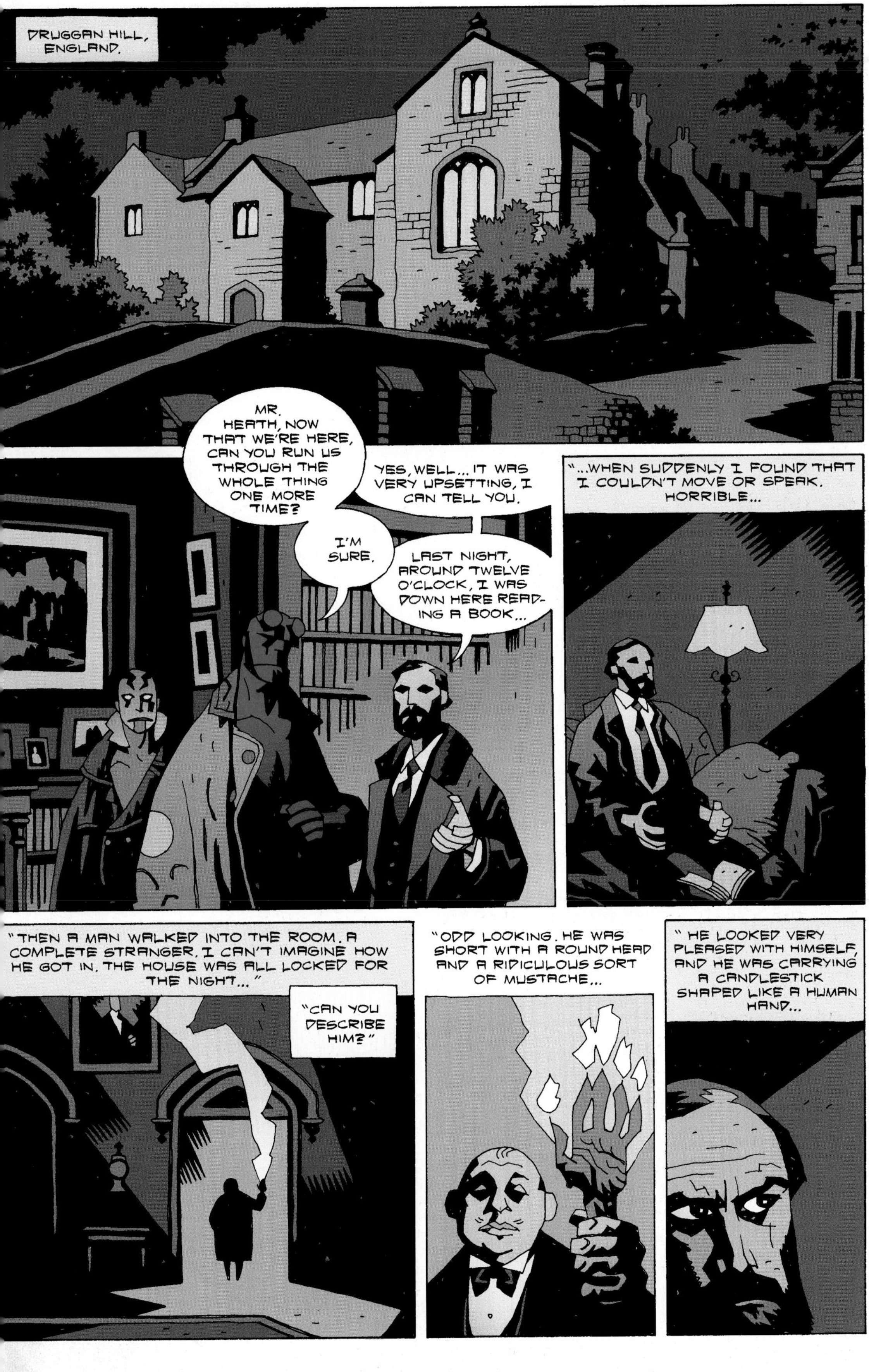
DRUGGAN HILL, ENGLAND.
MR. HEATH, NOW THAT WE'RE HERE, CAN YOU RUN US THROUGH THE WHOLE THING ONE MORE TIME?
YES, WELL... IT WAS VERY UPSETTING, I CAN TELL YOU.
I'M SURE.
LAST NIGHT, AROUND TWELVE O'CLOCK, I WAS DOWN HERE READ-ING A BOOK...
"...WHEN SUDDENLY I FOUND THAT I COULDN'T MOVE OR SPEAK. HORRIBLE...
"THEN A MAN WALKED INTO THE ROOM. A COMPLETE STRANGER. I CAN'T IMAGINE HOW HE GOT IN. THE HOUSE WAS ALL LOCKED FOR THE NIGHT..."
"CAN YOU DESCRIBE HIM?"
"ODD LOOKING. HE WAS SHORT WITH A ROUND HEAD AND A RIDICULOUS SORT OF MUSTACHE...
" HE LOOKED VERY PLEASED WITH HIMSELF, AND HE WAS CARRYING A CANDLESTICK SHAPED LIKE A HUMAN HAND...

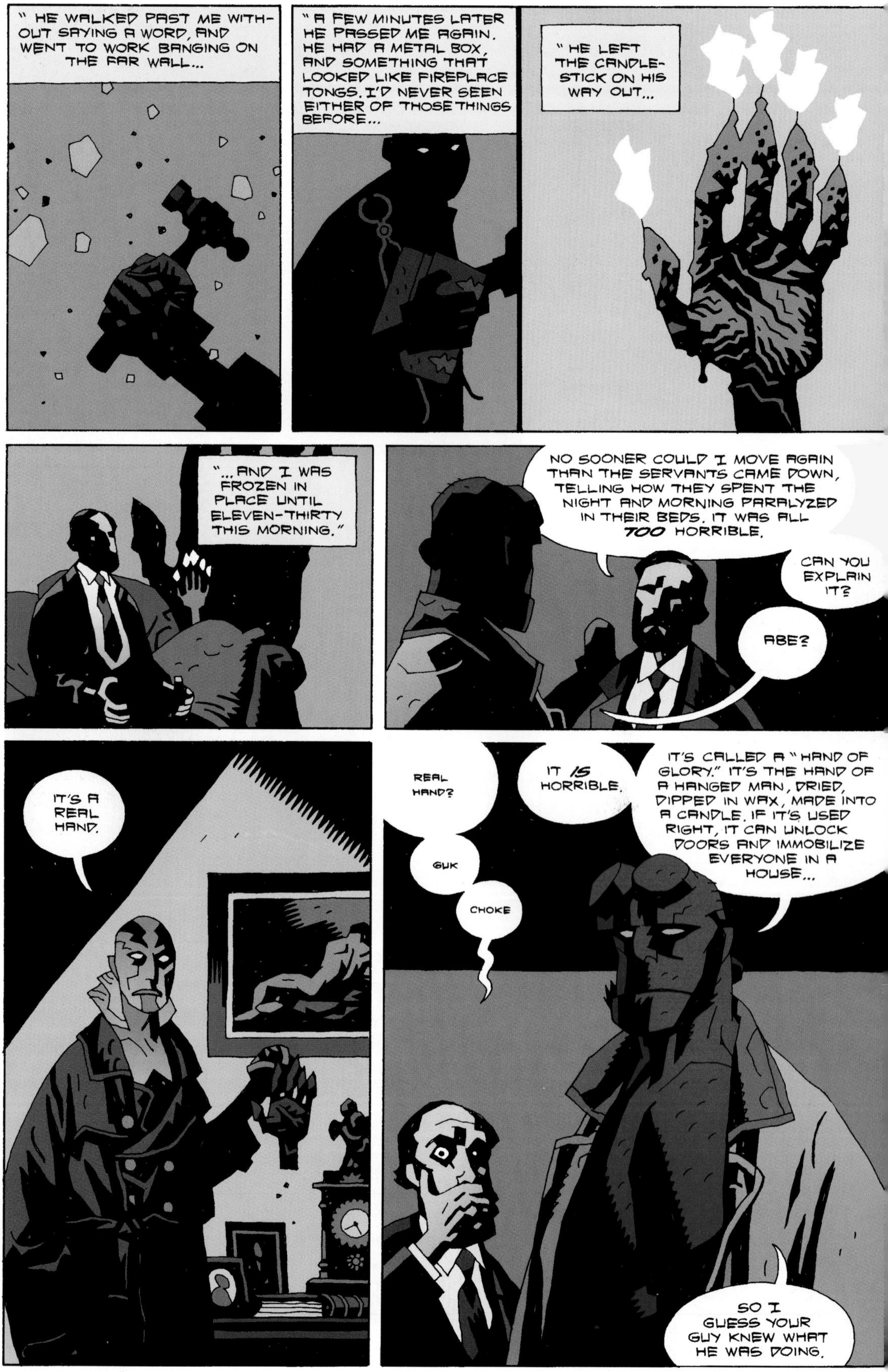
" HE WALKED PAST ME WITHOUT SAYING A WORD, AND WENT TO WORK BANGING ON THE FAR WALL...
" A FEW MINUTES LATER HE PASSED ME AGAIN. HE HAD A METAL BOX, AND SOMETHING THAT LOOKED LIKE FIREPLACE TONGS. I'D NEVER SEEN EITHER OF THOSE THINGS BEFORE...
" HE LEFT THE CANDLESTICK ON HIS WAY OUT...
"... AND I WAS FROZEN IN PLACE UNTIL ELEVEN-THIRTY THIS MORNING."
NO SOONER COULD I MOVE AGAIN THAN THE SERVANTS CAME DOWN, TELLING HOW THEY SPENT THE NIGHT AND MORNING PARALYZED IN THEIR BEDS. IT WAS ALL *TOO* HORRIBLE.
CAN YOU EXPLAIN IT?
ABE?
IT'S A REAL HAND.
REAL HAND?
GUK
CHOKE
IT *IS* HORRIBLE.
IT'S CALLED A "HAND OF GLORY." IT'S THE HAND OF A HANGED MAN, DRIED, DIPPED IN WAX, MADE INTO A CANDLE. IF IT'S USED RIGHT, IT CAN UNLOCK DOORS AND IMMOBILIZE EVERYONE IN A HOUSE...
SO I GUESS YOUR GUY KNEW WHAT HE WAS DOING.

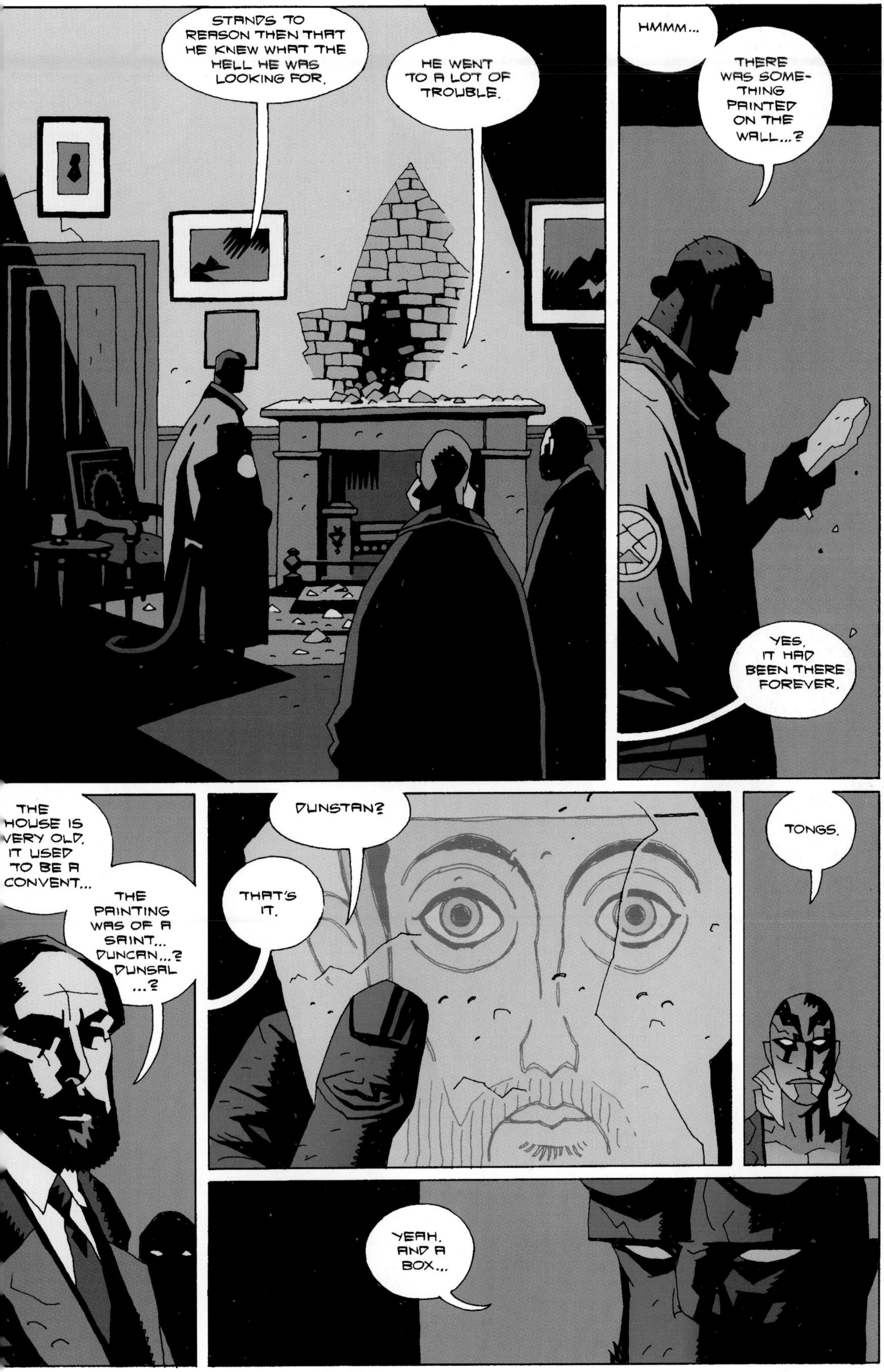

STANDS TO REASON THEN THAT HE KNEW WHAT THE HELL HE WAS LOOKING FOR.
HE WENT TO A LOT OF TROUBLE.
HMMM...
THERE WAS SOME-THING PAINTED ON THE WALL...?
YES, IT HAD BEEN THERE FOREVER.
THE HOUSE IS VERY OLD, IT USED TO BE A CONVENT...
THE PAINTING WAS OF A SAINT... DUNCAN...? DUNSAL ...?
DUNSTAN?
THAT'S IT.
TONGS.
YEAH. AND A BOX...

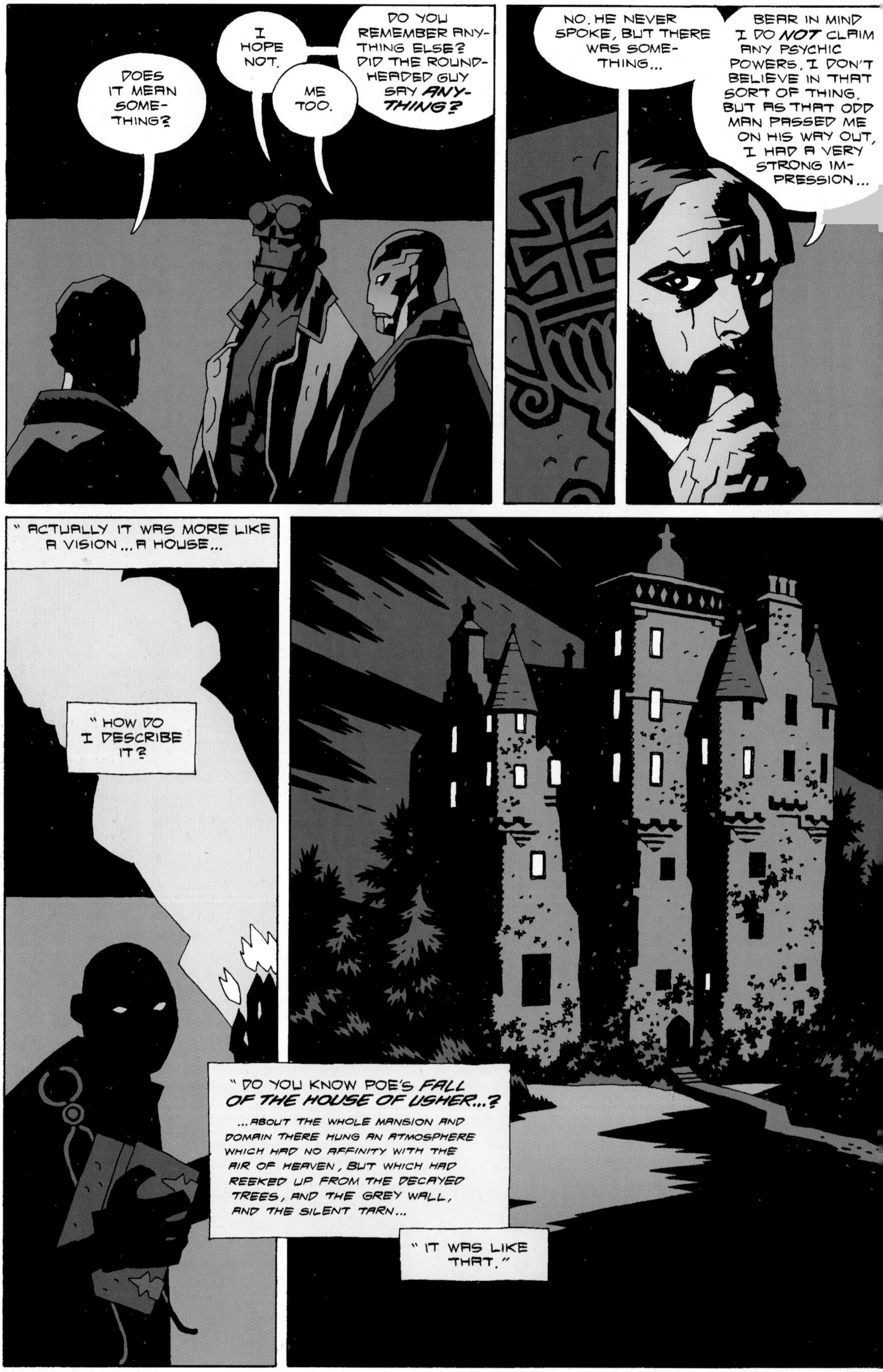
DOES IT MEAN SOME-THING?
I HOPE NOT.
ME TOO.
DO YOU REMEMBER ANY-THING ELSE? DID THE ROUND-HEADED GUY SAY *ANY-THING?*
NO. HE NEVER SPOKE, BUT THERE WAS SOME-THING...
BEAR IN MIND I DO *NOT* CLAIM ANY PSYCHIC POWERS. I DON'T BELIEVE IN THAT SORT OF THING. BUT AS THAT ODD MAN PASSED ME ON HIS WAY OUT, I HAD A VERY STRONG IM-PRESSION...
" ACTUALLY IT WAS MORE LIKE A VISION... A HOUSE...
" HOW DO I DESCRIBE IT?
" DO YOU KNOW POE'S *FALL OF THE HOUSE OF USHER...?*
...ABOUT THE WHOLE MANSION AND DOMAIN THERE HUNG AN ATMOSPHERE WHICH HAD NO AFFINITY WITH THE AIR OF HEAVEN, BUT WHICH HAD REEKED UP FROM THE DECAYED TREES, AND THE GREY WALL, AND THE SILENT TARN...
" IT WAS LIKE THAT."

ACCORDING TO THE LEGEND, DUNSTAN WORKED IN A BLACKSMITH'S SHOP IN MAYFIELD...

LOCKMABEN, SCOTLAND.

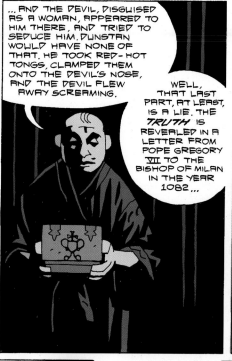

...AND THE DEVIL, DISGUISED AS A WOMAN, APPEARED TO HIM THERE, AND TRIED TO SEDUCE HIM. DUNSTAN WOULD HAVE NONE OF THAT. HE TOOK RED-HOT TONGS, CLAMPED THEM ONTO THE DEVIL'S NOSE, AND THE DEVIL FLEW AWAY SCREAMING.

WELL, THAT LAST PART, AT LEAST, IS A LIE. THE *TRUTH* IS REVEALED IN A LETTER FROM POPE GREGORY VII TO THE BISHOP OF MILAN IN THE YEAR 1082...

"...HOW DUNSTAN WOULD NOT LET THE DEVIL GO, BUT PUT HIS HEAD ON AN ANVIL AND STRUCK IT WITH A HAMMER, AND HOW HE PUT THE DEVIL IN A BOX AND LOCKED IT, AND PUT HOLY SEALS UPON IT, AND HID IT."

AND NOW HERE IS THAT BOX.

IT'S NOT VERY BIG...

MY HUSBAND AND I ARE VERY PLEASED, MR. BROMHEAD.

AND WE *ARE* AWARE THAT WE OWE YOU A FINAL PAYMENT.

BUT THE TRUTH IS WE HAVE NO MONEY LEFT TO GIVE YOU.

INSTEAD, WILL YOU ACCEPT THE DEED TO THIS HOUSE, AND ALL OUR WORLDLY GOODS?

GLADLY, COUNTESS.

FROM THIS DAY FORWARD MY HUSBAND AND I BELONG TO SATAN.

I'M SURE HE WILL TAKE GOOD CARE OF YOU.

WHAT ABOUT THE KEY?

A COMPLETELY SEPARATE ITEM FROM THE BOX. EXPENSIVE TO LOCATE AND "ACQUIRE"...

MY GIFT TO YOU BOTH.

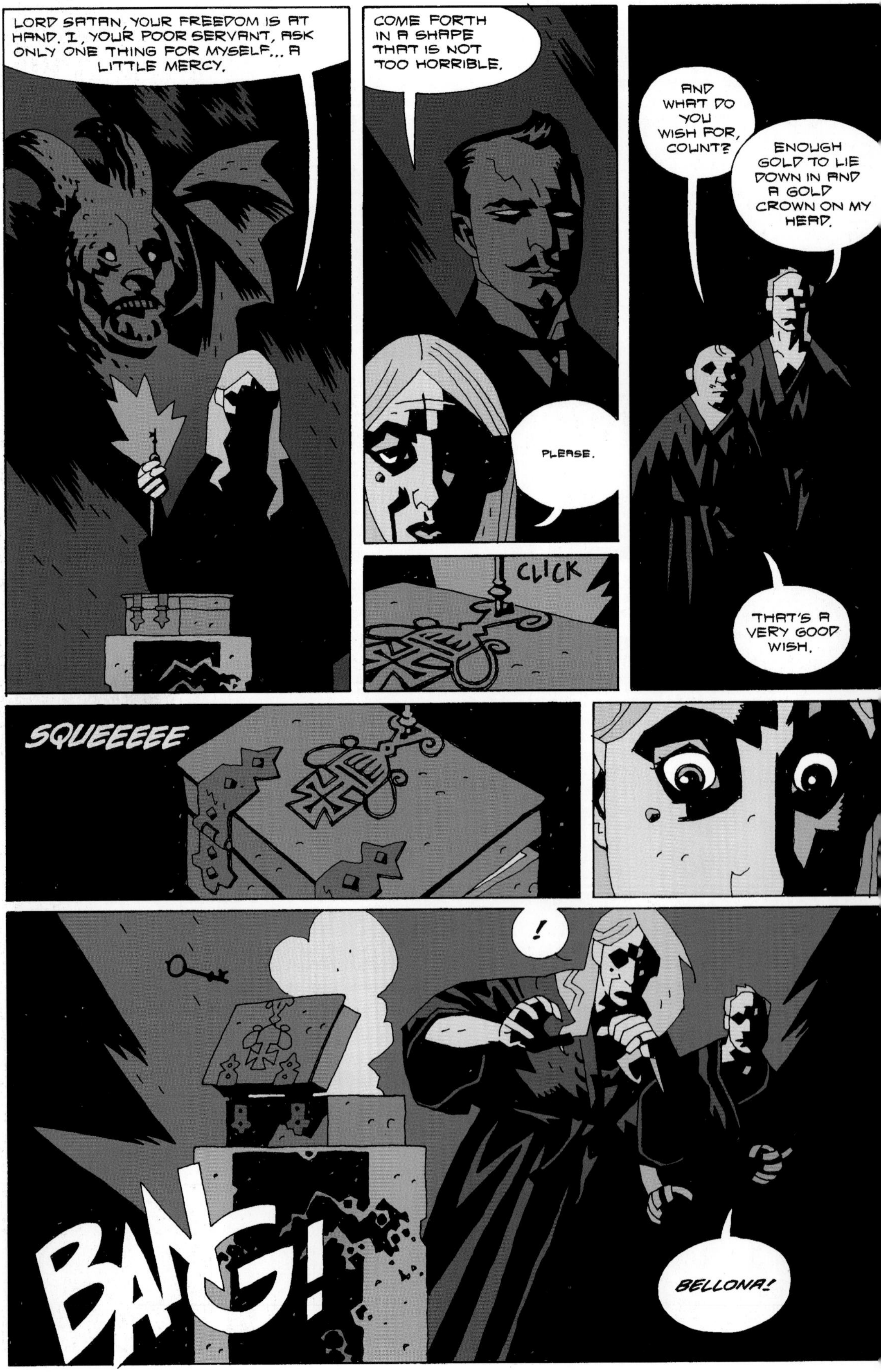
LORD SATAN, YOUR FREEDOM IS AT HAND. I, YOUR POOR SERVANT, ASK ONLY ONE THING FOR MYSELF... A LITTLE MERCY.
COME FORTH IN A SHAPE THAT IS NOT TOO HORRIBLE.
PLEASE.
AND WHAT DO YOU WISH FOR, COUNT?
ENOUGH GOLD TO LIE DOWN IN AND A GOLD CROWN ON MY HEAD.
THAT'S A VERY GOOD WISH.
CLICK
SQUEEEEEE
!
BANG!
BELLONA!

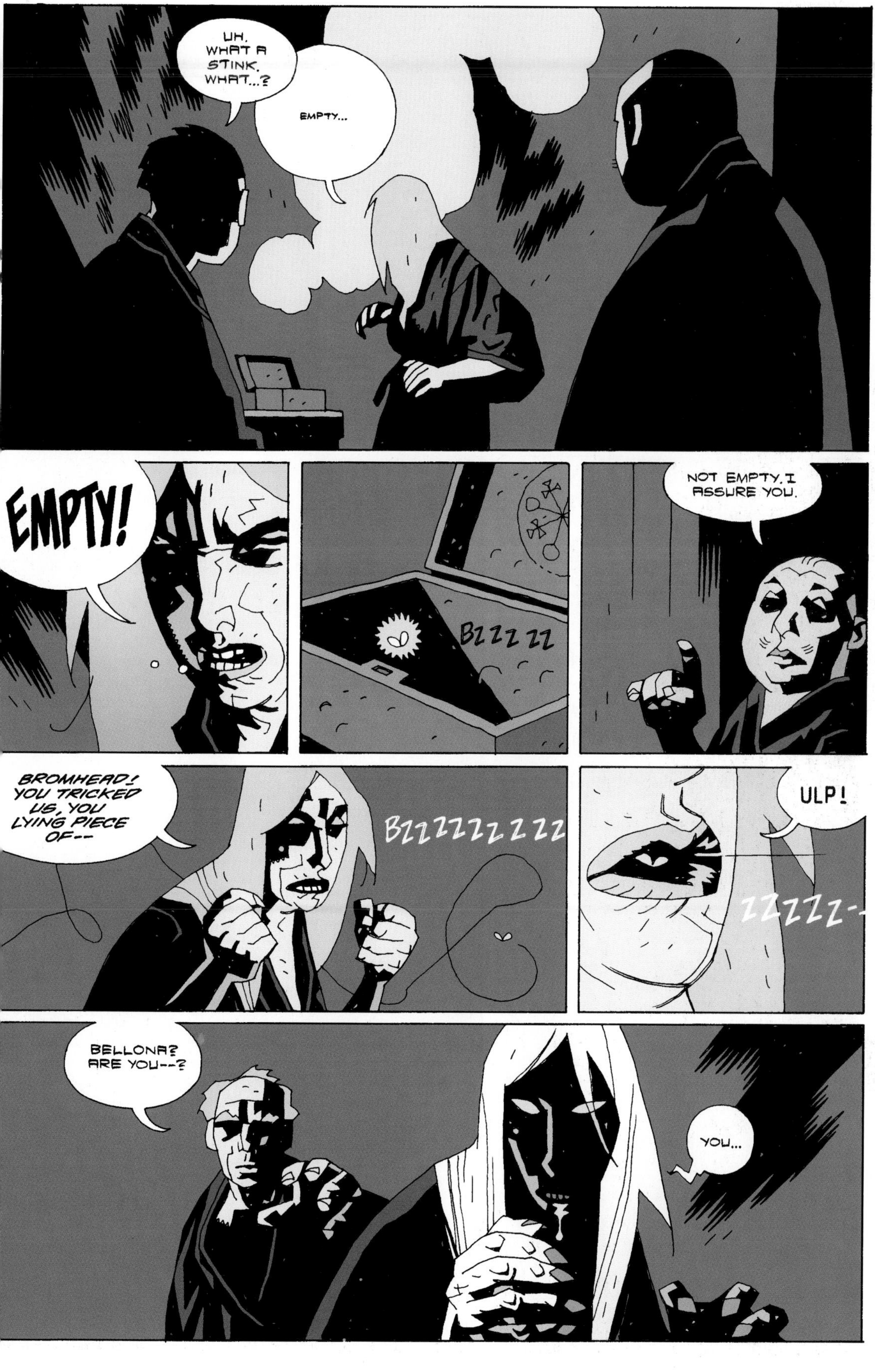

UH. WHAT A STINK. WHAT...?
EMPTY...
EMPTY!
BZZZZZ
NOT EMPTY, I ASSURE YOU.
BROMHEAD! YOU TRICKED US, YOU LYING PIECE OF--
BZZZZZZZZZ
ULP!
ZZZZZ--
BELLONA? ARE YOU--?
YOU...

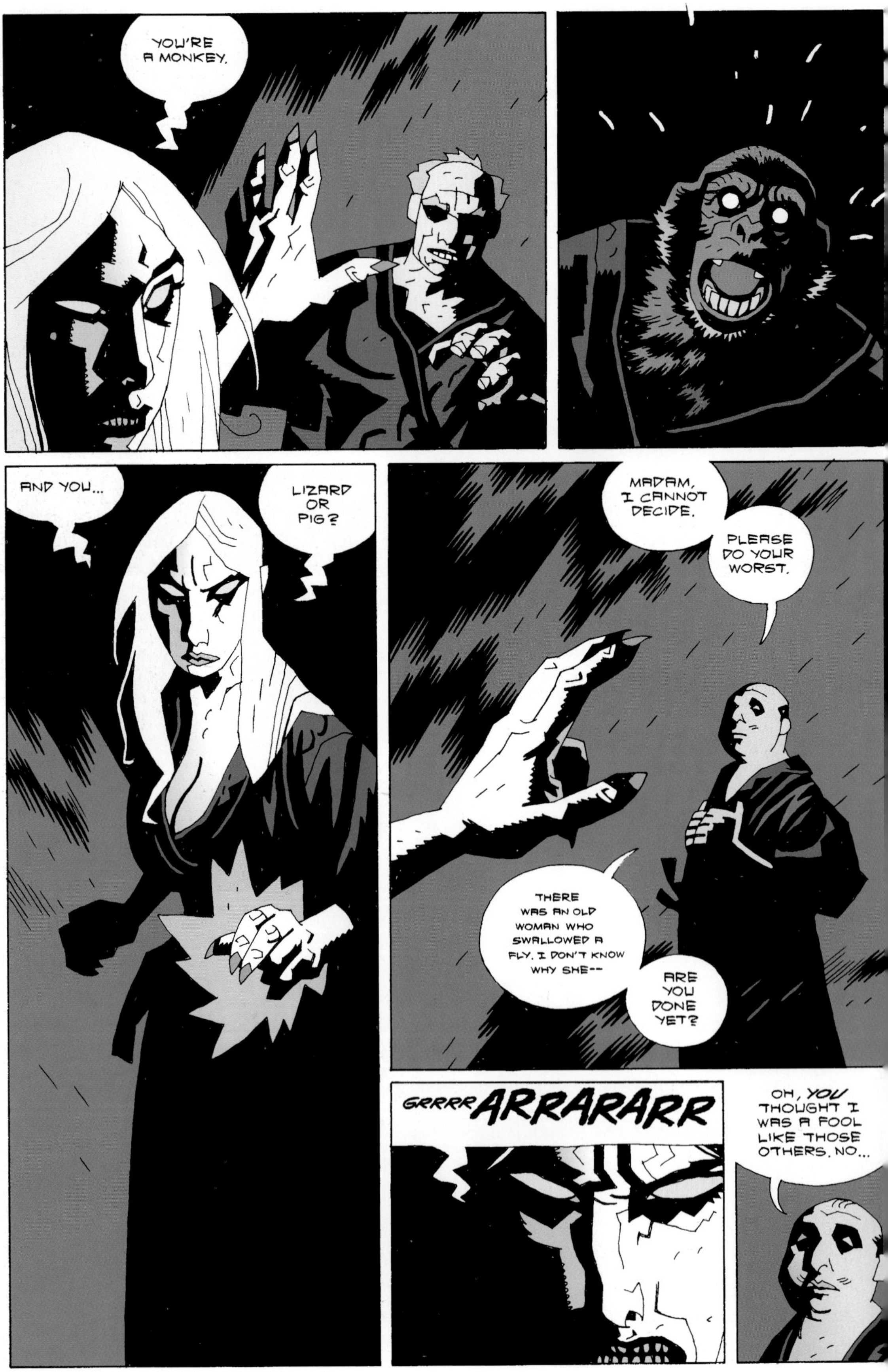
YOU'RE A MONKEY.
AND YOU...
LIZARD OR PIG?
MADAM, I CANNOT DECIDE.
PLEASE DO YOUR WORST.
THERE WAS AN OLD WOMAN WHO SWALLOWED A FLY. I DON'T KNOW WHY SHE--
ARE YOU DONE YET?
GRRRR ARRARARR
OH, YOU THOUGHT I WAS A FOOL LIKE THOSE OTHERS. NO...

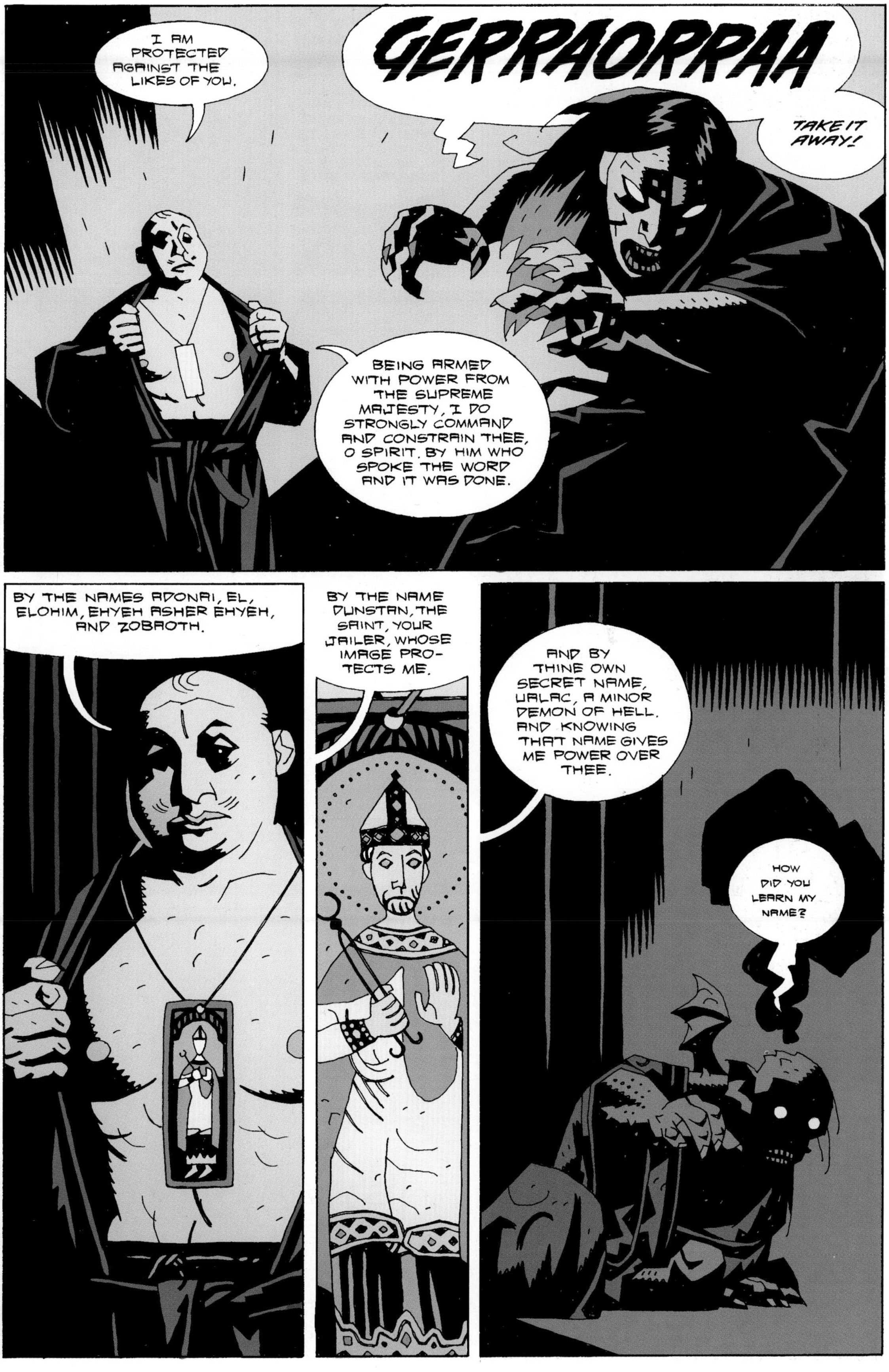
I AM PROTECTED AGAINST THE LIKES OF YOU.
GERRAORRAA
TAKE IT AWAY!
BEING ARMED WITH POWER FROM THE SUPREME MAJESTY, I DO STRONGLY COMMAND AND CONSTRAIN THEE, O SPIRIT. BY HIM WHO SPOKE THE WORD AND IT WAS DONE.
BY THE NAMES ADONAI, EL, ELOHIM, EHYEH ASHER EHYEH, AND ZOBAOTH.
BY THE NAME DUNSTAN, THE SAINT, YOUR JAILER, WHOSE IMAGE PROTECTS ME.
AND BY THINE OWN SECRET NAME, UALAC, A MINOR DEMON OF HELL. AND KNOWING THAT NAME GIVES ME POWER OVER THEE.
HOW DID YOU LEARN MY NAME?

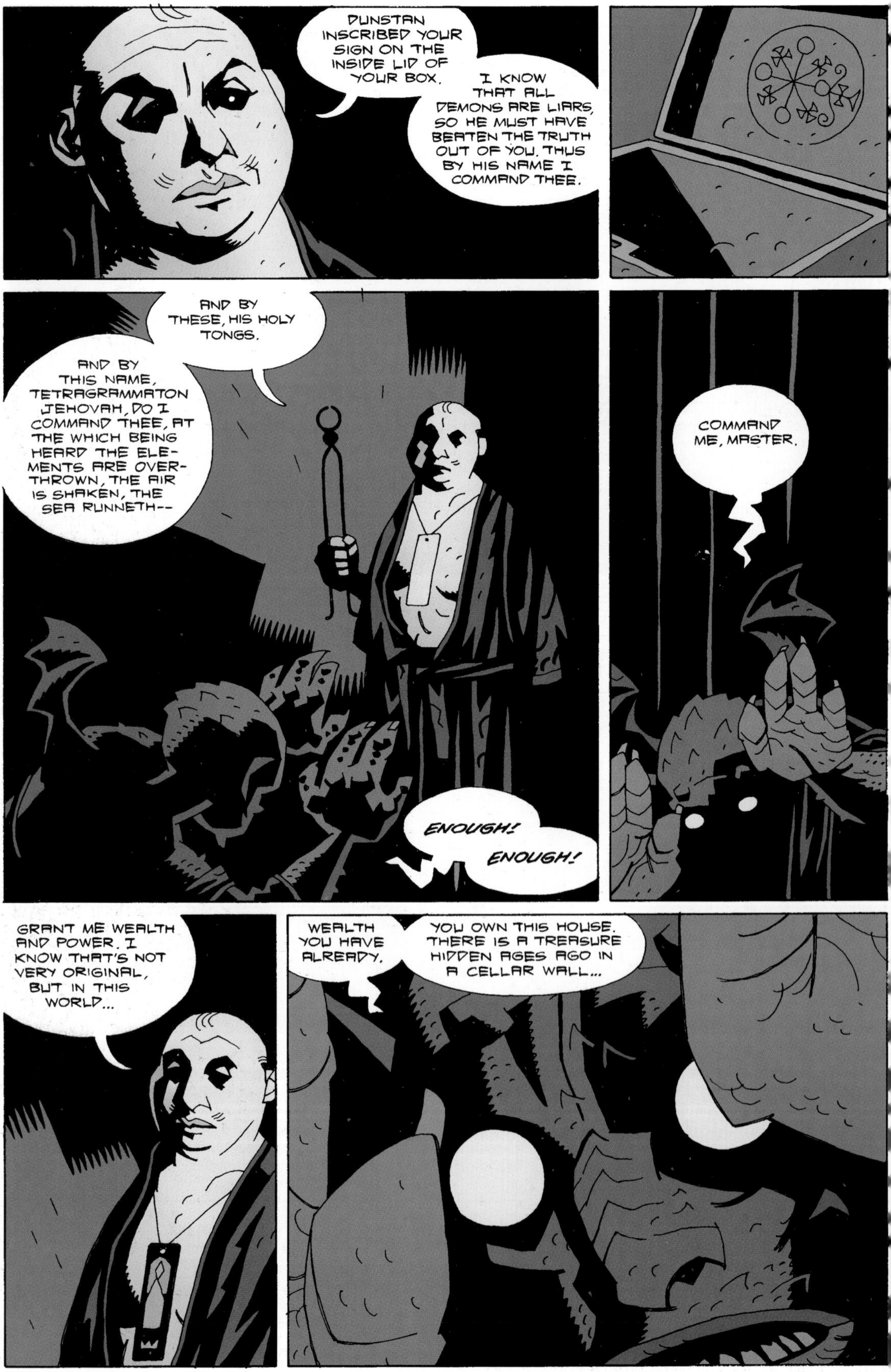
DUNSTAN INSCRIBED YOUR SIGN ON THE INSIDE LID OF YOUR BOX.
I KNOW THAT ALL DEMONS ARE LIARS, SO HE MUST HAVE BEATEN THE TRUTH OUT OF YOU. THUS BY HIS NAME I COMMAND THEE.
AND BY THESE, HIS HOLY TONGS.
AND BY THIS NAME, TETRAGRAMMATON JEHOVAH, DO I COMMAND THEE, AT THE WHICH BEING HEARD THE ELE-MENTS ARE OVER-THROWN, THE AIR IS SHAKEN, THE SEA RUNNETH--
ENOUGH! ENOUGH!
COMMAND ME, MASTER.
GRANT ME WEALTH AND POWER. I KNOW THAT'S NOT VERY ORIGINAL, BUT IN THIS WORLD...
WEALTH YOU HAVE ALREADY.
YOU OWN THIS HOUSE. THERE IS A TREASURE HIDDEN AGES AGO IN A CELLAR WALL...

THERE IS WEALTH ENOUGH THERE TO *BUY* EARTHLY POWER IF THAT IS WHAT YOU DESIRE.

BUT I CAN GRANT YOU *GREATER* POWER THAN THAT.

TELL ME.

THE GREAT BEAST, HARBINGER OF APOCALYPSE, IS ALIVE NOW IN THE WORLD.

HE HAS DENIED HIS FATE, BUT HE HAS NEVER GIVEN UP HIS CROWN. IT IS INVISIBLE TO HIM, AND TO ALL MEN, BUT HE WEARS IT...

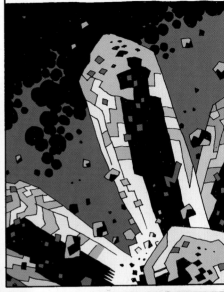

"...AND HIS IS THE POWER TO LOOSE AND CONTROL THE GREATER FURIES OF DESTRUCTIVE NATURE. EVEN THE REGENTS OF HELL MUST BOW BEFORE THAT..."

EVEN IN MY PRISON I HAVE HEARD THEM WHISPER HIS SECRET NAME...

ANUNG UN RAMA.

HIS SECRET NAME...

CAN YOU BRING HIM HERE?

MASTER...

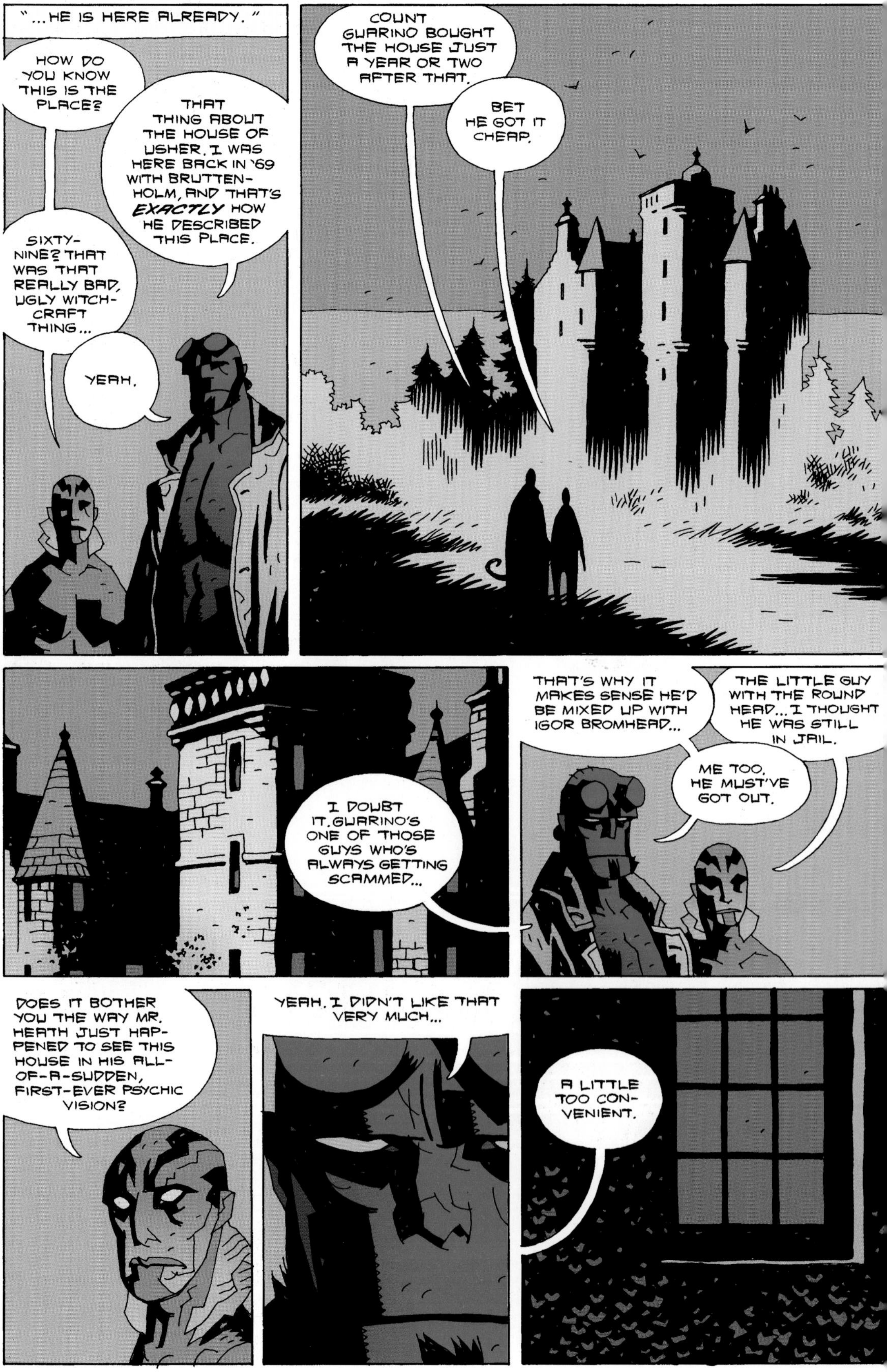
"...HE IS HERE ALREADY."
HOW DO YOU KNOW THIS IS THE PLACE?
THAT THING ABOUT THE HOUSE OF USHER. I WAS HERE BACK IN '69 WITH BRUTTENHOLM, AND THAT'S EXACTLY HOW HE DESCRIBED THIS PLACE.
SIXTY-NINE? THAT WAS THAT REALLY BAD, UGLY WITCHCRAFT THING...
YEAH.
COUNT GUARINO BOUGHT THE HOUSE JUST A YEAR OR TWO AFTER THAT.
BET HE GOT IT CHEAP.
I DOUBT IT. GUARINO'S ONE OF THOSE GUYS WHO'S ALWAYS GETTING SCAMMED...
THAT'S WHY IT MAKES SENSE HE'D BE MIXED UP WITH IGOR BROMHEAD...
THE LITTLE GUY WITH THE ROUND HEAD... I THOUGHT HE WAS STILL IN JAIL.
ME TOO. HE MUST'VE GOT OUT.
DOES IT BOTHER YOU THE WAY MR. HEATH JUST HAPPENED TO SEE THIS HOUSE IN HIS ALL-OF-A-SUDDEN, FIRST-EVER PSYCHIC VISION?
YEAH. I DIDN'T LIKE THAT VERY MUCH...
A LITTLE TOO CONVENIENT.

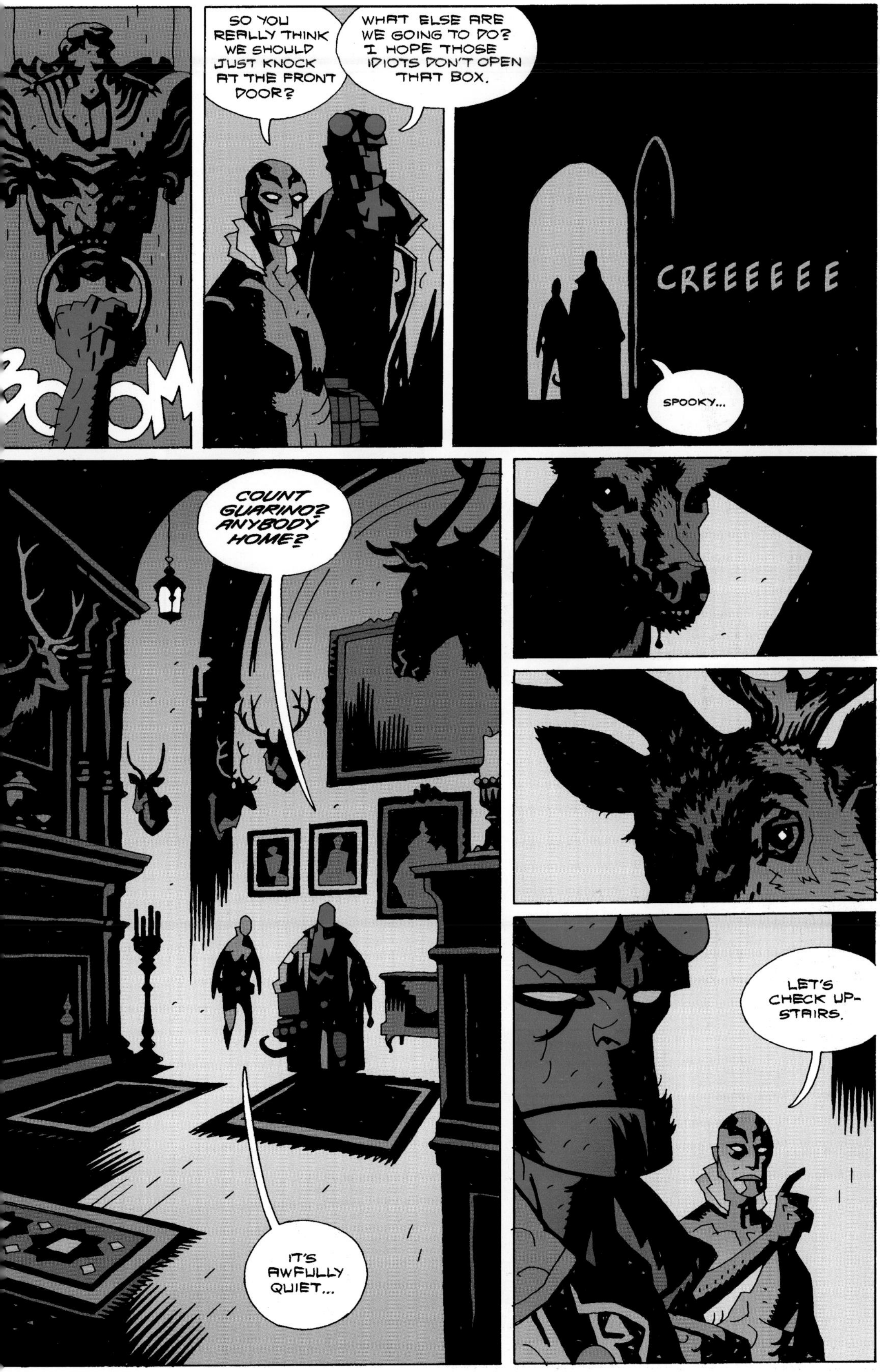
BOOM
SO YOU REALLY THINK WE SHOULD JUST KNOCK AT THE FRONT DOOR?
WHAT ELSE ARE WE GOING TO DO? I HOPE THOSE IDIOTS DON'T OPEN THAT BOX.
CREEEEEEE
SPOOKY...
COUNT GUARINO? ANYBODY HOME?
IT'S AWFULLY QUIET...
LET'S CHECK UP-STAIRS.

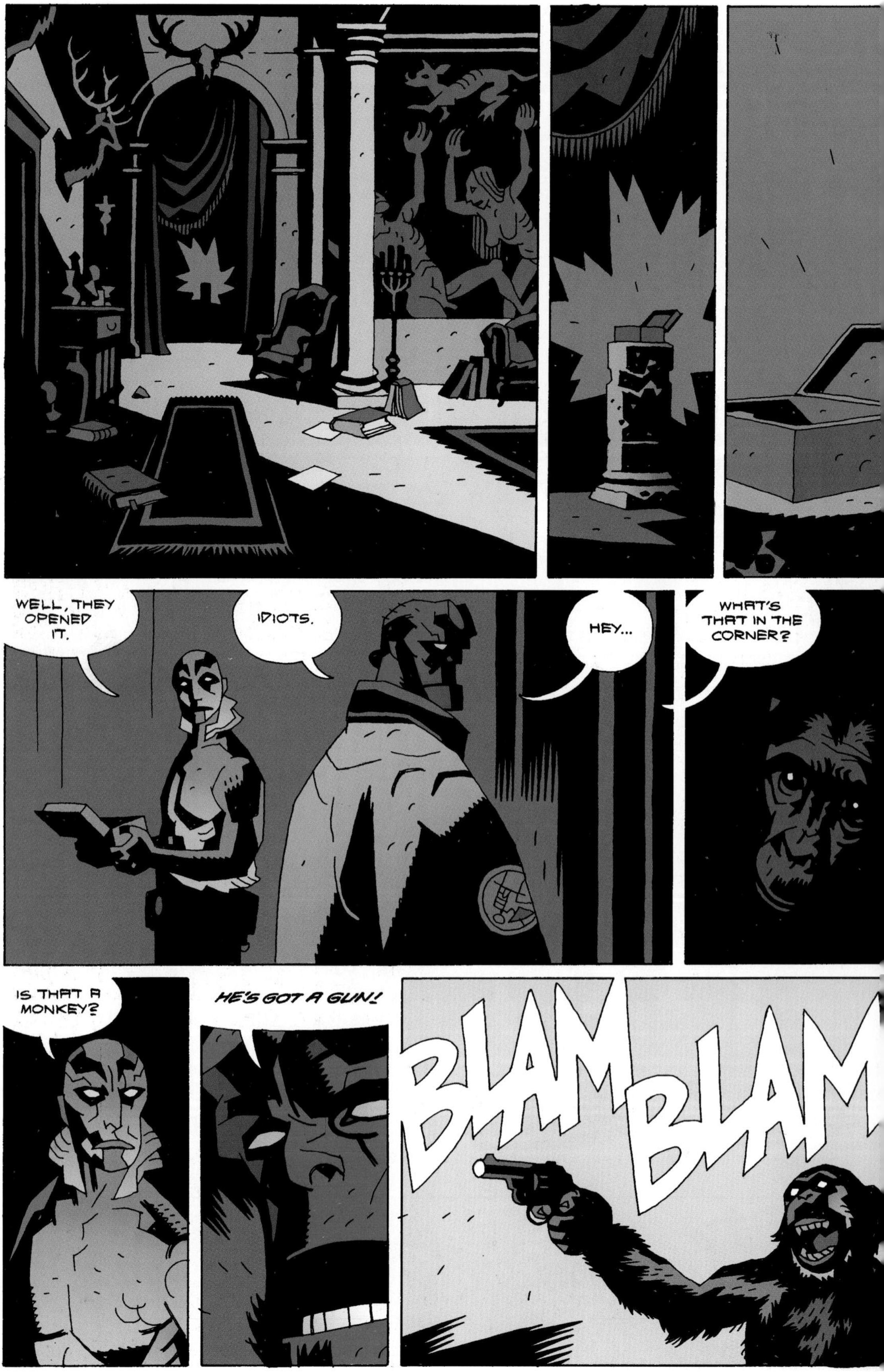
WELL, THEY OPENED IT.
IDIOTS.
HEY...
WHAT'S THAT IN THE CORNER?
IS THAT A MONKEY?
HE'S GOT A GUN!
BLAM
BLAM
BLAM
BLAM

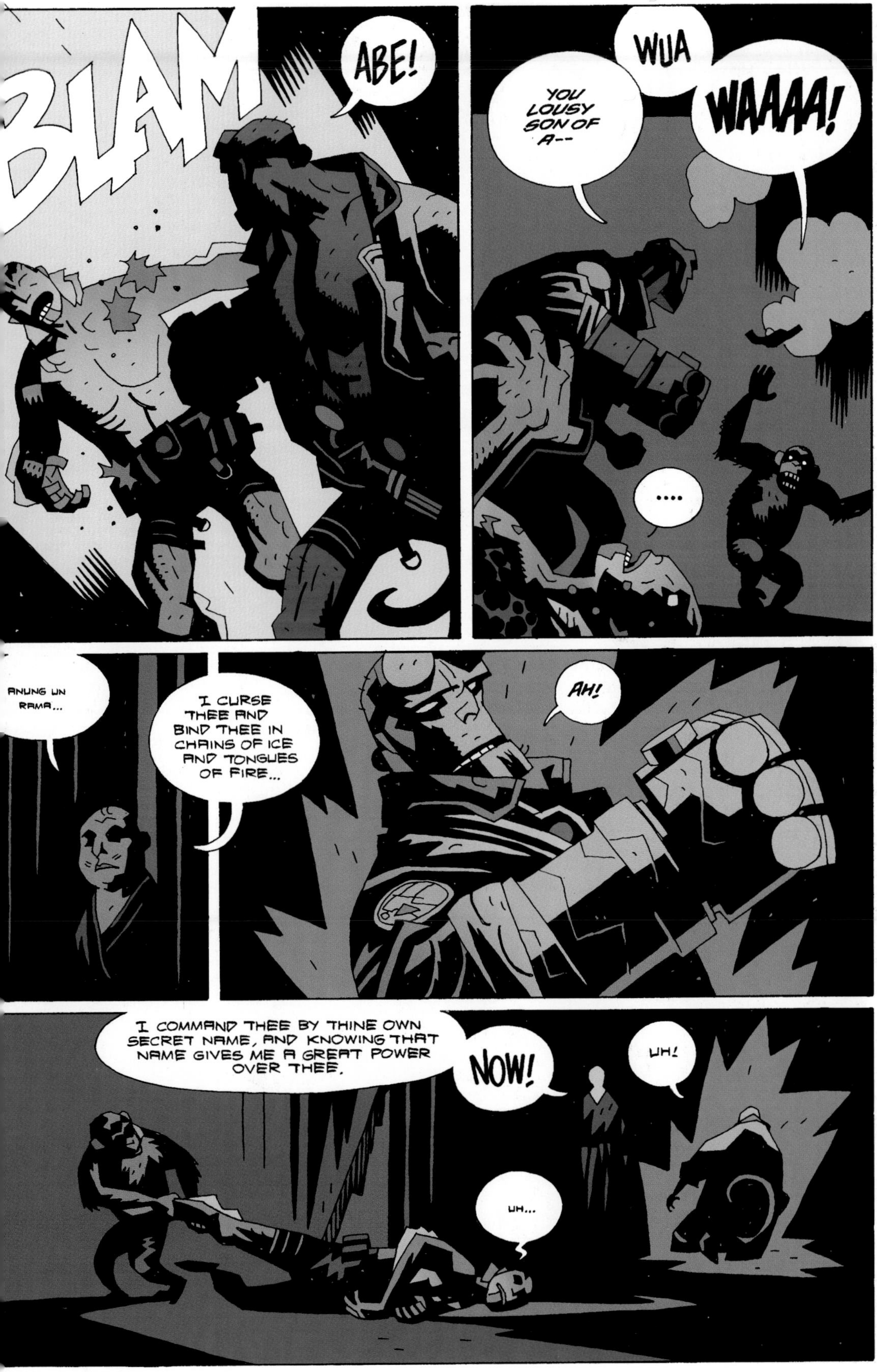
BLAM
ABE!
YOU LOUSY SON OF A--
WUA
WAAAA!
....
ANUNG UN RAMA...
I CURSE THEE AND BIND THEE IN CHAINS OF ICE AND TONGUES OF FIRE...
AH!
I COMMAND THEE BY THINE OWN SECRET NAME, AND KNOWING THAT NAME GIVES ME A GREAT POWER OVER THEE.
NOW!
UH!
UH...

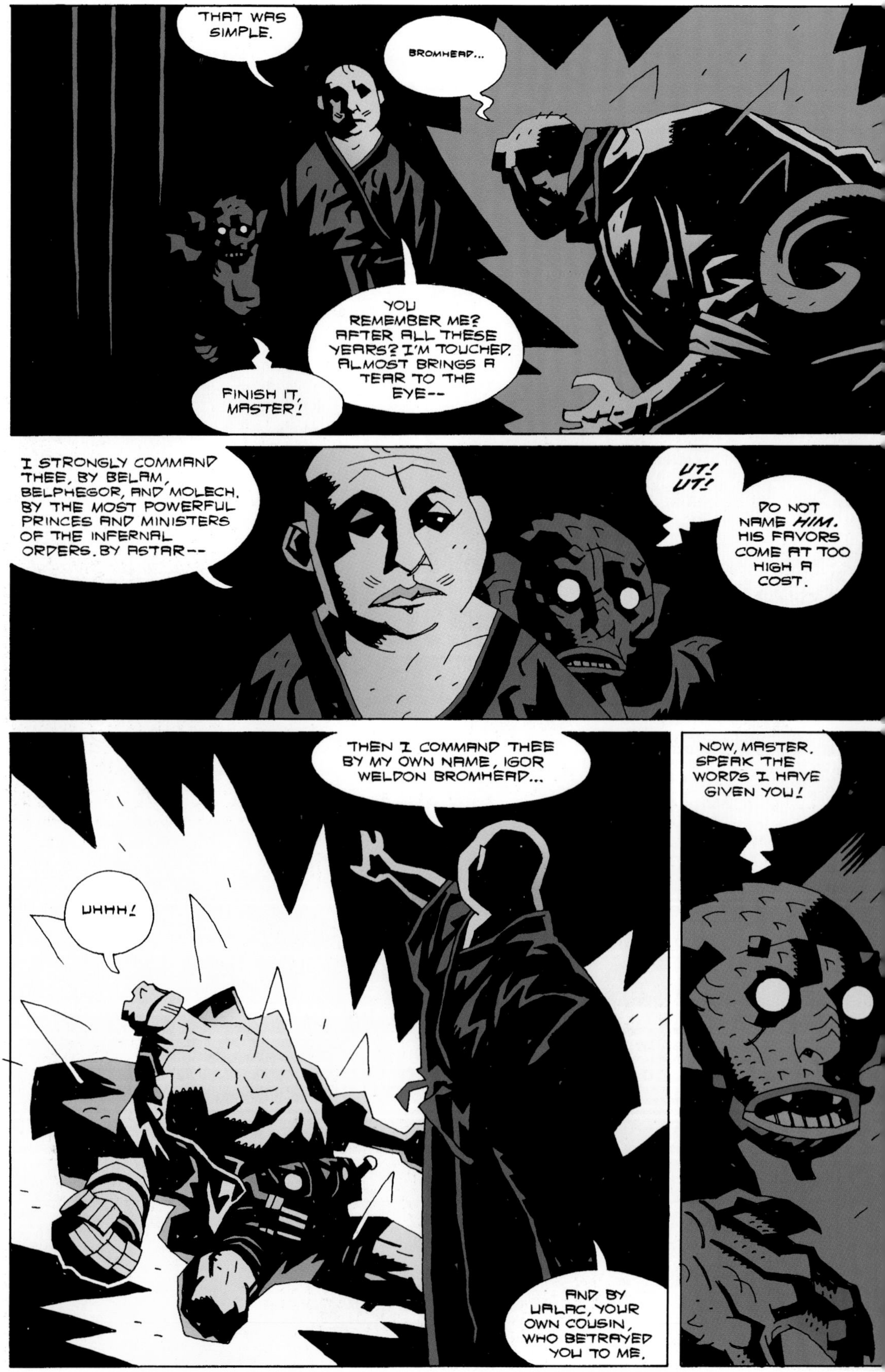
THAT WAS SIMPLE.
BROMHEAD...
YOU REMEMBER ME? AFTER ALL THESE YEARS? I'M TOUCHED. ALMOST BRINGS A TEAR TO THE EYE--
FINISH IT, MASTER!
I STRONGLY COMMAND THEE, BY BELAM, BELPHEGOR, AND MOLECH. BY THE MOST POWERFUL PRINCES AND MINISTERS OF THE INFERNAL ORDERS. BY ASTAR--
UT! UT!
DO NOT NAME HIM. HIS FAVORS COME AT TOO HIGH A COST.
THEN I COMMAND THEE BY MY OWN NAME, IGOR WELDON BROMHEAD...
UHHH!
AND BY VALAC, YOUR OWN COUSIN, WHO BETRAYED YOU TO ME.
NOW, MASTER, SPEAK THE WORDS I HAVE GIVEN YOU!

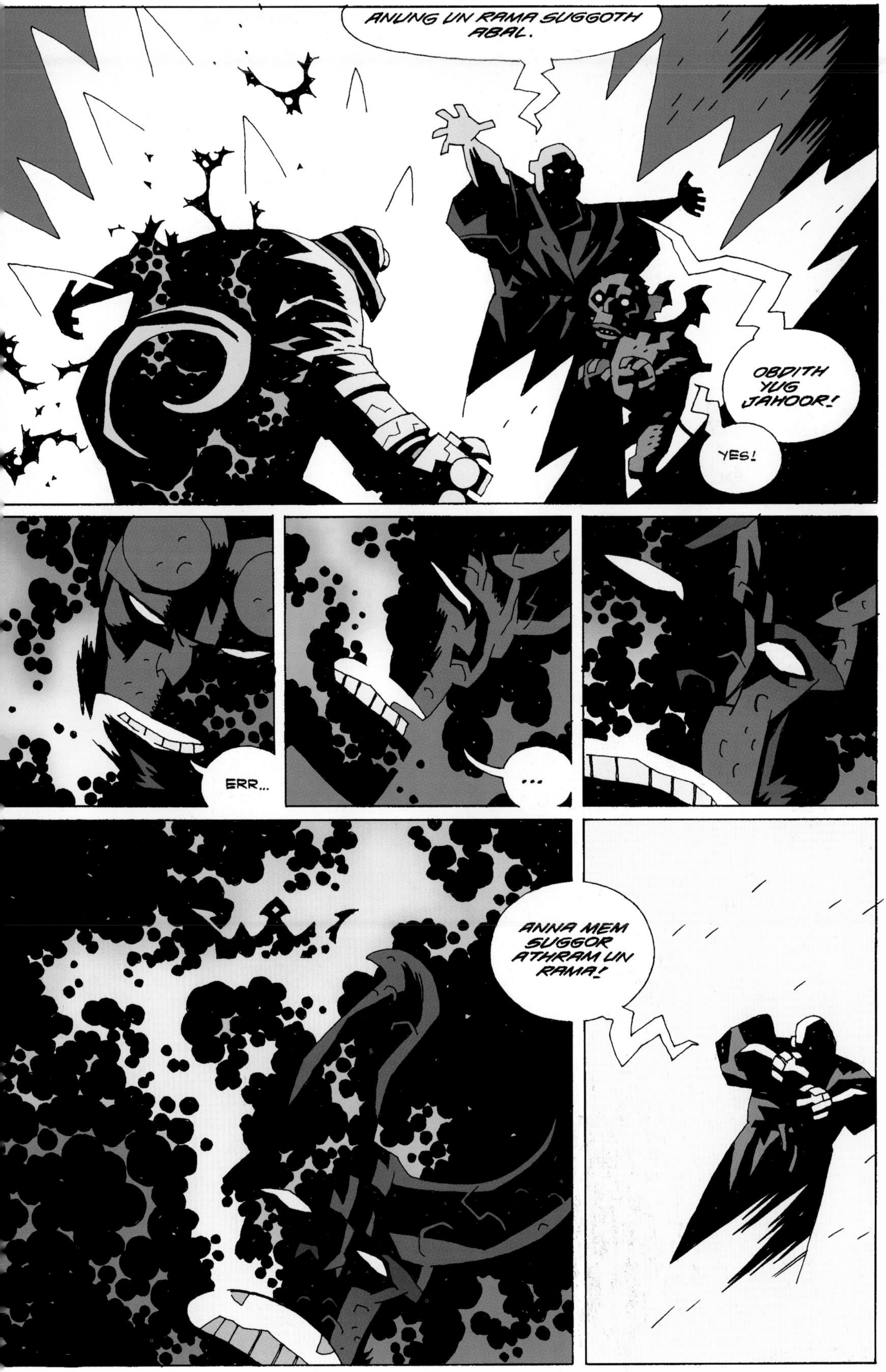
ANUNG UN RAMA SUGGOTH ABAL.
OBDITH YUG JAHOOR!
YES!
ERR...
...
ANNA MEM SUGGOR ATHRAM UN RAMA!

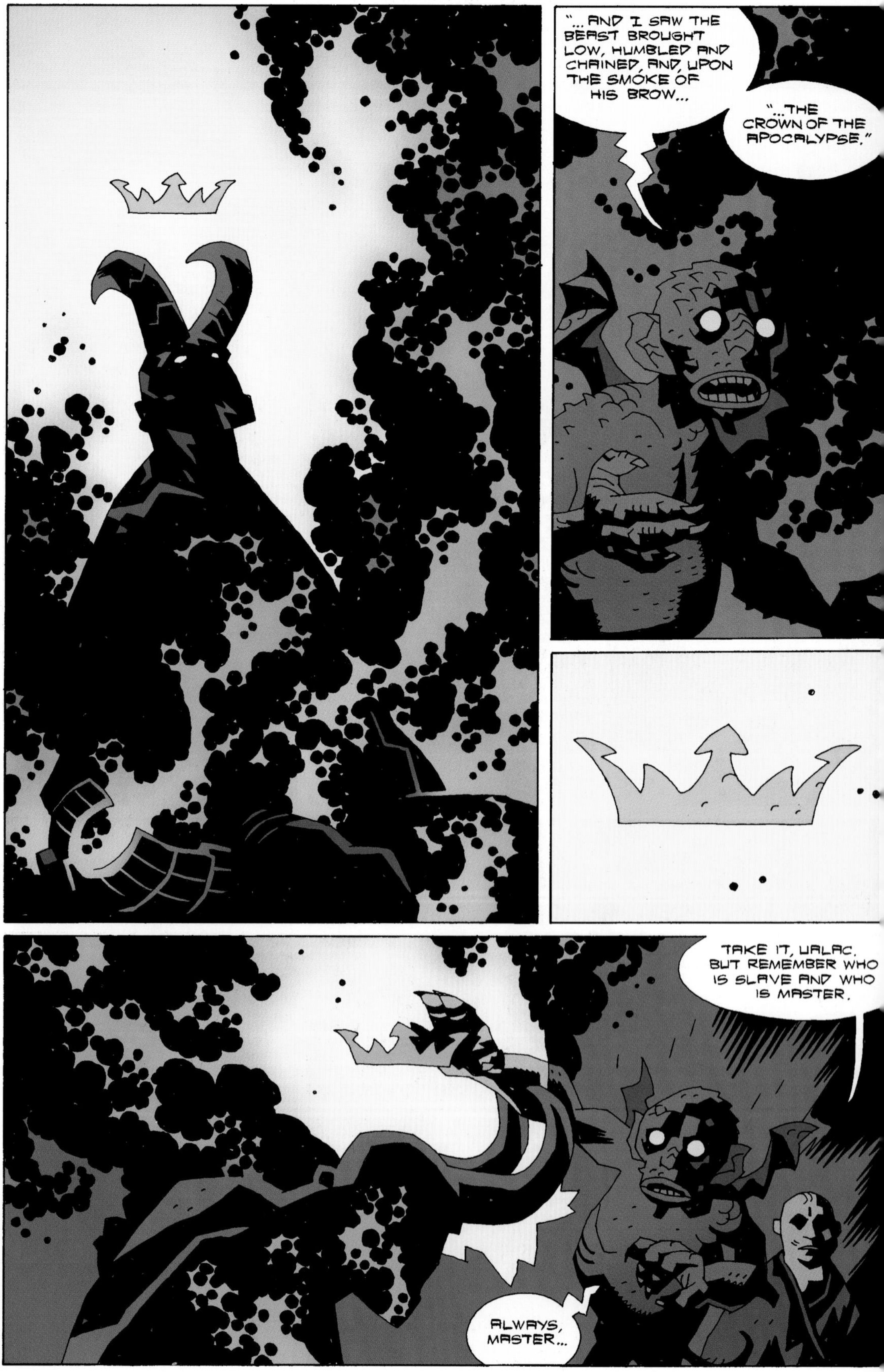
"...AND I SAW THE BEAST BROUGHT LOW, HUMBLED AND CHAINED, AND, UPON THE SMOKE OF HIS BROW...
"...THE CROWN OF THE APOCALYPSE."
TAKE IT, URLAC, BUT REMEMBER WHO IS SLAVE AND WHO IS MASTER.
ALWAYS, MASTER...

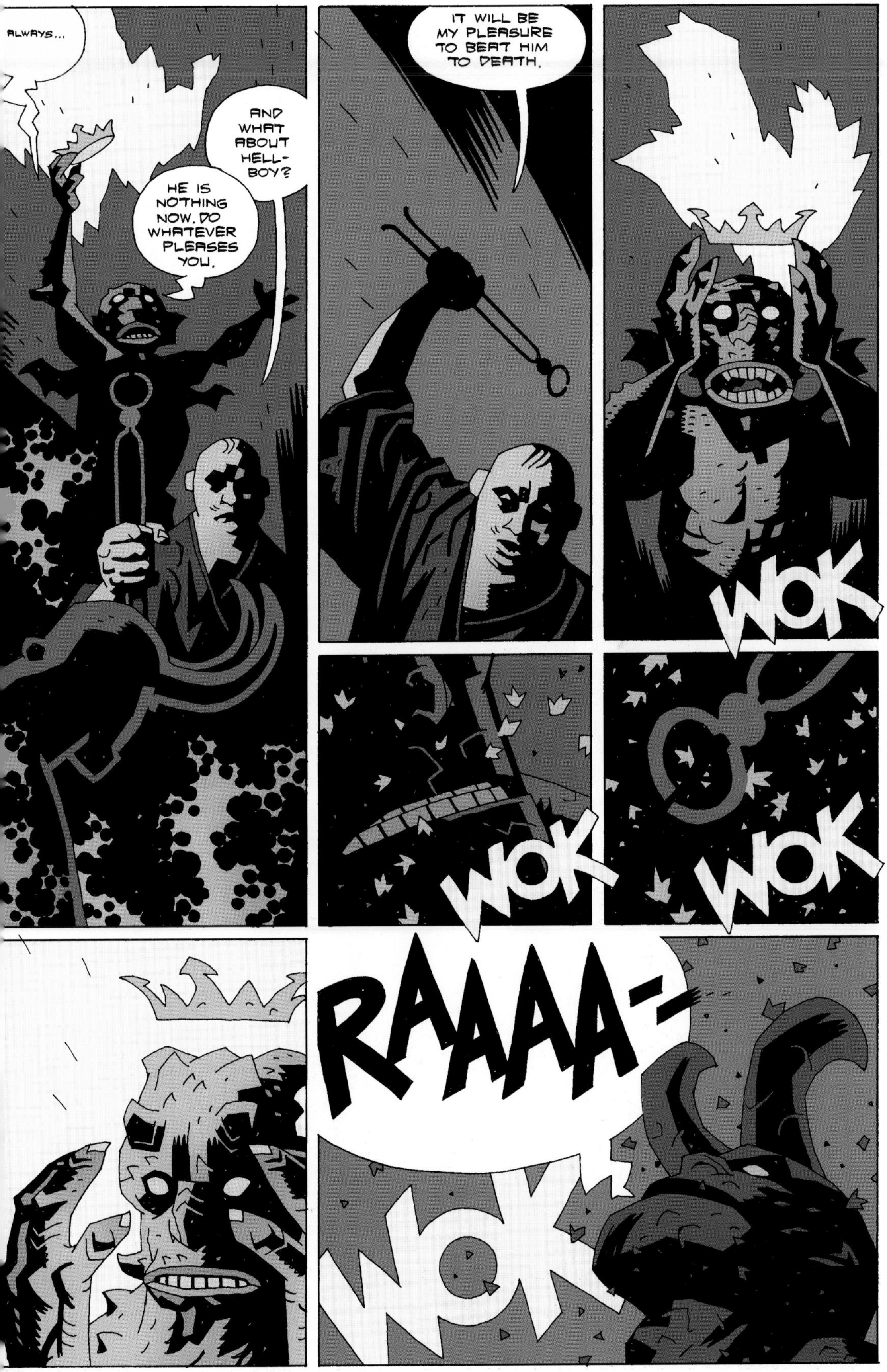
ALWAYS...
AND WHAT ABOUT HELL-BOY?
HE IS NOTHING NOW. DO WHATEVER PLEASES YOU.
IT WILL BE MY PLEASURE TO BEAT HIM TO DEATH.
WOK
WOK
WOK
RAAAA-
WOK

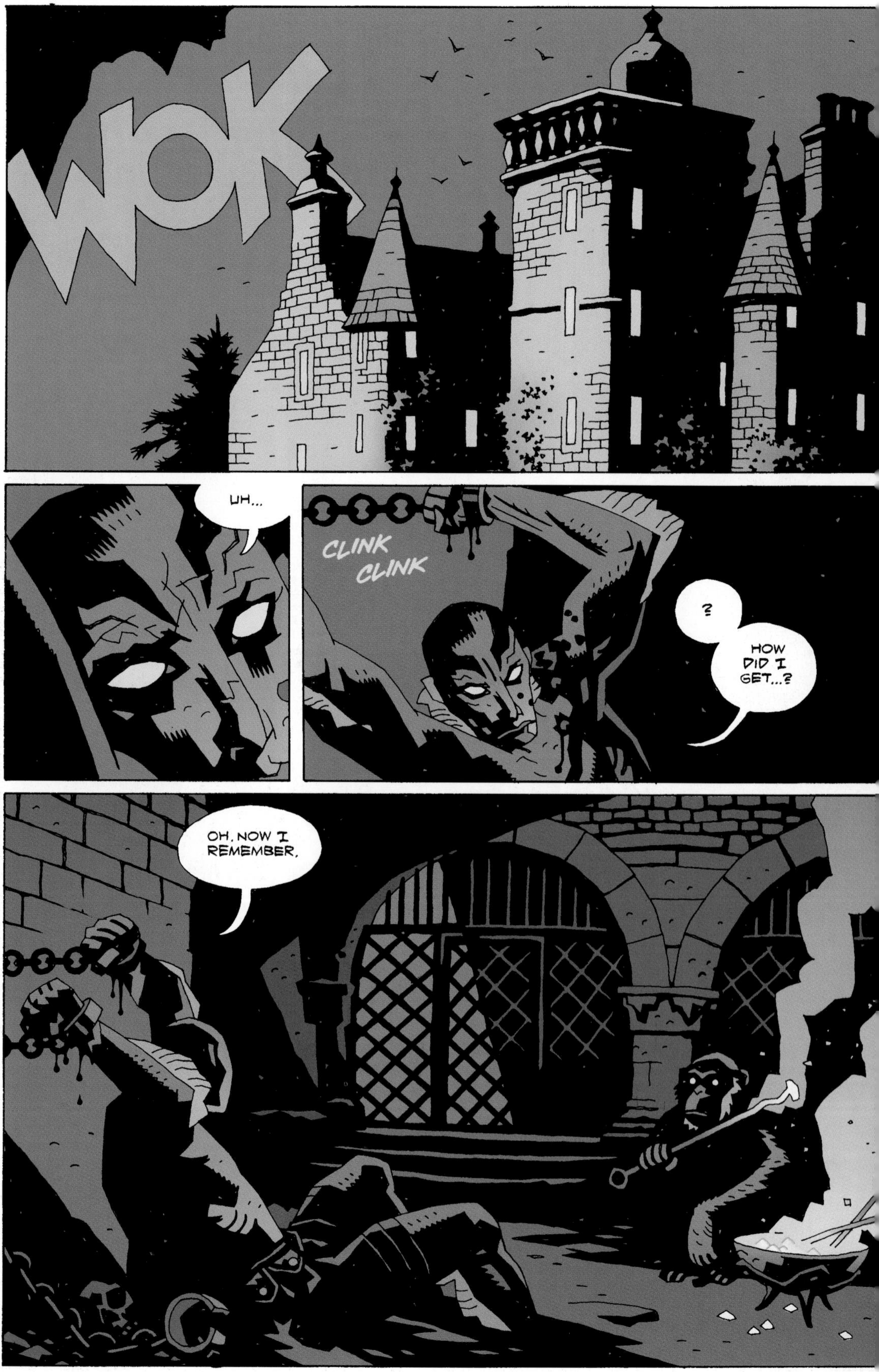
WOK
UH...
CLINK
CLINK
?
HOW DID I GET...?
OH, NOW I REMEMBER.

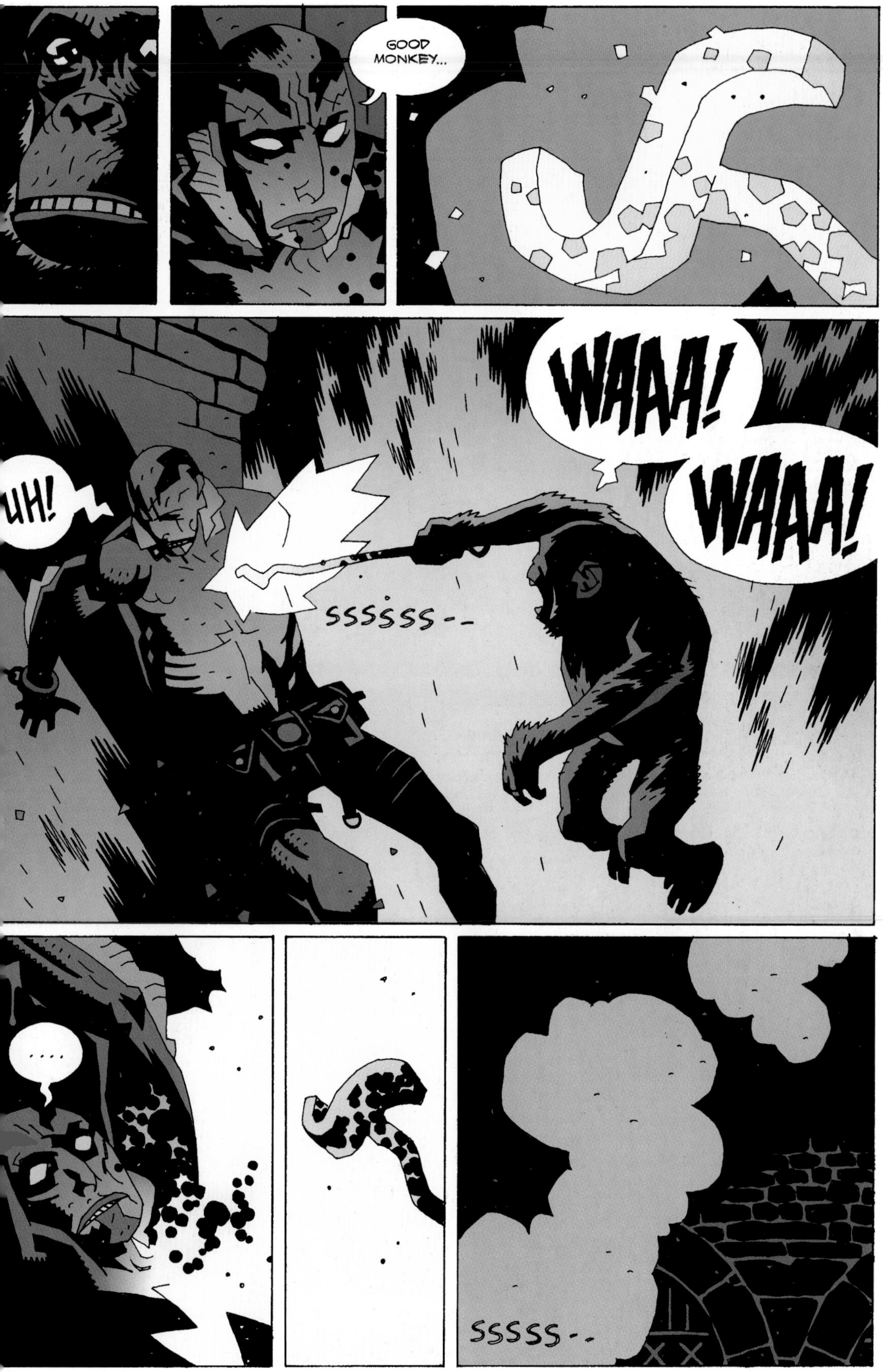
GOOD MONKEY...
WAAA!
WAAA!
UH!
SSSSSS--
....
SSSSS--

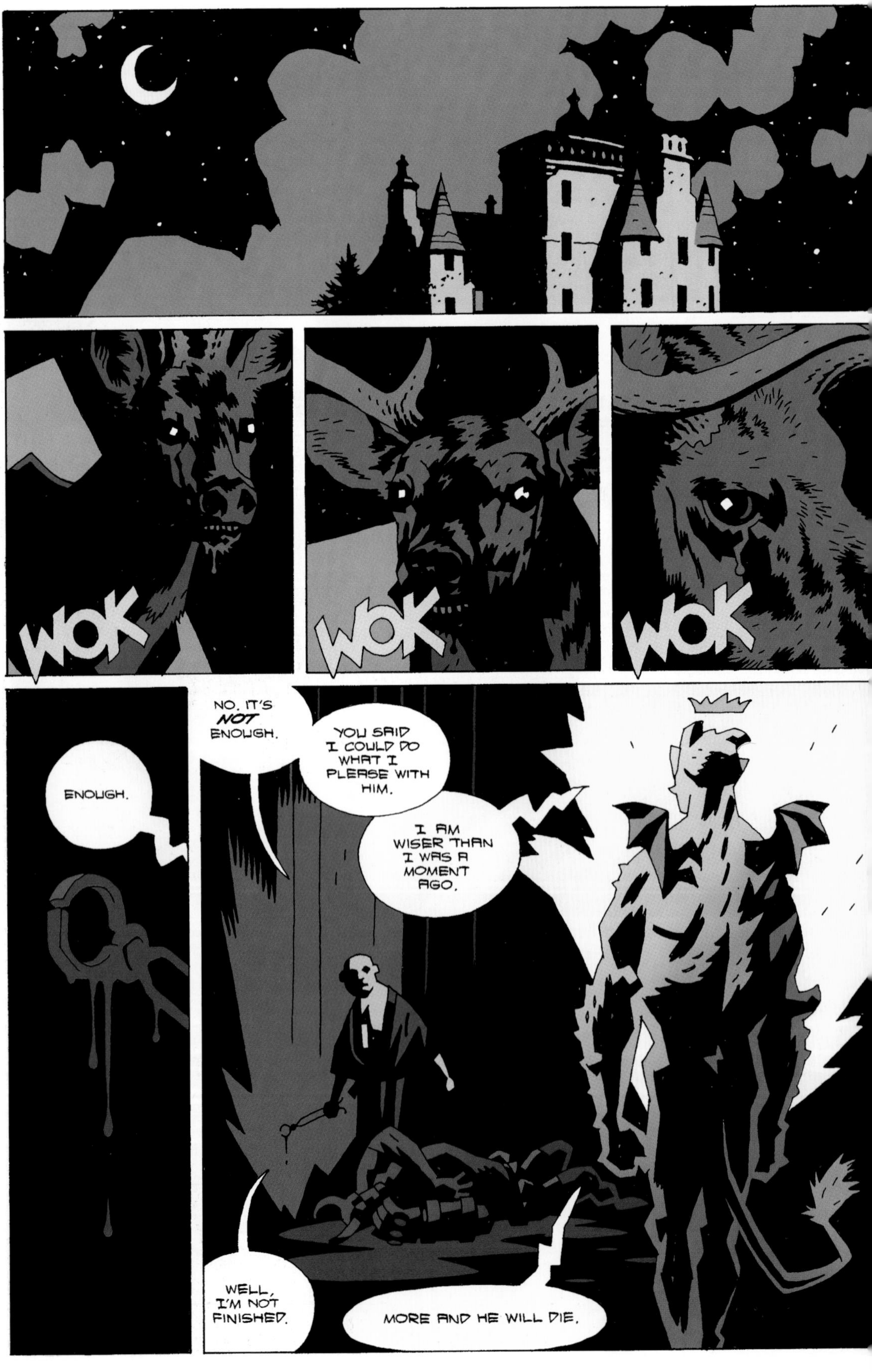
WOK
WOK
WOK
ENOUGH.
NO. IT'S *NOT* ENOUGH.
YOU SAID I COULD DO WHAT I PLEASE WITH HIM.
I AM WISER THAN I WAS A MOMENT AGO.
WELL, I'M NOT FINISHED.
MORE AND HE WILL DIE.

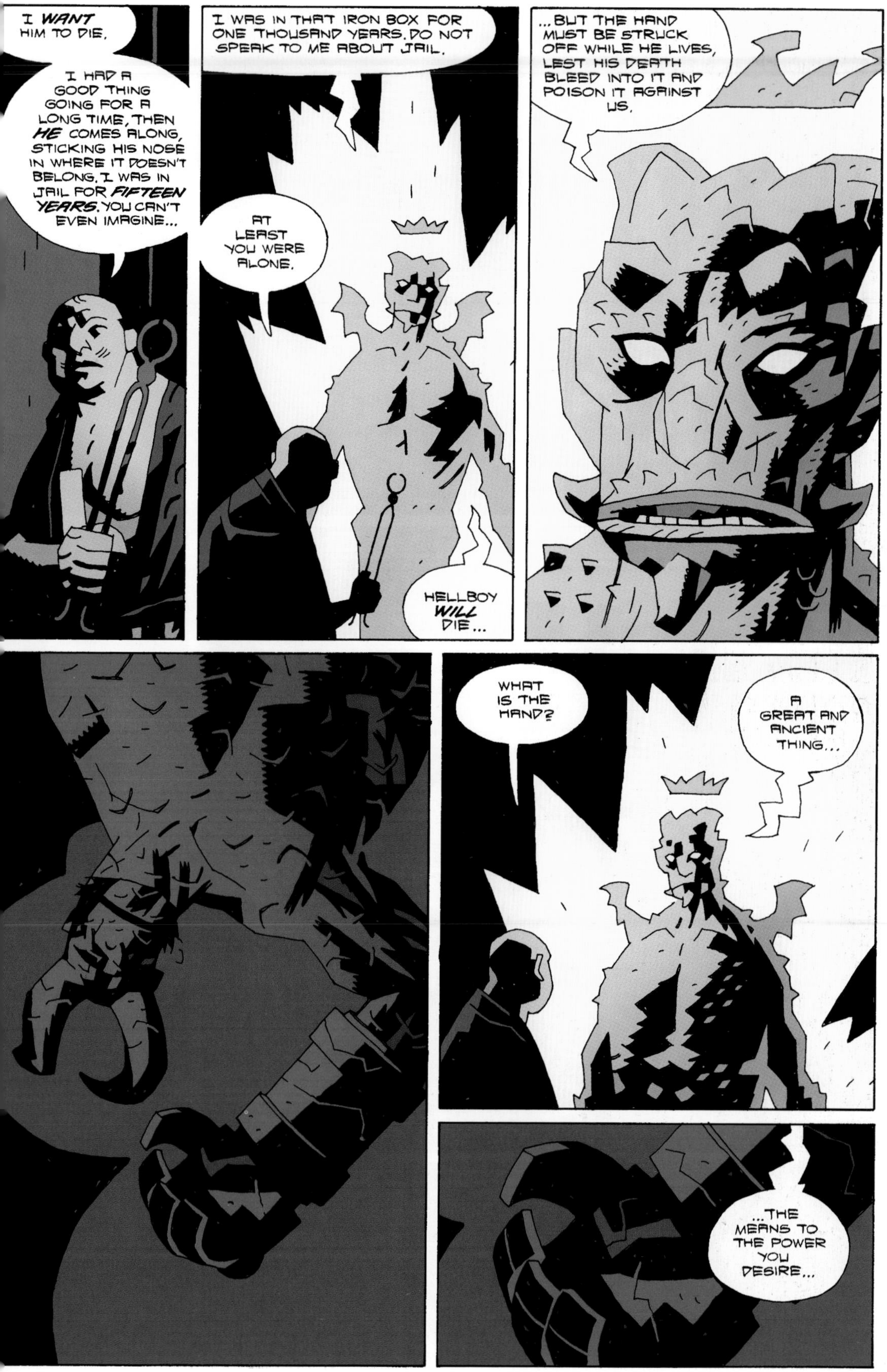

I WANT HIM TO DIE.
I HAD A GOOD THING GOING FOR A LONG TIME, THEN HE COMES ALONG, STICKING HIS NOSE IN WHERE IT DOESN'T BELONG. I WAS IN JAIL FOR FIFTEEN YEARS. YOU CAN'T EVEN IMAGINE...
I WAS IN THAT IRON BOX FOR ONE THOUSAND YEARS. DO NOT SPEAK TO ME ABOUT JAIL.
AT LEAST YOU WERE ALONE.
HELLBOY WILL DIE...
...BUT THE HAND MUST BE STRUCK OFF WHILE HE LIVES, LEST HIS DEATH BLEED INTO IT AND POISON IT AGAINST US.
WHAT IS THE HAND?
A GREAT AND ANCIENT THING...
...THE MEANS TO THE POWER YOU DESIRE...

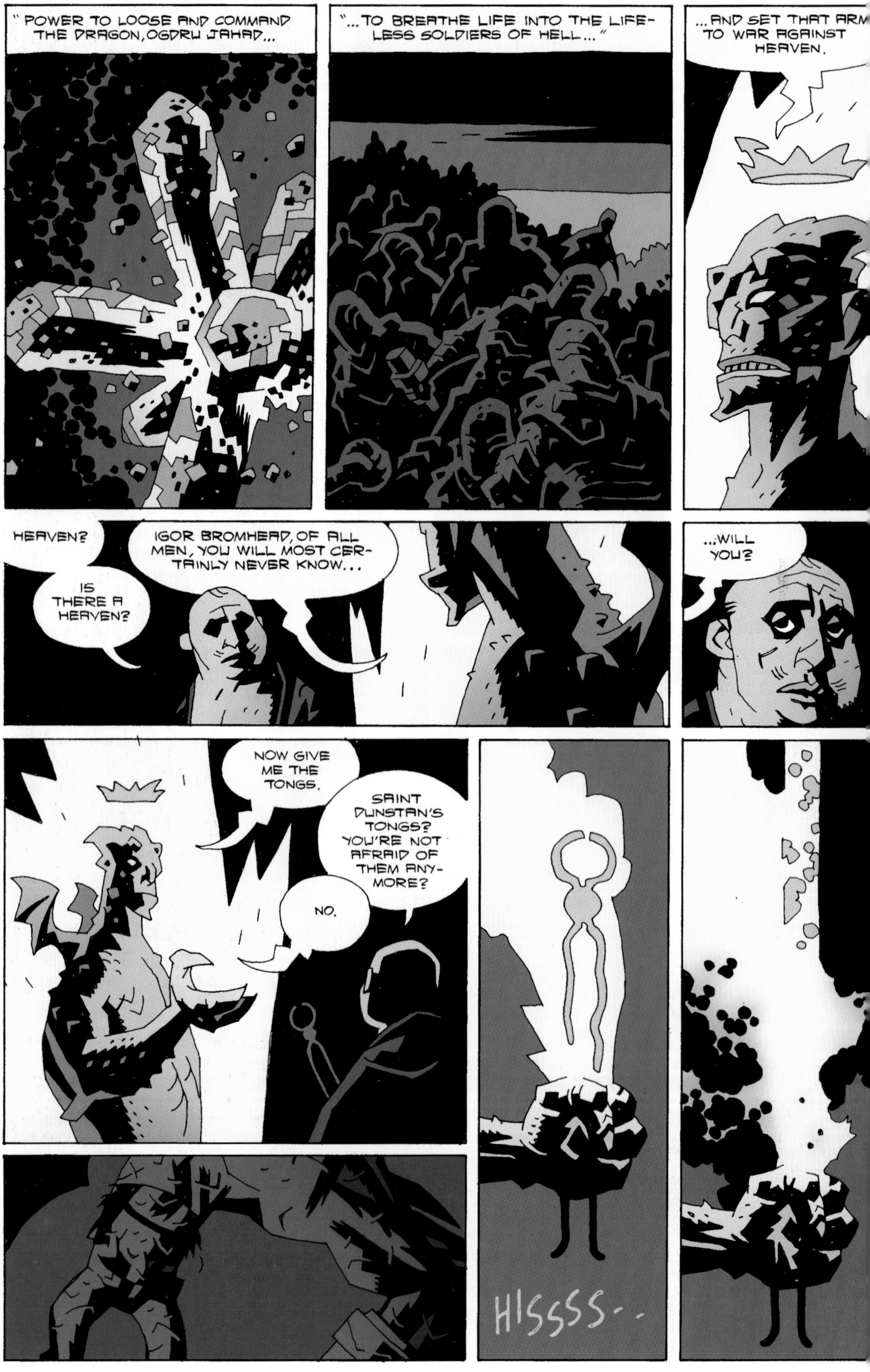
"POWER TO LOOSE AND COMMAND THE DRAGON, OGDRU JAHAD...
"...TO BREATHE LIFE INTO THE LIFE-LESS SOLDIERS OF HELL..."
...AND SET THAT ARM
TO WAR AGAINST HEAVEN.
HEAVEN?
IS THERE A HEAVEN?
IGOR BROMHEAD, OF ALL MEN, YOU WILL MOST CERTAINLY NEVER KNOW...
...WILL YOU?
NOW GIVE ME THE TONGS.
SAINT DUNSTAN'S TONGS? YOU'RE NOT AFRAID OF THEM ANYMORE?
NO.
HISSSS...

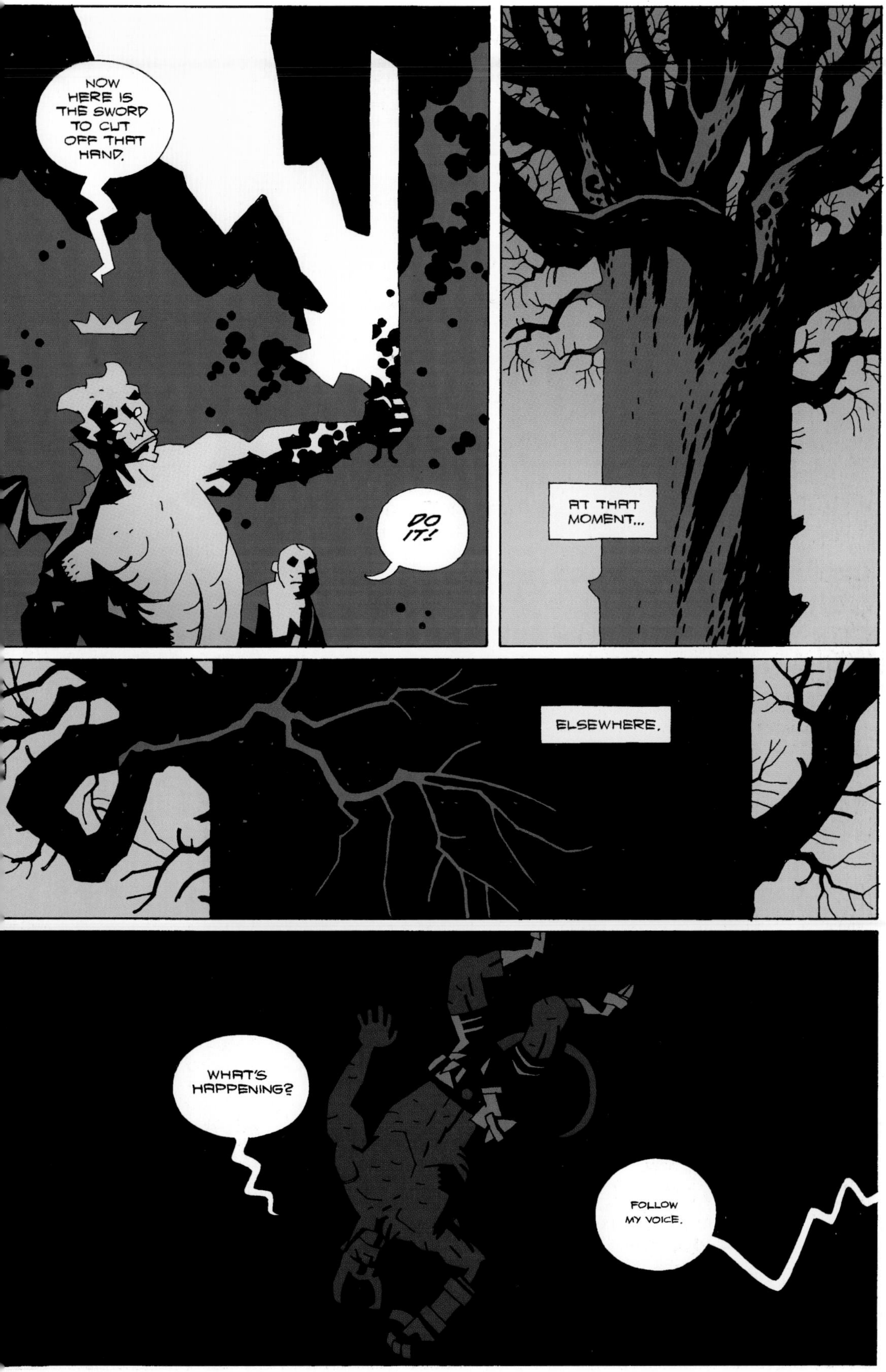
NOW HERE IS THE SWORD TO CUT OFF THAT HAND.
DO IT!
AT THAT MOMENT...
ELSEWHERE.
WHAT'S HAPPENING?
FOLLOW MY VOICE.

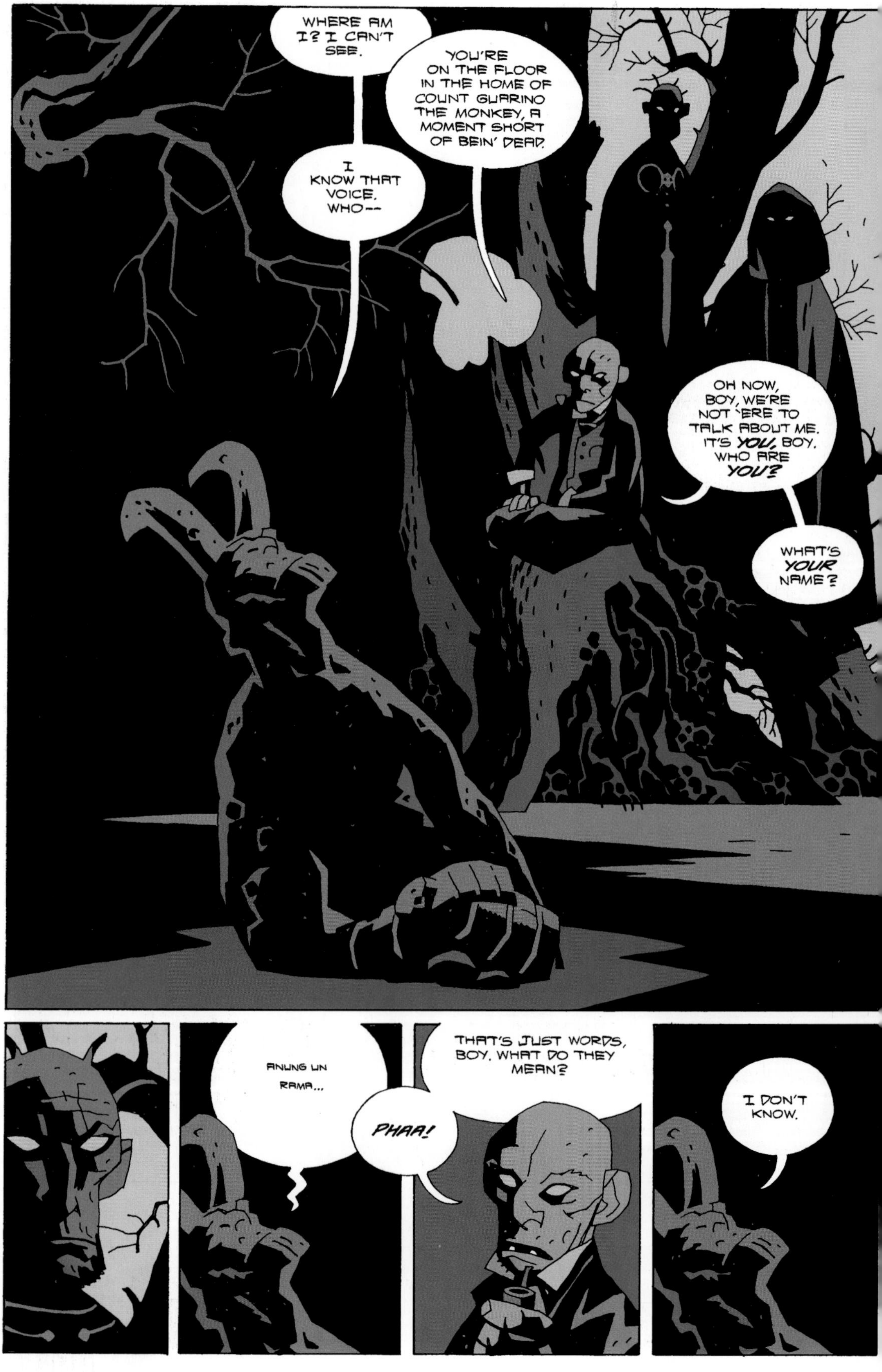
WHERE AM I? I CAN'T SEE.
YOU'RE ON THE FLOOR IN THE HOME OF COUNT GUARINO THE MONKEY, A MOMENT SHORT OF BEIN' DEAD.
I KNOW THAT VOICE. WHO--
OH NOW, BOY, WE'RE NOT 'ERE TO TALK ABOUT ME. IT'S YOU, BOY. WHO ARE YOU?
WHAT'S YOUR NAME?
ANUNG UN RAMA...
THAT'S JUST WORDS, BOY. WHAT DO THEY MEAN?
PHAA!
I DON'T KNOW.

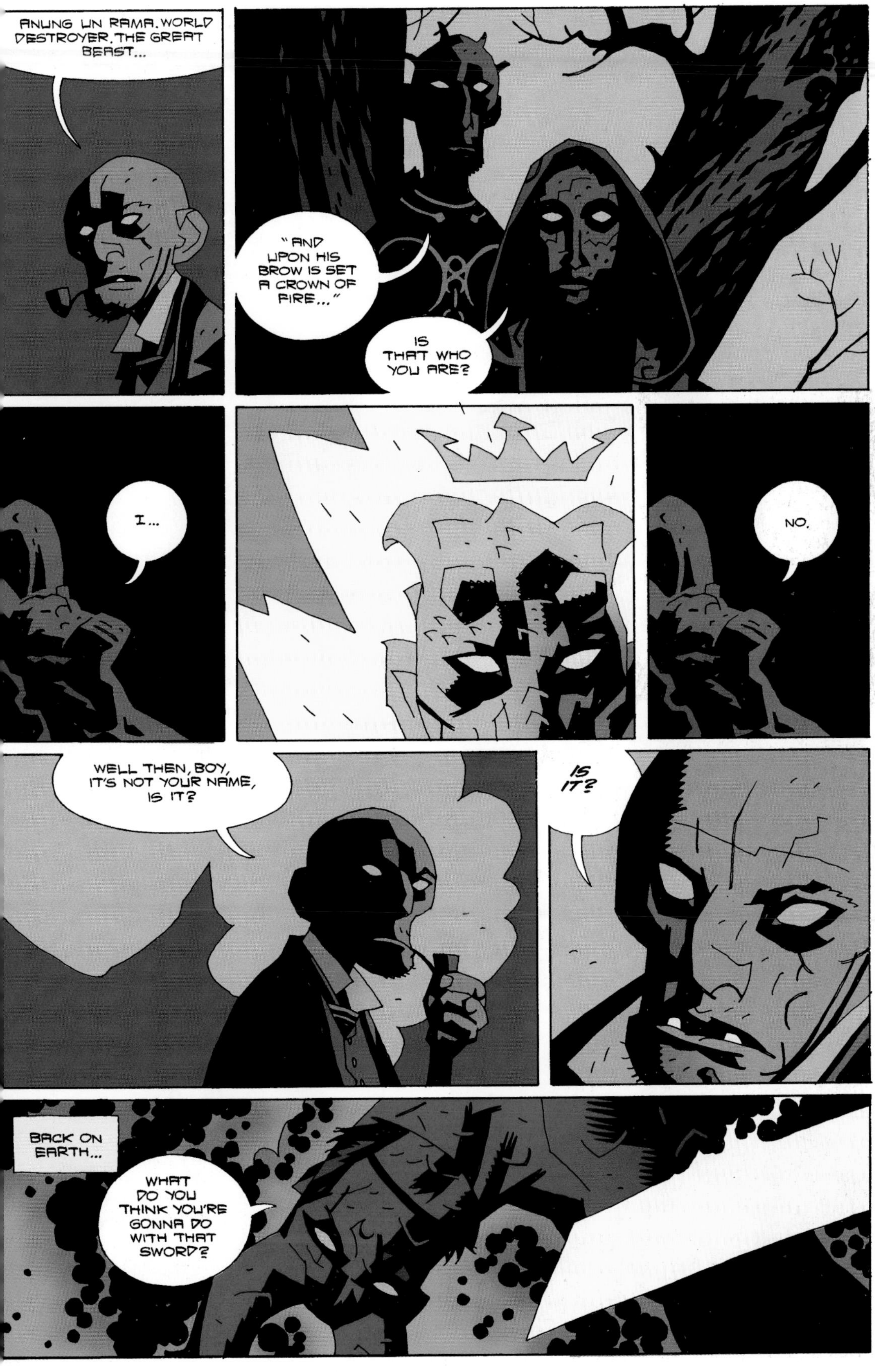

ANUNG UN RAMA. WORLD DESTROYER. THE GREAT BEAST...
"AND UPON HIS BROW IS SET A CROWN OF FIRE..."
IS THAT WHO YOU ARE?
I...
NO.
WELL THEN, BOY, IT'S NOT YOUR NAME, IS IT?
IS IT?
BACK ON EARTH...
WHAT DO YOU THINK YOU'RE GONNA DO WITH THAT SWORD?

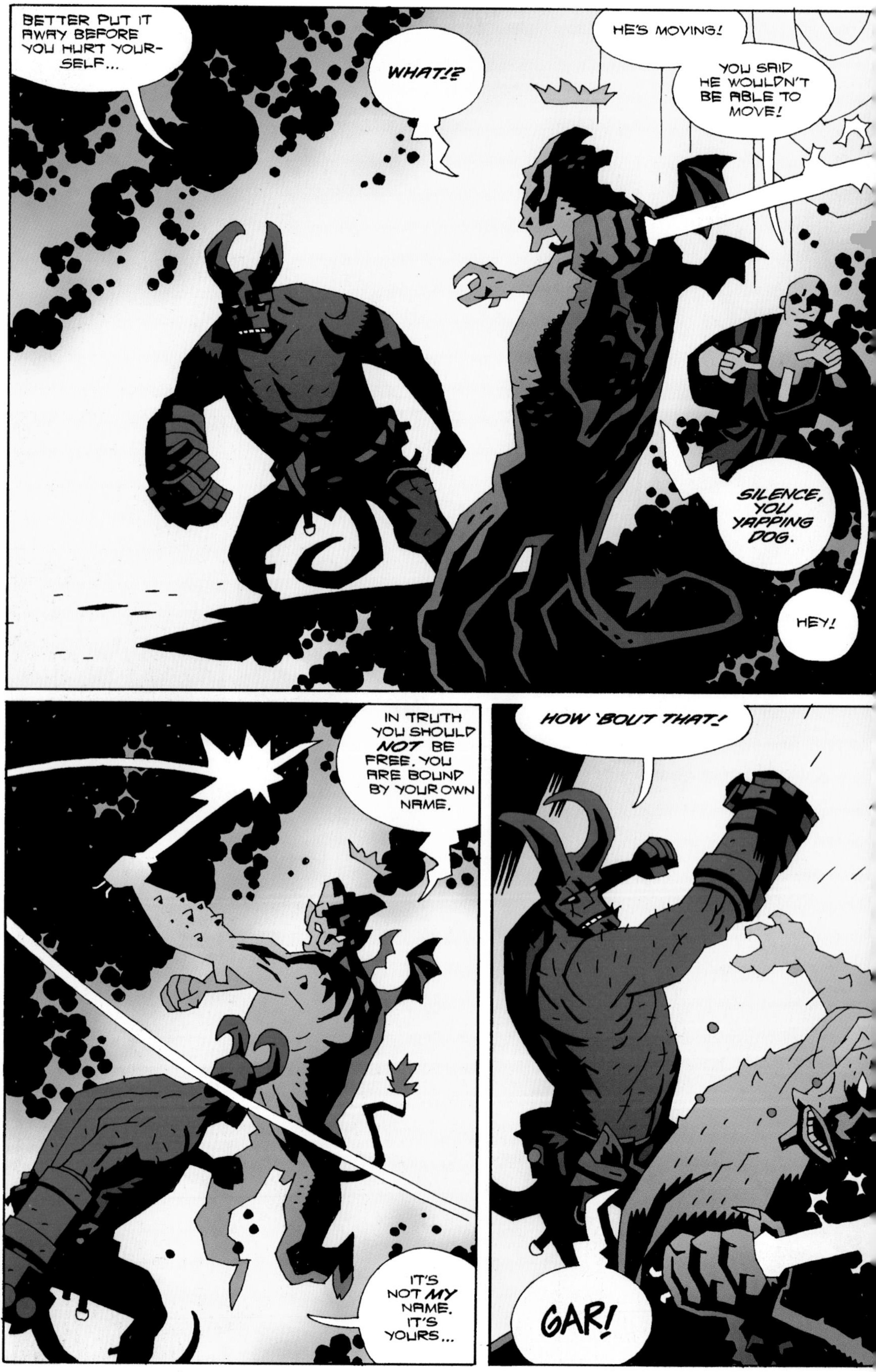

BETTER PUT IT AWAY BEFORE YOU HURT YOUR-SELF...
WHAT!?
HE'S MOVING!
YOU SAID HE WOULDN'T BE ABLE TO MOVE!
SILENCE, YOU YAPPING DOG.
HEY!
IN TRUTH YOU SHOULD NOT BE FREE. YOU ARE BOUND BY YOUR OWN NAME.
IT'S NOT MY NAME. IT'S YOURS...
HOW 'BOUT THAT!
GAR!

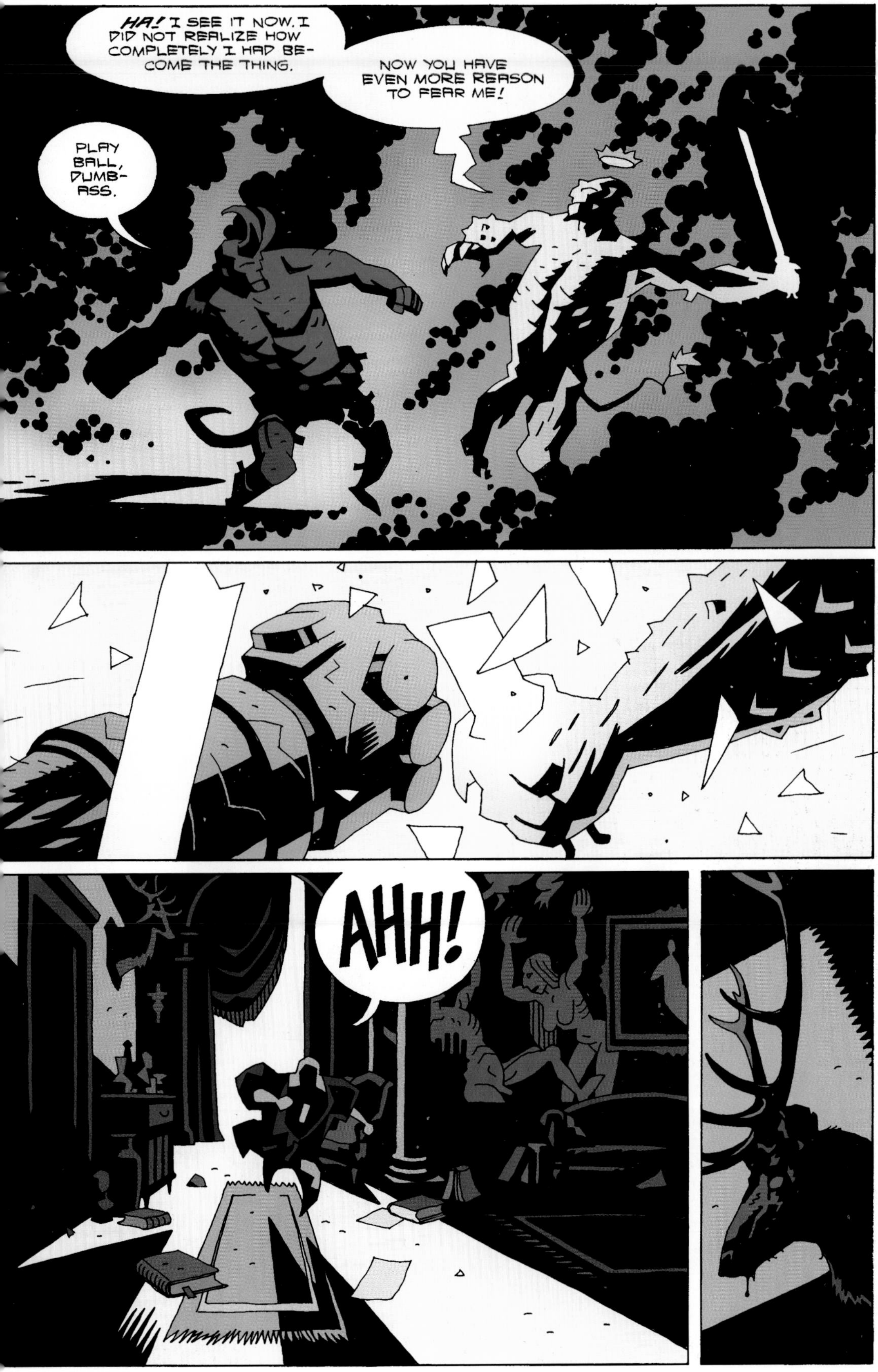
HA! I SEE IT NOW. I DID NOT REALIZE HOW COMPLETELY I HAD BE-COME THE THING.
NOW YOU HAVE EVEN MORE REASON TO FEAR ME!
PLAY BALL, DUMB-ASS.
AHH!

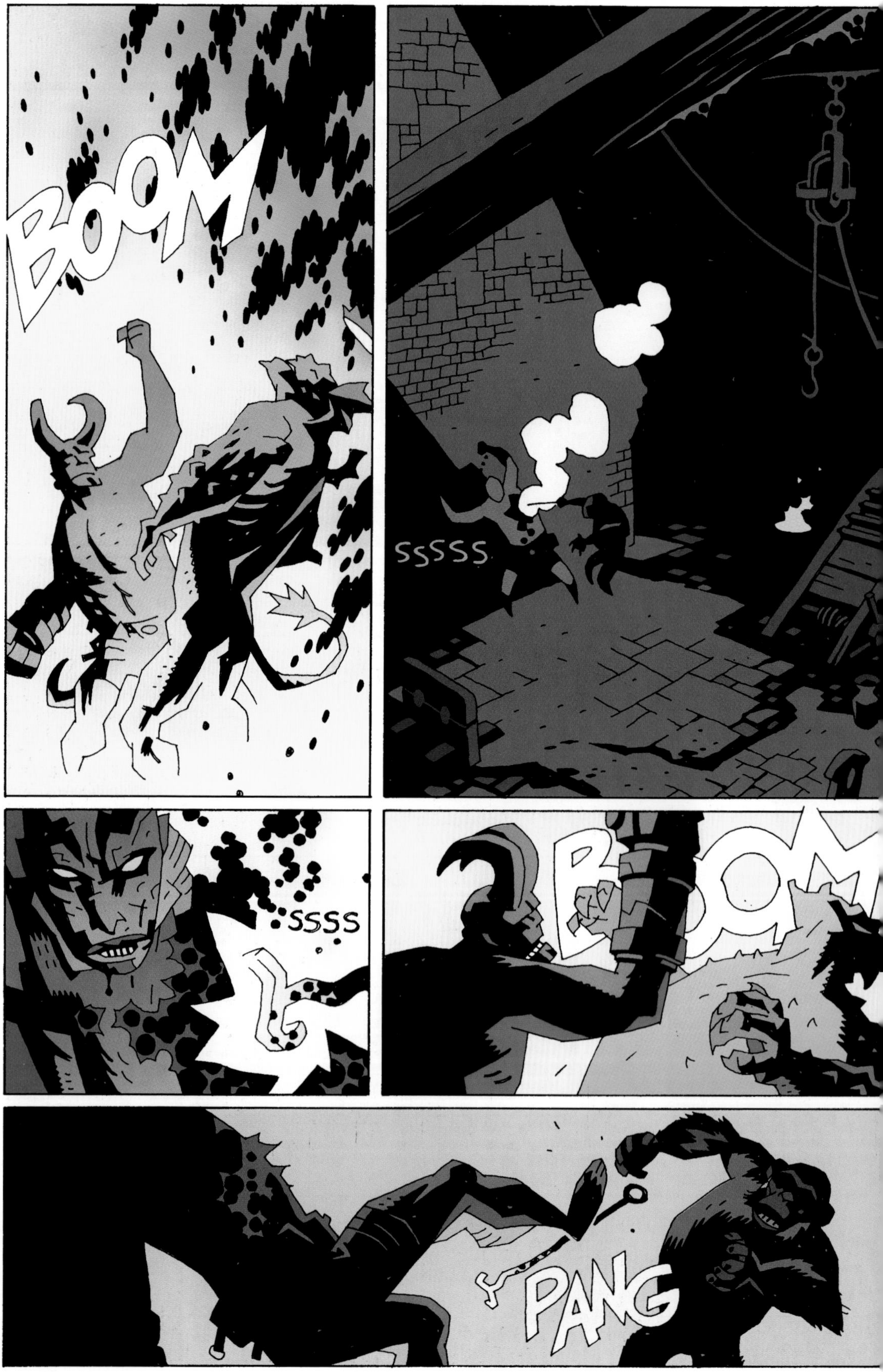
BOOM
SSSSS
SSSS
BOOM
PANG

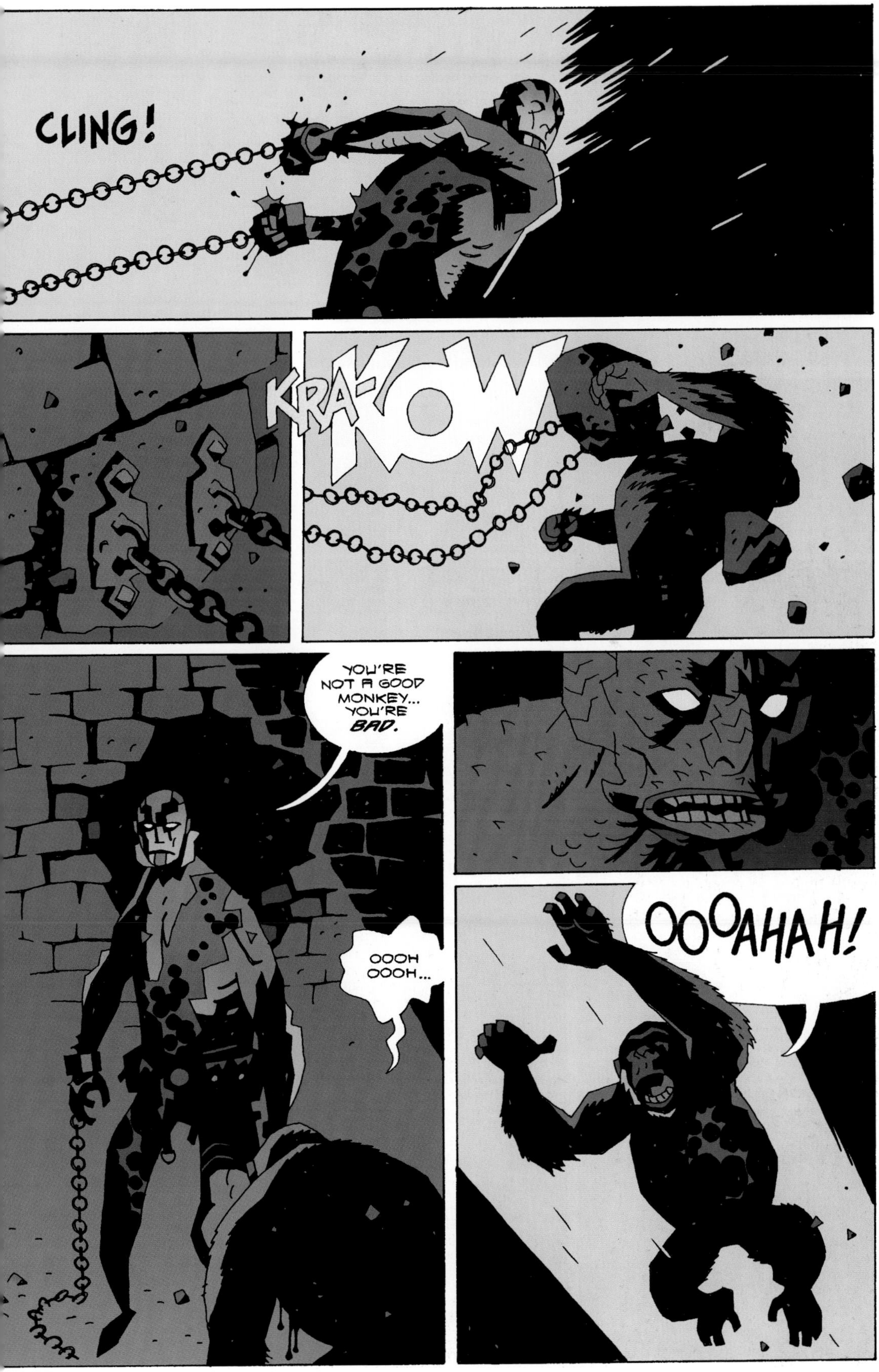
CLING!
KRA-KOW
YOU'RE NOT A GOOD MONKEY... YOU'RE BAD.
OOOH OOOH...
OOOAHAH!

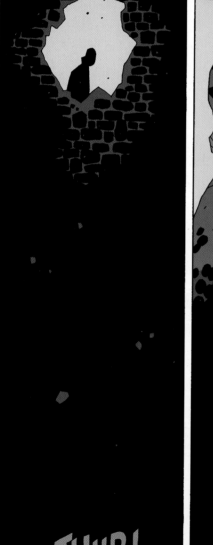

THUD!

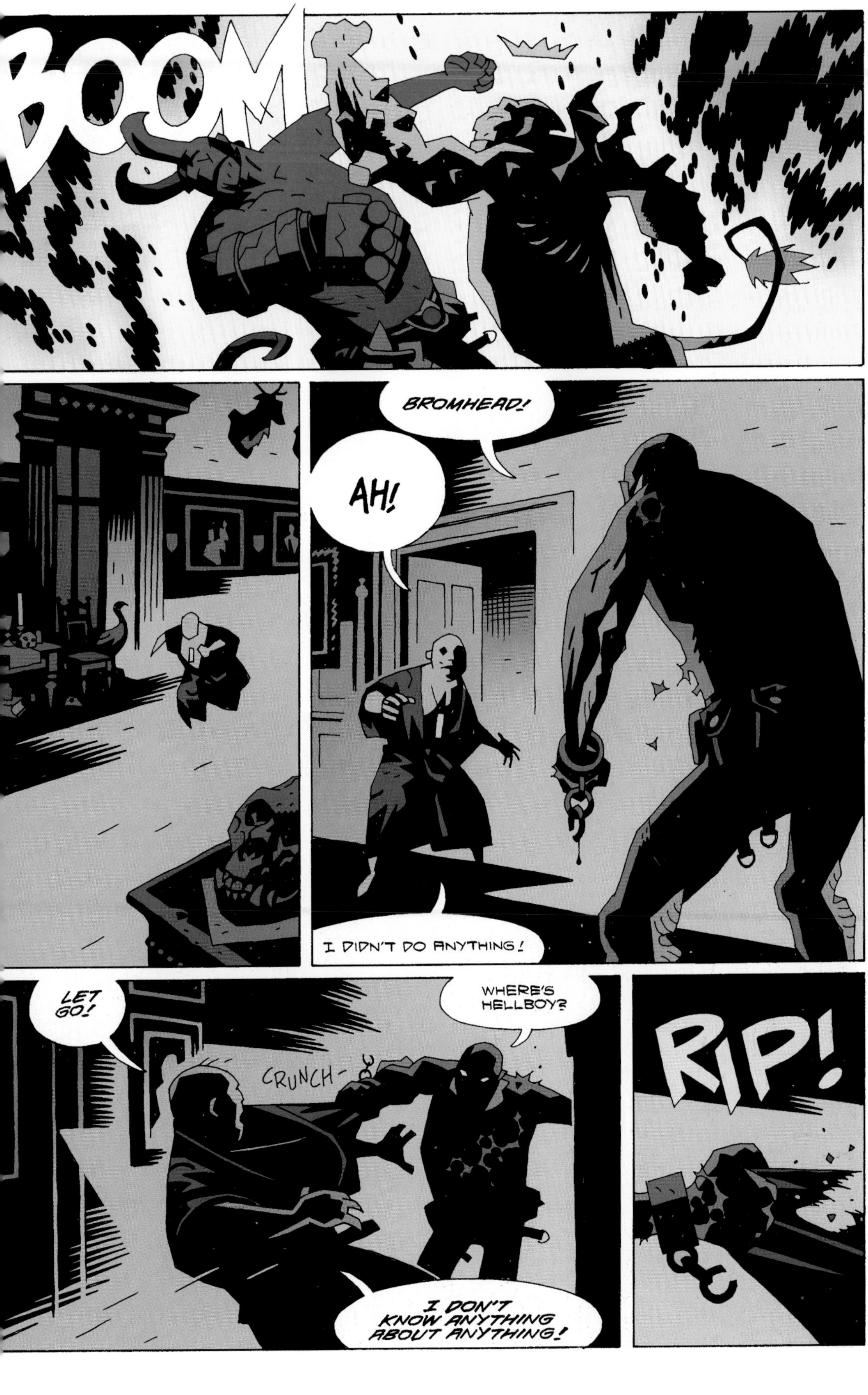
BOOM
BROMHEAD!
AH!
I DIDN'T DO ANYTHING!
LET GO!
CRUNCH-
WHERE'S HELLBOY?
I DON'T KNOW ANYTHING ABOUT ANYTHING!
RIP!

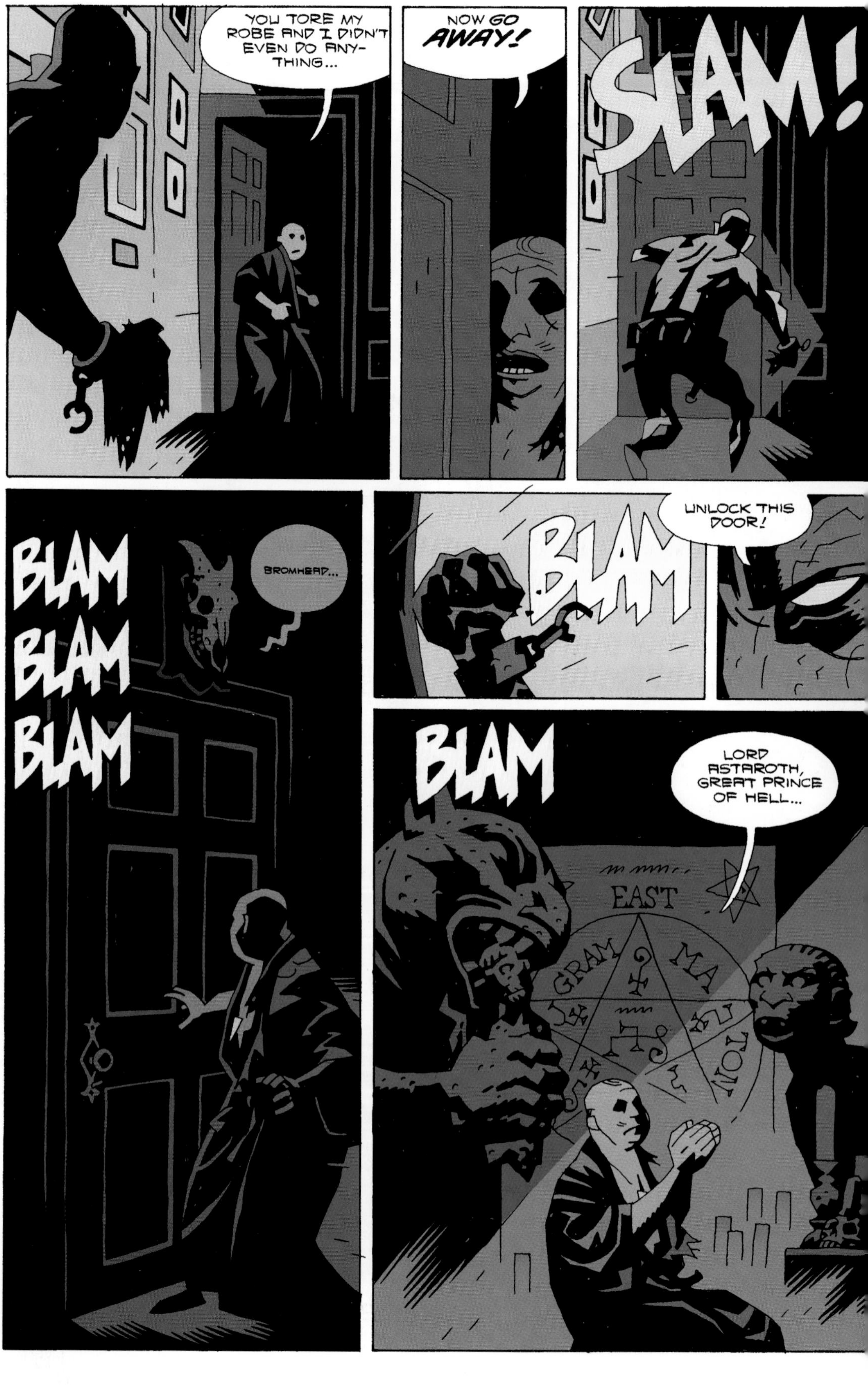
YOU TORE MY ROBE AND I DIDN'T EVEN DO ANY-THING...
NOW GO AWAY!
SLAM!
BLAM BLAM BLAM
BROMHEAD...
BLAM
UNLOCK THIS DOOR!
BLAM
LORD ASTAROTH, GREAT PRINCE OF HELL...
EAST
GRAM
MA
TON

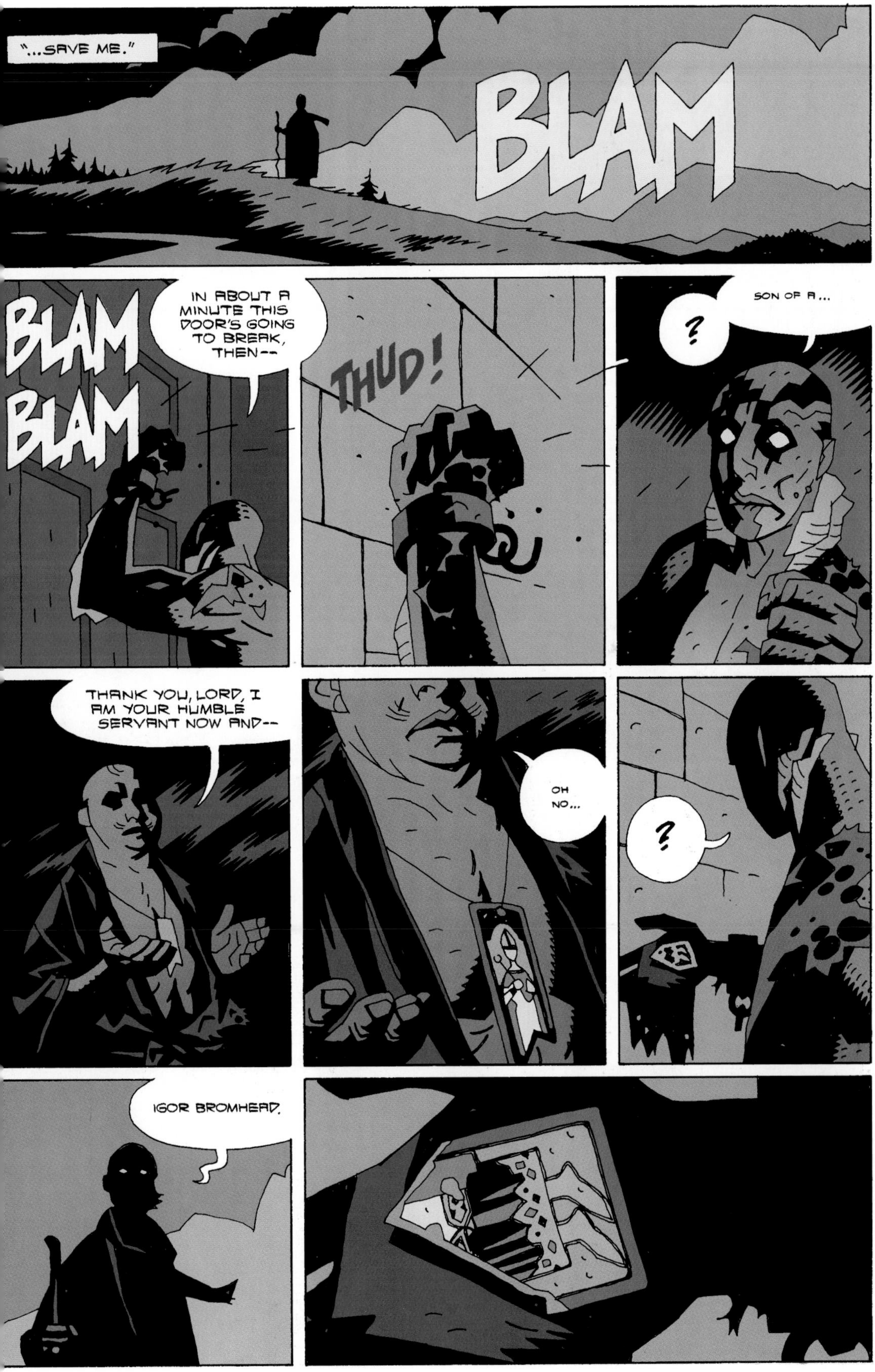
"...SAVE ME."
BLAM
BLAM
BLAM
IN ABOUT A MINUTE THIS DOOR'S GOING TO BREAK, THEN--
THUD!
SON OF A...
?
THANK YOU, LORD, I AM YOUR HUMBLE SERVANT NOW AND--
OH NO...
?
IGOR BROMHEAD.

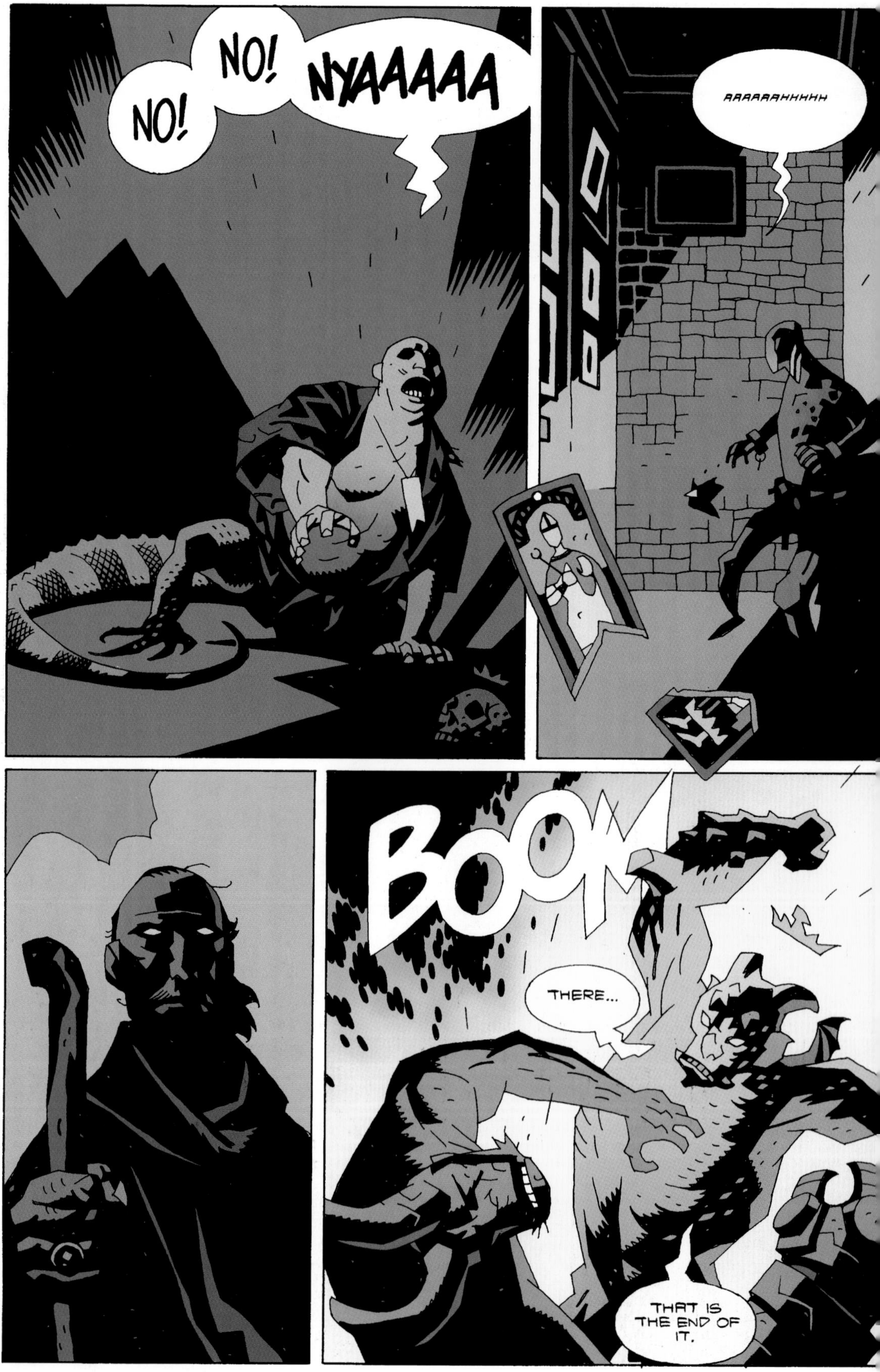
NO!
NO!
NYAAAAA
AAAAAAHHHHH
BOOM
THERE...
THAT IS THE END OF IT.

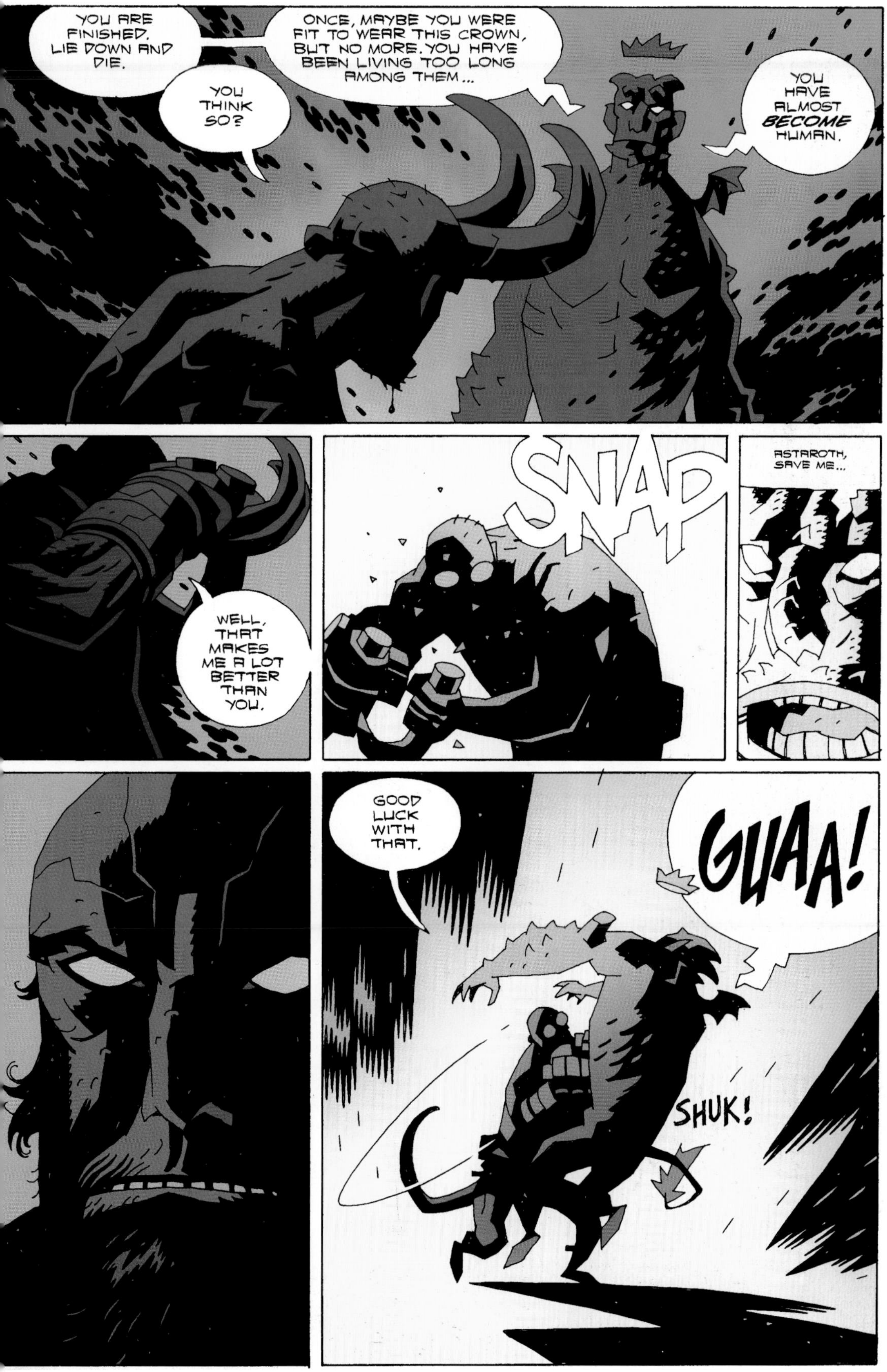

YOU ARE FINISHED. LIE DOWN AND DIE.
YOU THINK SO?
ONCE, MAYBE YOU WERE FIT TO WEAR THIS CROWN, BUT NO MORE. YOU HAVE BEEN LIVING TOO LONG AMONG THEM...
YOU HAVE ALMOST *BECOME* HUMAN.
WELL, THAT MAKES ME A LOT BETTER THAN YOU.
SNAP
ASTAROTH, SAVE ME...
GOOD LUCK WITH THAT.
GUAA!
SHUK!

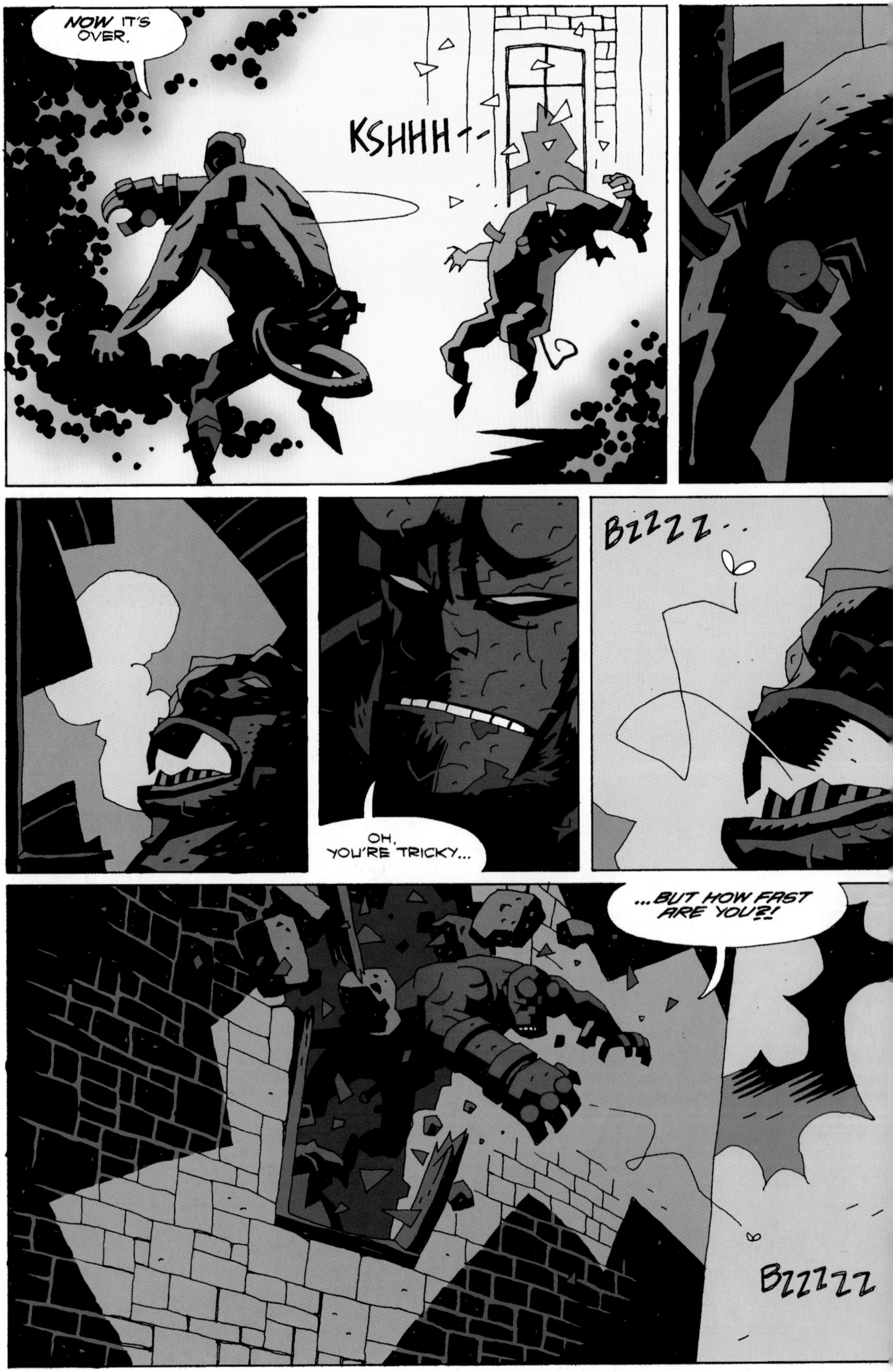
NOW IT'S OVER.
KSHHH--
OH, YOU'RE TRICKY...
BZZZZ..
...BUT HOW FAST ARE YOU?!
BZZZZZ

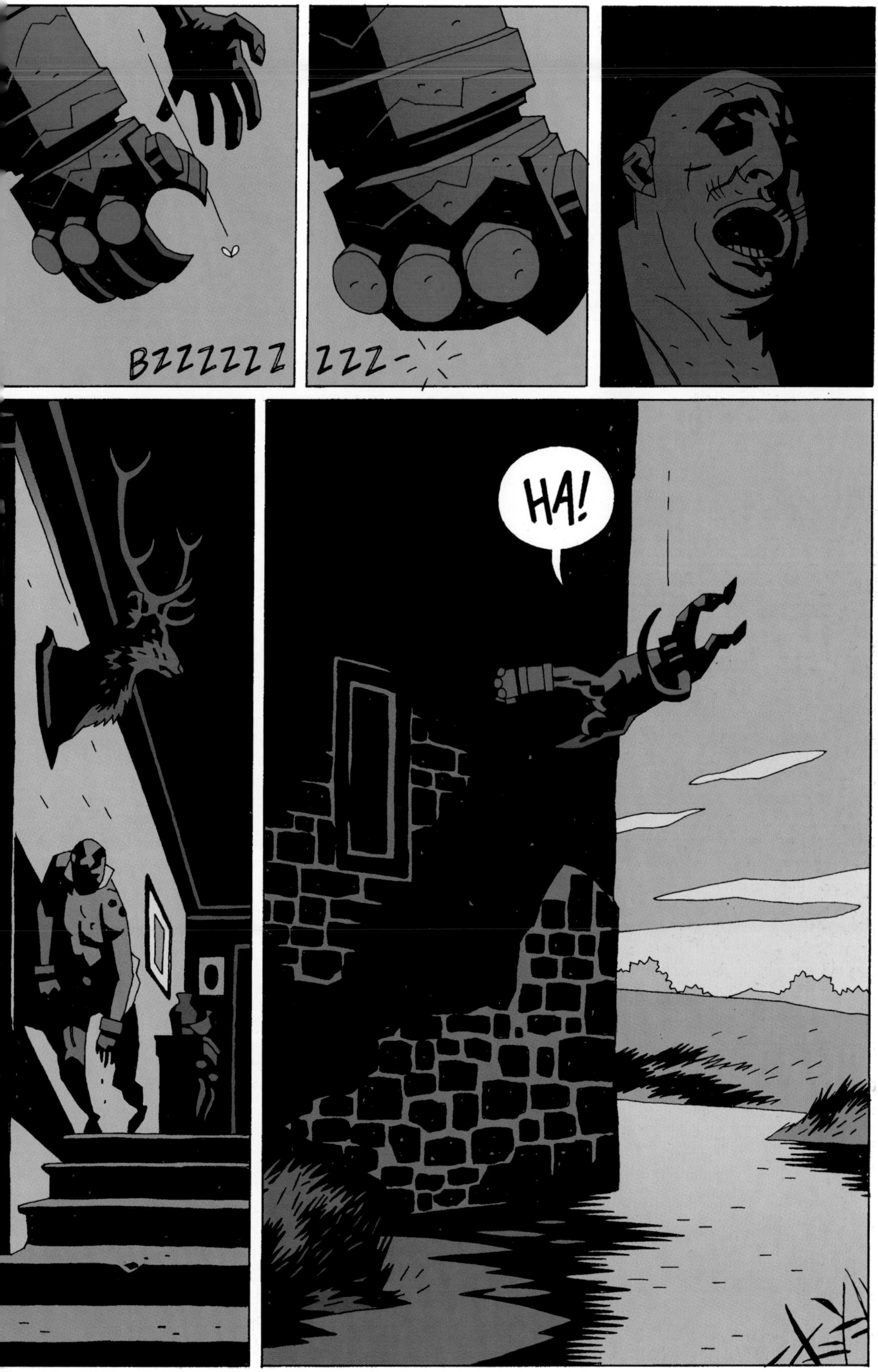
BZZZZZZ
ZZZ-
HA!

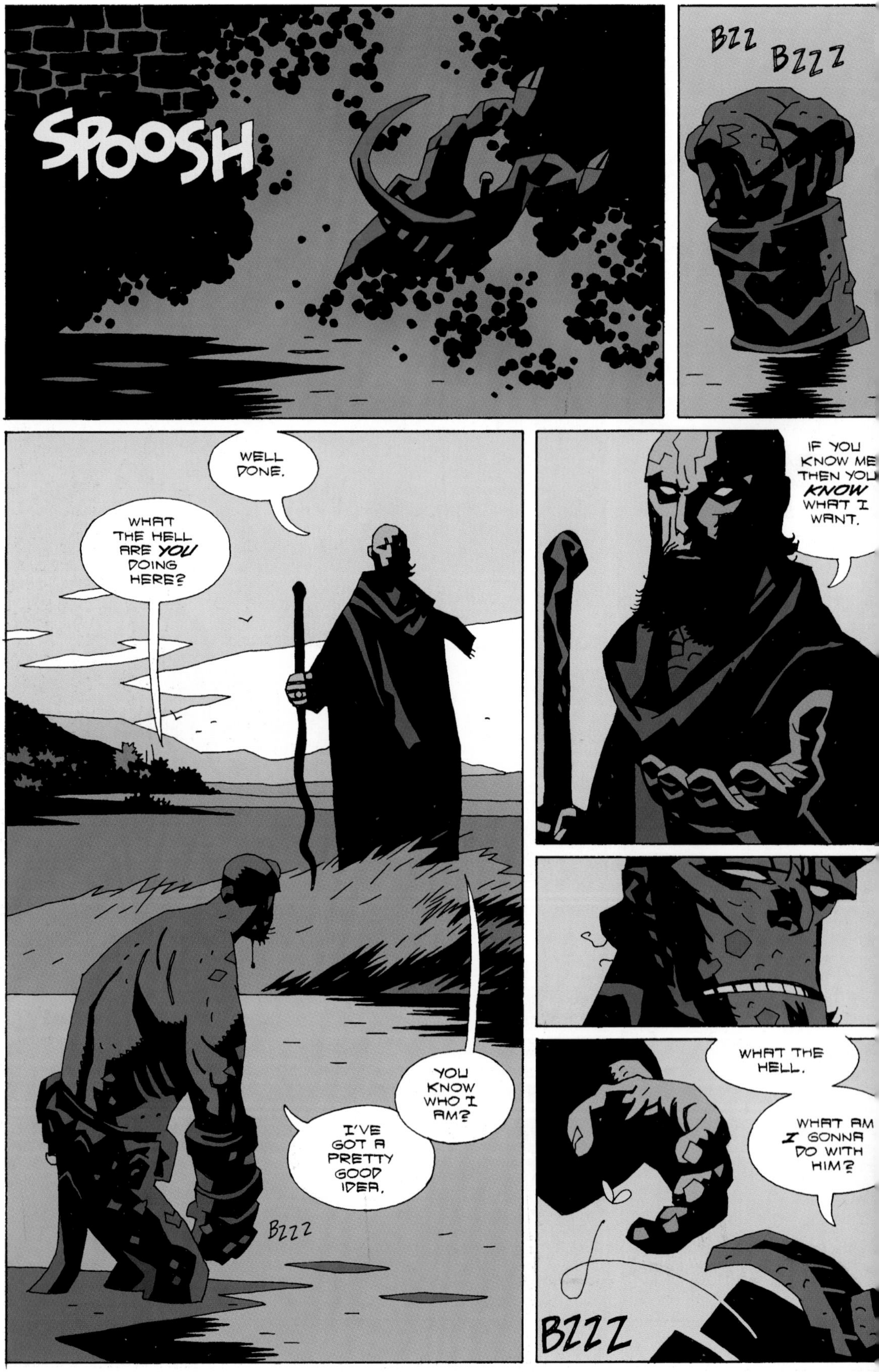
SPOOSH
BZZ BZZZ
WELL DONE.
WHAT THE HELL ARE YOU DOING HERE?
YOU KNOW WHO I AM?
I'VE GOT A PRETTY GOOD IDEA.
BZZZ
IF YOU KNOW ME THEN YOU KNOW WHAT I WANT.
WHAT THE HELL.
WHAT AM I GONNA DO WITH HIM?
BZZZ

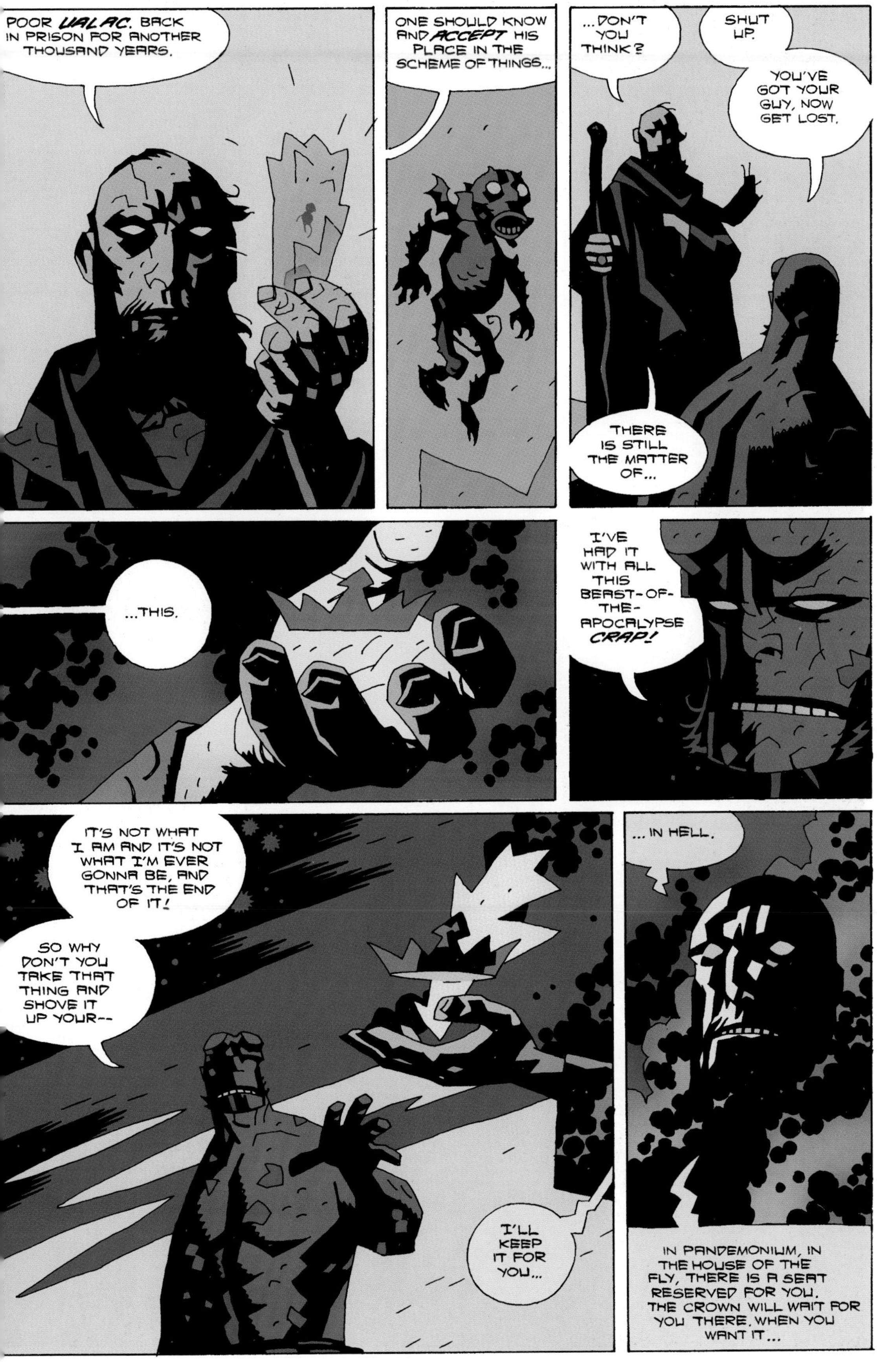
POOR VALAC. BACK IN PRISON FOR ANOTHER THOUSAND YEARS.
ONE SHOULD KNOW AND ACCEPT HIS PLACE IN THE SCHEME OF THINGS...
...DON'T YOU THINK?
SHUT UP.
YOU'VE GOT YOUR GUY, NOW GET LOST.
THERE IS STILL THE MATTER OF...
...THIS.
I'VE HAD IT WITH ALL THIS BEAST-OF-THE-APOCALYPSE CRAP!
IT'S NOT WHAT I AM AND IT'S NOT WHAT I'M EVER GONNA BE, AND THAT'S THE END OF IT!
SO WHY DON'T YOU TAKE THAT THING AND SHOVE IT UP YOUR--
I'LL KEEP IT FOR YOU...
...IN HELL.
IN PANDEMONIUM, IN THE HOUSE OF THE FLY, THERE IS A SEAT RESERVED FOR YOU. THE CROWN WILL WAIT FOR YOU THERE, WHEN YOU WANT IT...

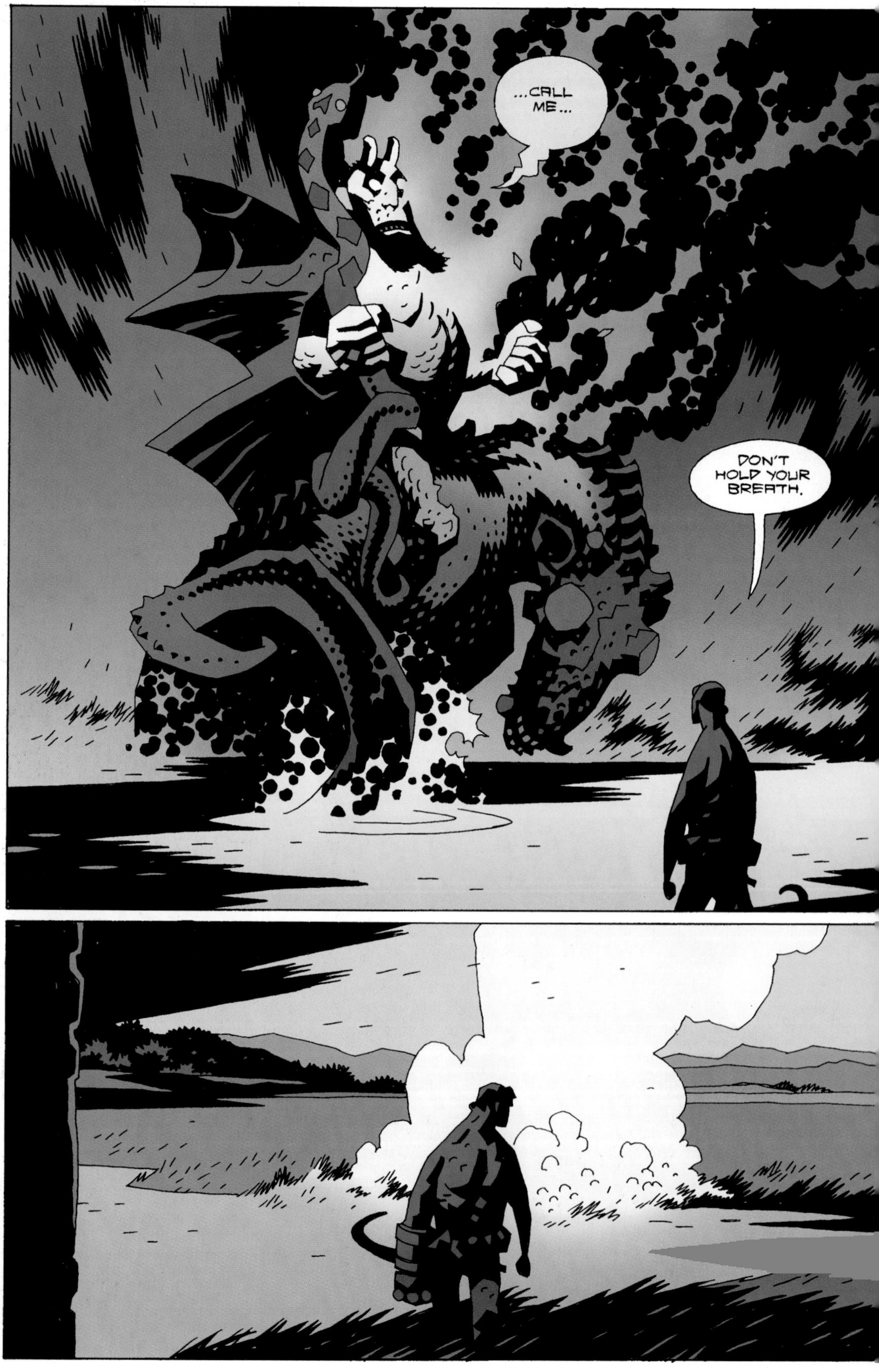
...CALL ME...
DON'T HOLD YOUR BREATH.

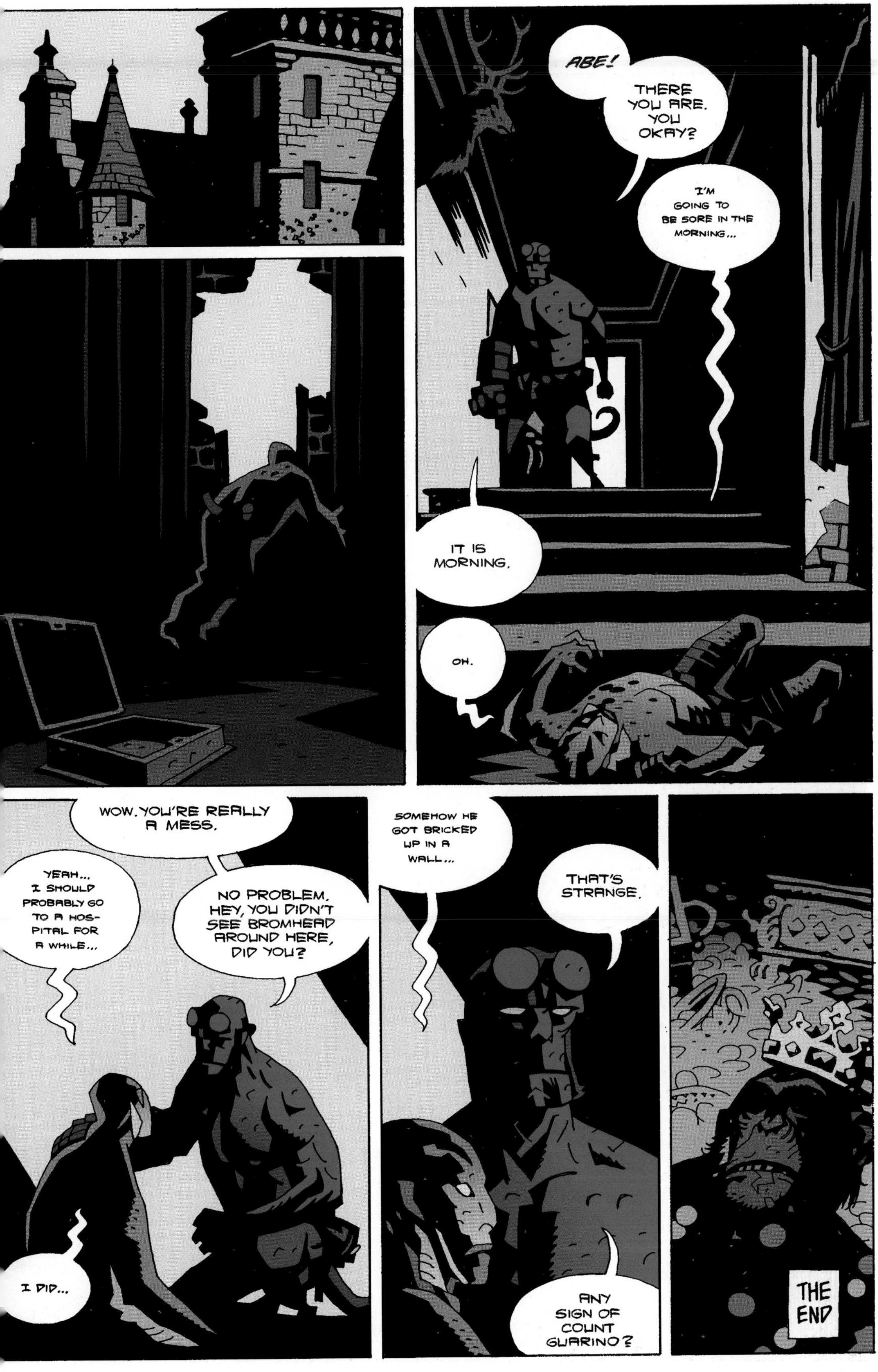
ABE!
THERE YOU ARE. YOU OKAY?
I'M GOING TO BE SORE IN THE MORNING...
IT IS MORNING.
OH.
WOW. YOU'RE REALLY A MESS.
YEAH... I SHOULD PROBABLY GO TO A HOS-PITAL FOR A WHILE...
NO PROBLEM. HEY, YOU DIDN'T SEE BROMHEAD AROUND HERE, DID YOU?
I DID...
SOMEHOW HE GOT BRICKED UP IN A WALL...
THAT'S STRANGE.
ANY SIGN OF COUNT GUARINO?
THE END

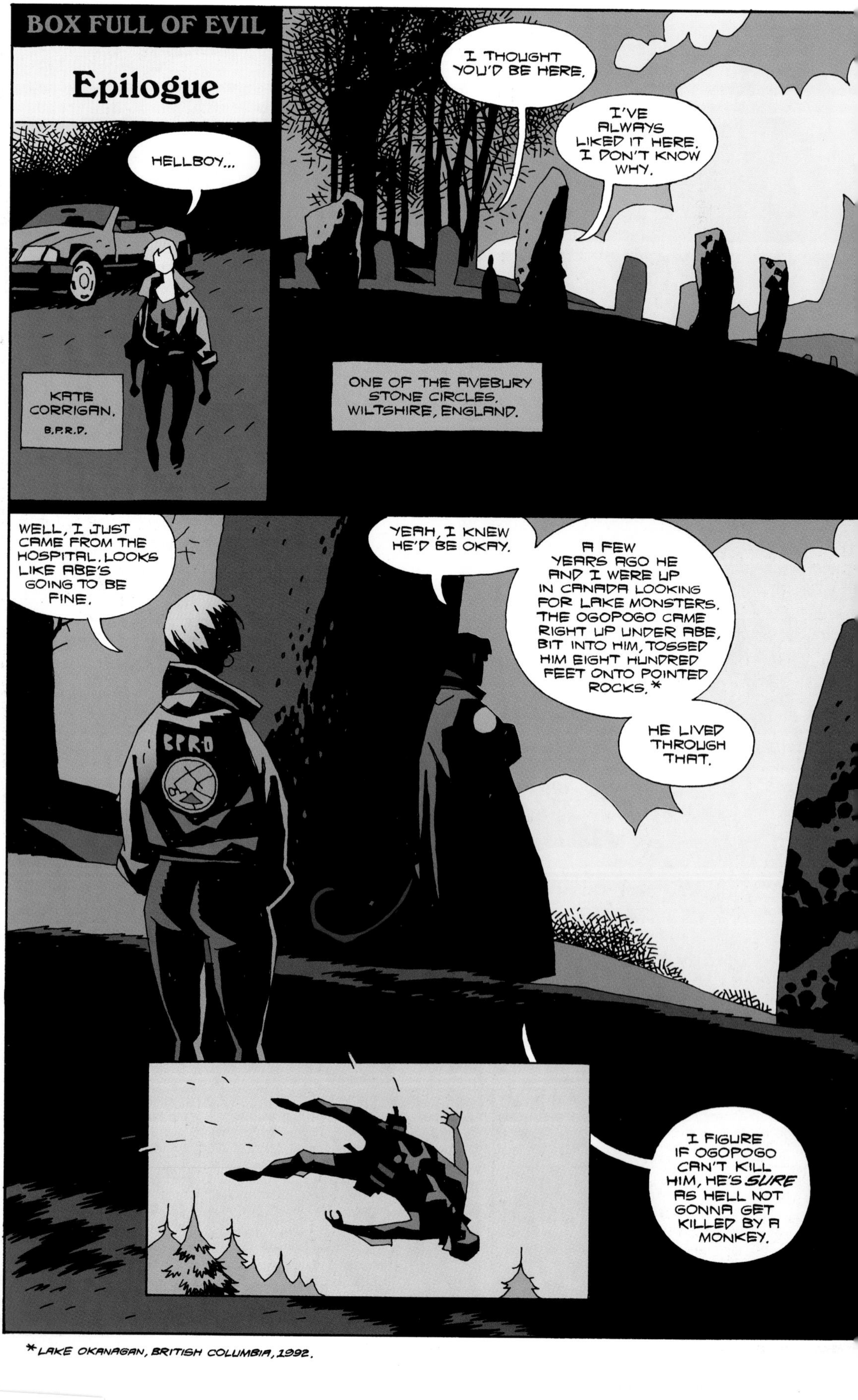
BOX FULL OF EVIL
Epilogue
HELLBOY...
KATE CORRIGAN. B.P.R.D.
I THOUGHT YOU'D BE HERE.
I'VE ALWAYS LIKED IT HERE. I DON'T KNOW WHY.
ONE OF THE AVEBURY STONE CIRCLES. WILTSHIRE, ENGLAND.
WELL, I JUST CAME FROM THE HOSPITAL. LOOKS LIKE ABE'S GOING TO BE FINE.
YEAH, I KNEW HE'D BE OKAY.
A FEW YEARS AGO HE AND I WERE UP IN CANADA LOOKING FOR LAKE MONSTERS. THE OGOPOGO CAME RIGHT UP UNDER ABE, BIT INTO HIM, TOSSED HIM EIGHT HUNDRED FEET ONTO POINTED ROCKS.*
HE LIVED THROUGH THAT.
BPRD
I FIGURE IF OGOPOGO CAN'T KILL HIM, HE'S *SURE* AS HELL NOT GONNA GET KILLED BY A MONKEY.

*LAKE OKANAGAN, BRITISH COLUMBIA, 1992.

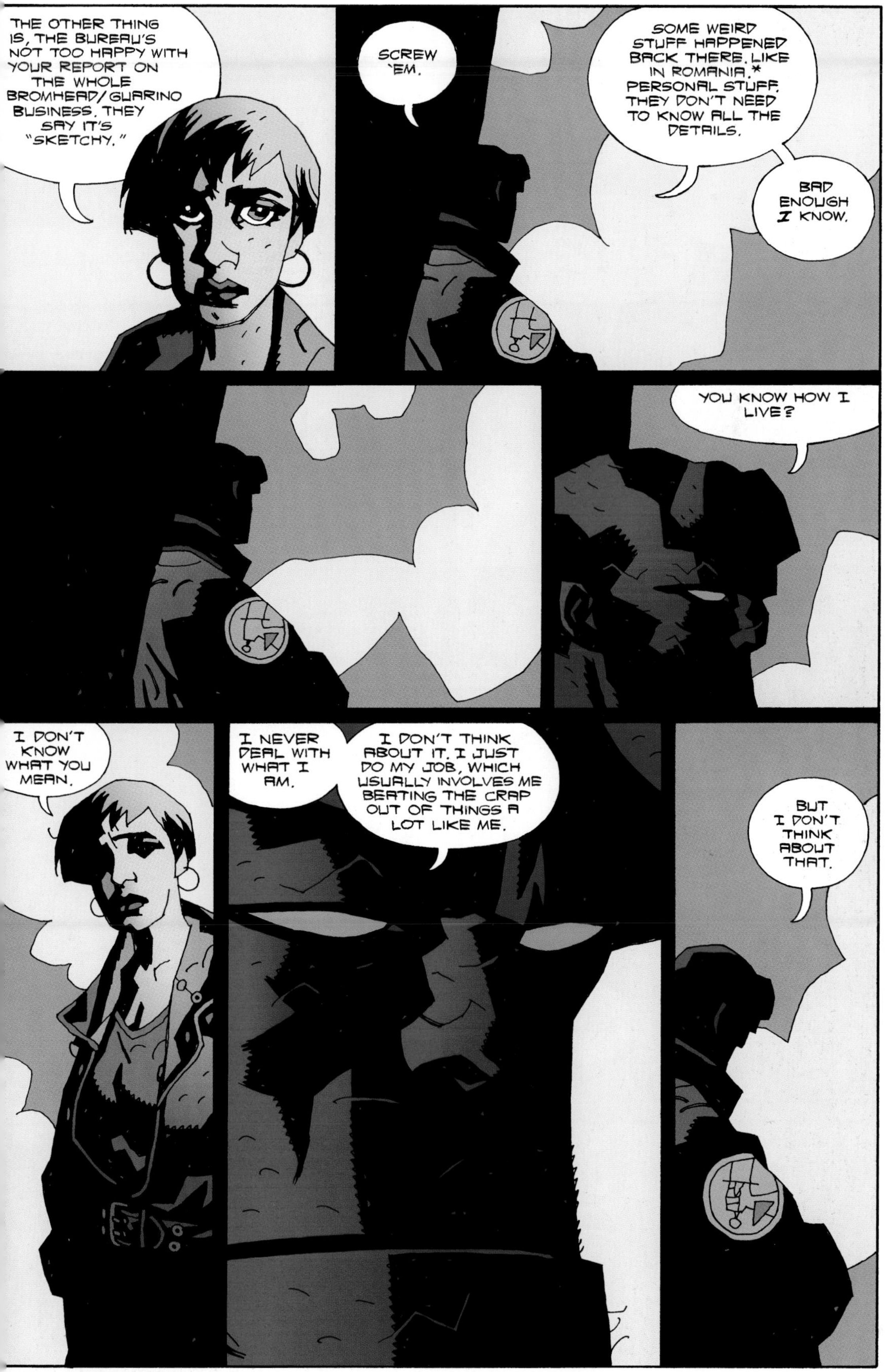
THE OTHER THING IS, THE BUREAU'S NOT TOO HAPPY WITH YOUR REPORT ON THE WHOLE BROMHEAD/GUARINO BUSINESS. THEY SAY IT'S "SKETCHY."
SCREW 'EM.
SOME WEIRD STUFF HAPPENED BACK THERE. LIKE IN ROMANIA.* PERSONAL STUFF. THEY DON'T NEED TO KNOW ALL THE DETAILS.
BAD ENOUGH I KNOW.
YOU KNOW HOW I LIVE?
I DON'T KNOW WHAT YOU MEAN.
I NEVER DEAL WITH WHAT I AM.
I DON'T THINK ABOUT IT. I JUST DO MY JOB, WHICH USUALLY INVOLVES ME BEATING THE CRAP OUT OF THINGS A LOT LIKE ME.
BUT I DON'T THINK ABOUT THAT.

*HELLBOY: WAKE THE DEVIL

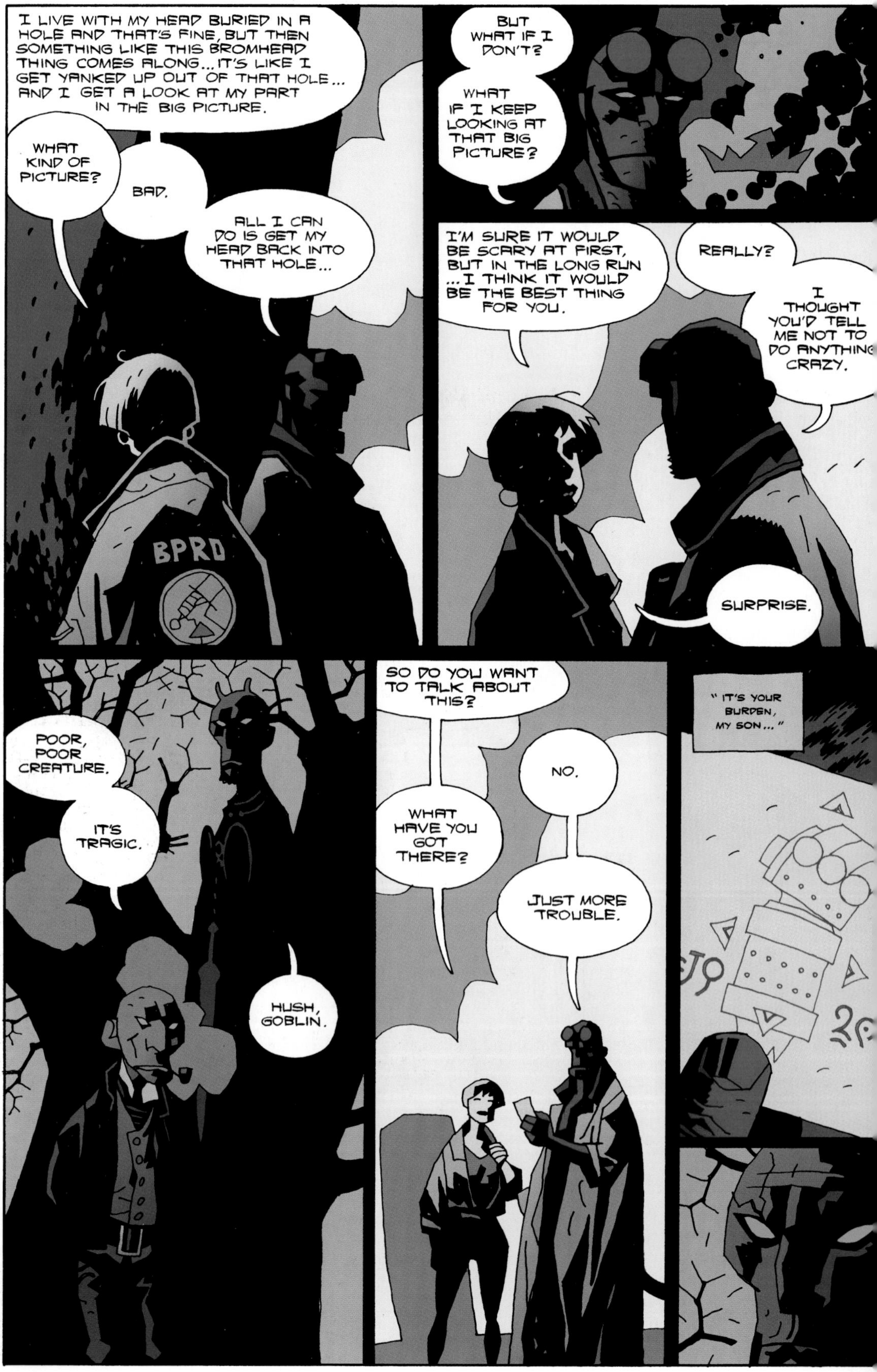
I LIVE WITH MY HEAD BURIED IN A HOLE AND THAT'S FINE, BUT THEN SOMETHING LIKE THIS BROMHEAD THING COMES ALONG... IT'S LIKE I GET YANKED UP OUT OF THAT HOLE... AND I GET A LOOK AT MY PART IN THE BIG PICTURE.
WHAT KIND OF PICTURE?
BAD.
ALL I CAN DO IS GET MY HEAD BACK INTO THAT HOLE...
BUT WHAT IF I DON'T?
WHAT IF I KEEP LOOKING AT THAT BIG PICTURE?
I'M SURE IT WOULD BE SCARY AT FIRST, BUT IN THE LONG RUN ...I THINK IT WOULD BE THE BEST THING FOR YOU.
REALLY?
I THOUGHT YOU'D TELL ME NOT TO DO ANYTHING CRAZY.
SURPRISE.
POOR, POOR CREATURE.
IT'S TRAGIC.
HUSH, GOBLIN.
SO DO YOU WANT TO TALK ABOUT THIS?
NO.
WHAT HAVE YOU GOT THERE?
JUST MORE TROUBLE.
"IT'S YOUR BURDEN, MY SON..."

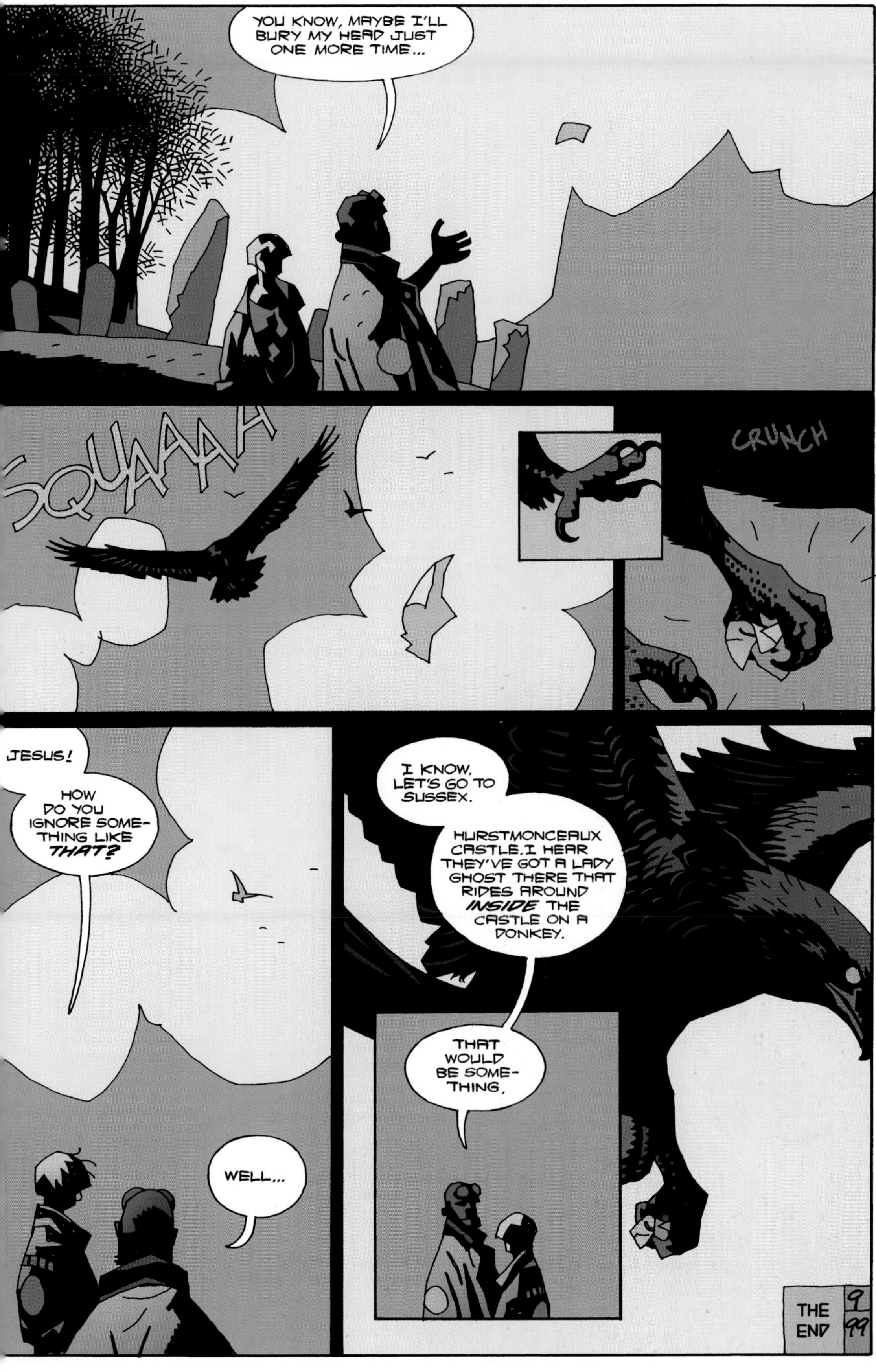
YOU KNOW, MAYBE I'LL BURY MY HEAD JUST ONE MORE TIME...
SQUAAAA
CRUNCH
JESUS!
HOW DO YOU IGNORE SOME-THING LIKE *THAT?*
WELL...
I KNOW. LET'S GO TO SUSSEX.
HURSTMONCEAUX CASTLE. I HEAR THEY'VE GOT A LADY GHOST THERE THAT RIDES AROUND *INSIDE* THE CASTLE ON A DONKEY.
THAT WOULD BE SOME-THING.
THE END
9
99

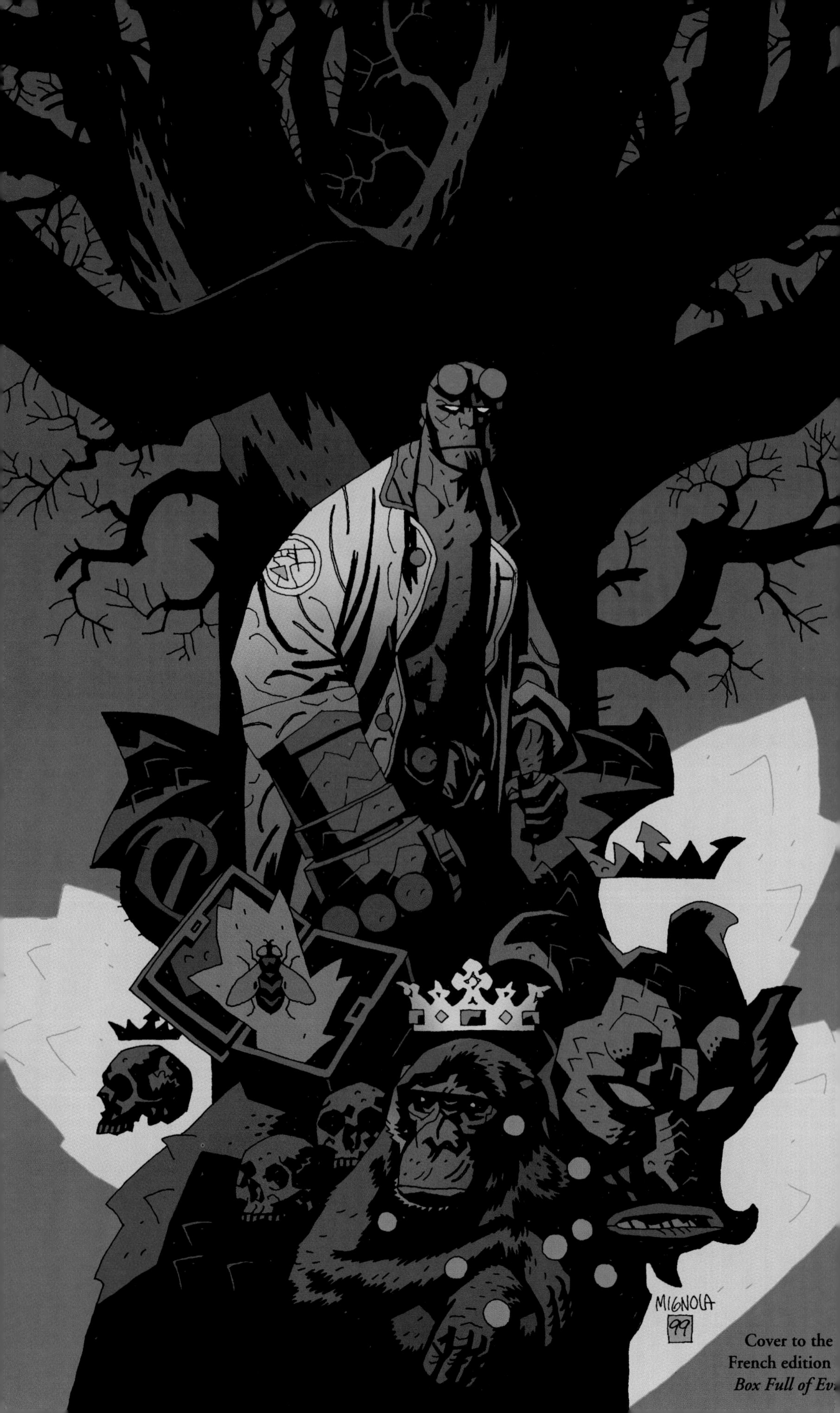
MIGNOLA
99

Cover to the
French edition
Box Full of Ev

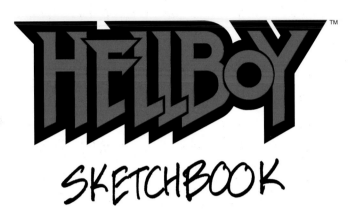

SKETCHBOOK

All of the drawings on the following pages were
done between 1993 and 1999.

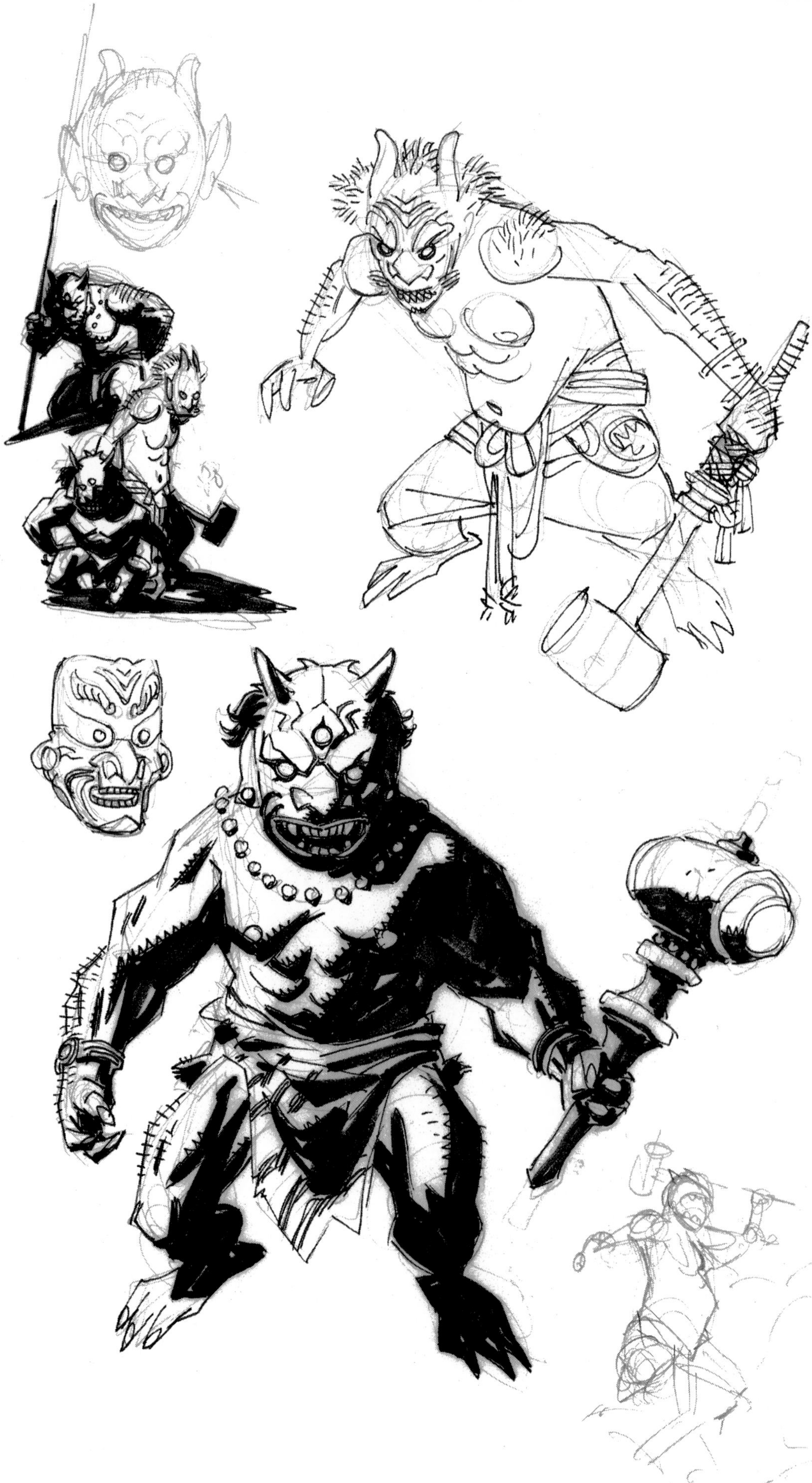

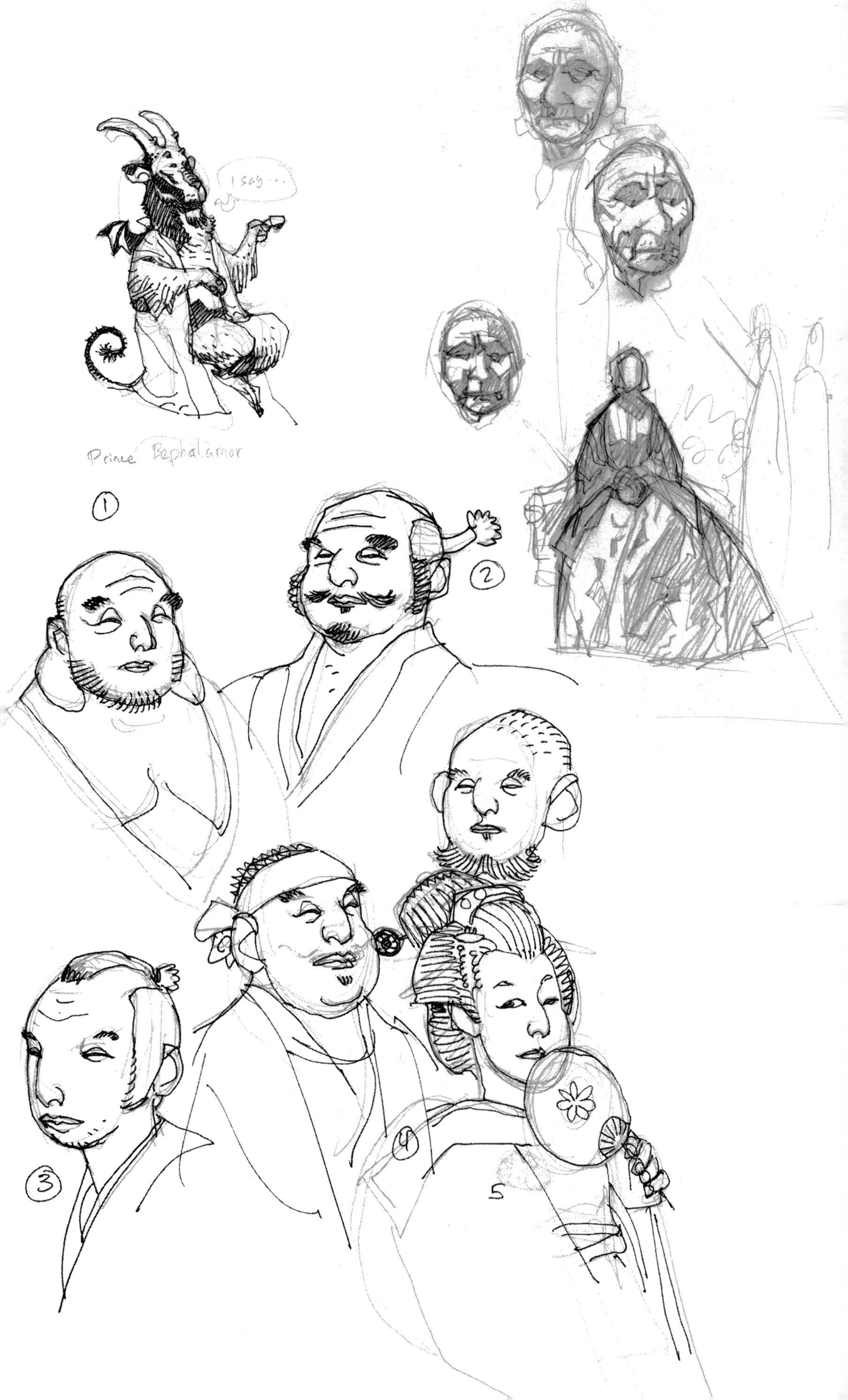

I say...
Prince Bephalamor
1
2
3
4
5

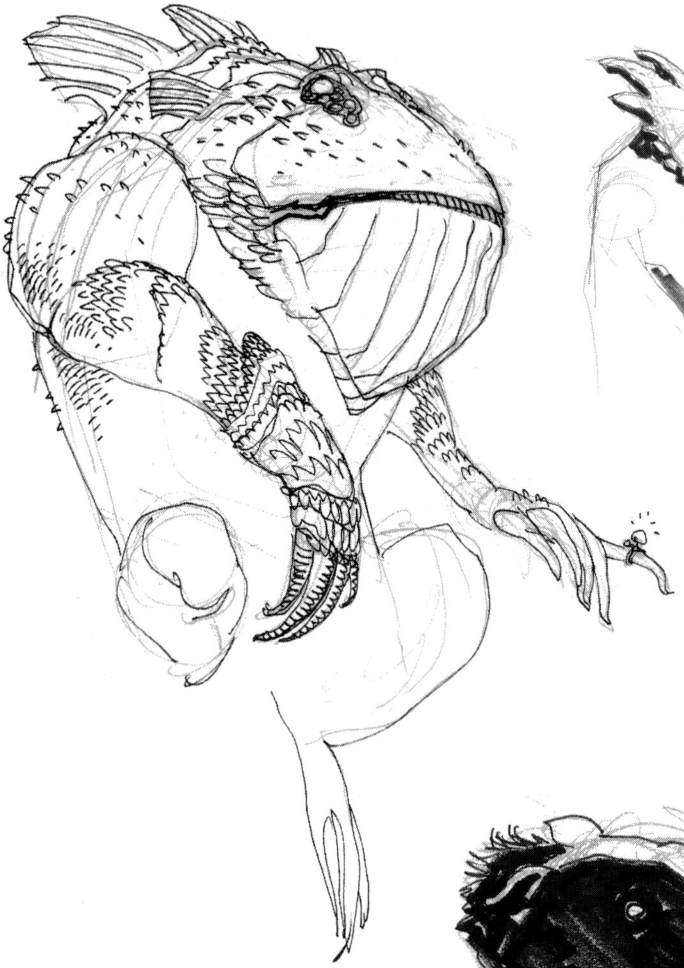
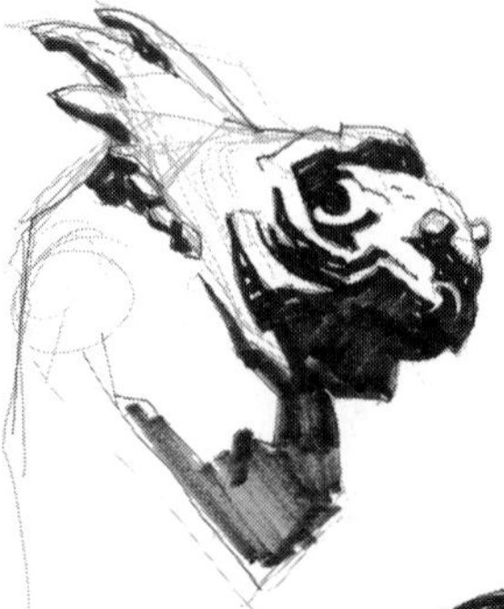
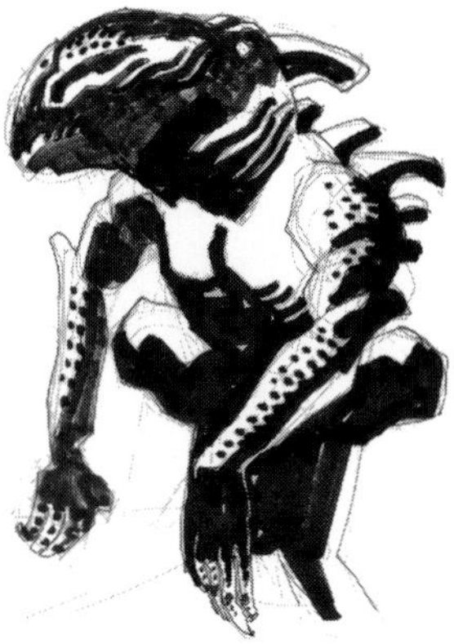
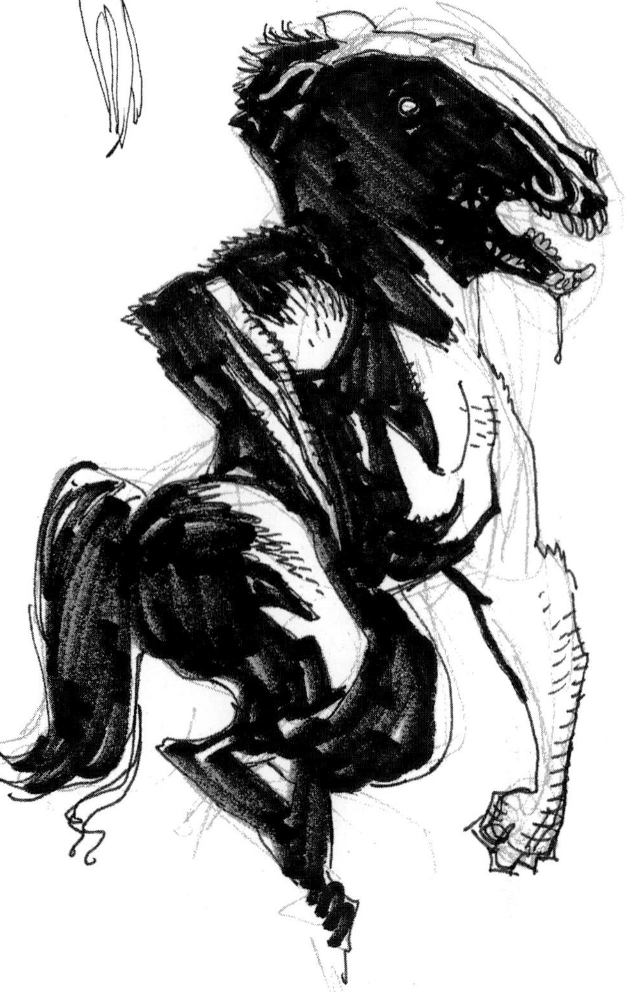

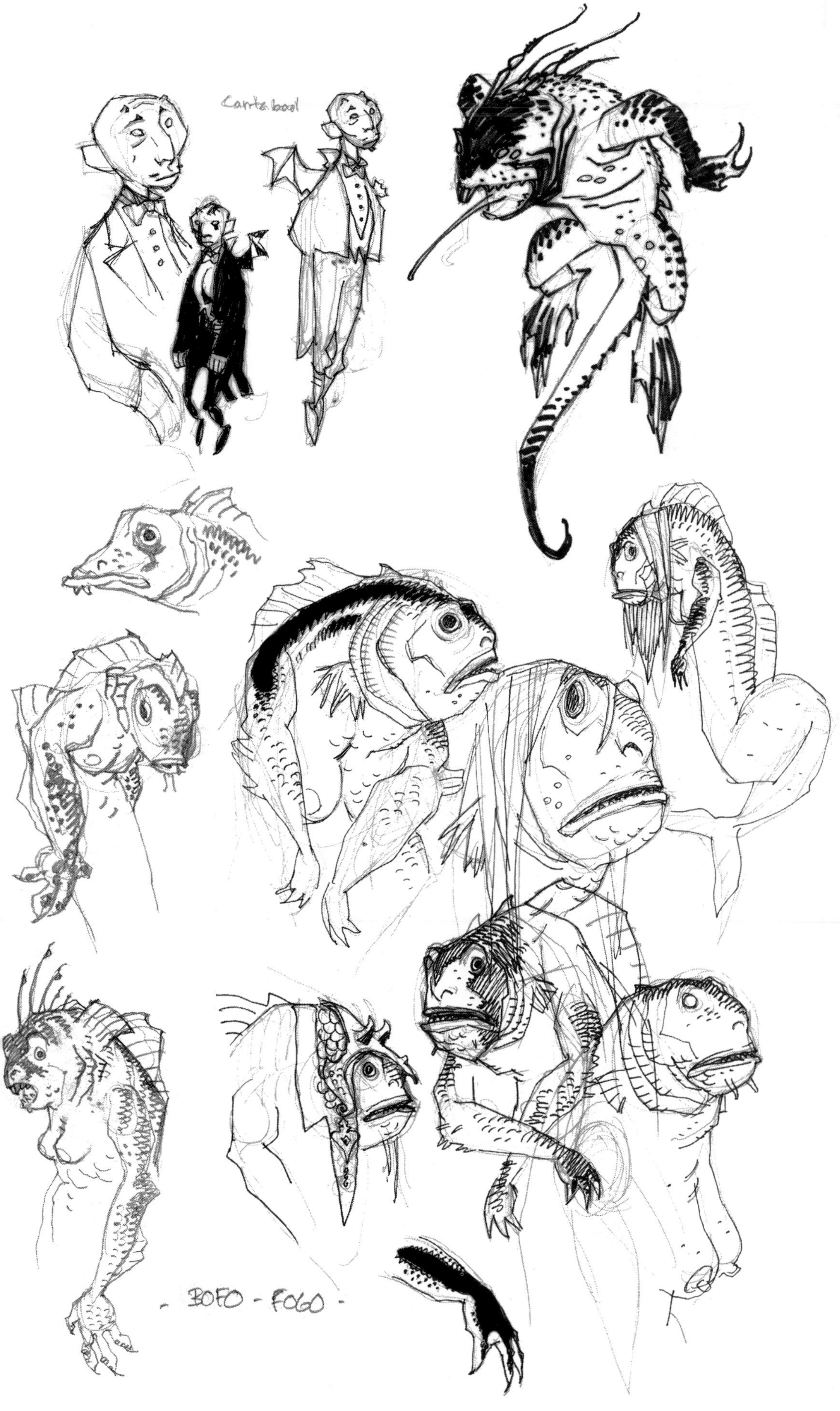
Cantabool
- BOFO - FOGO -

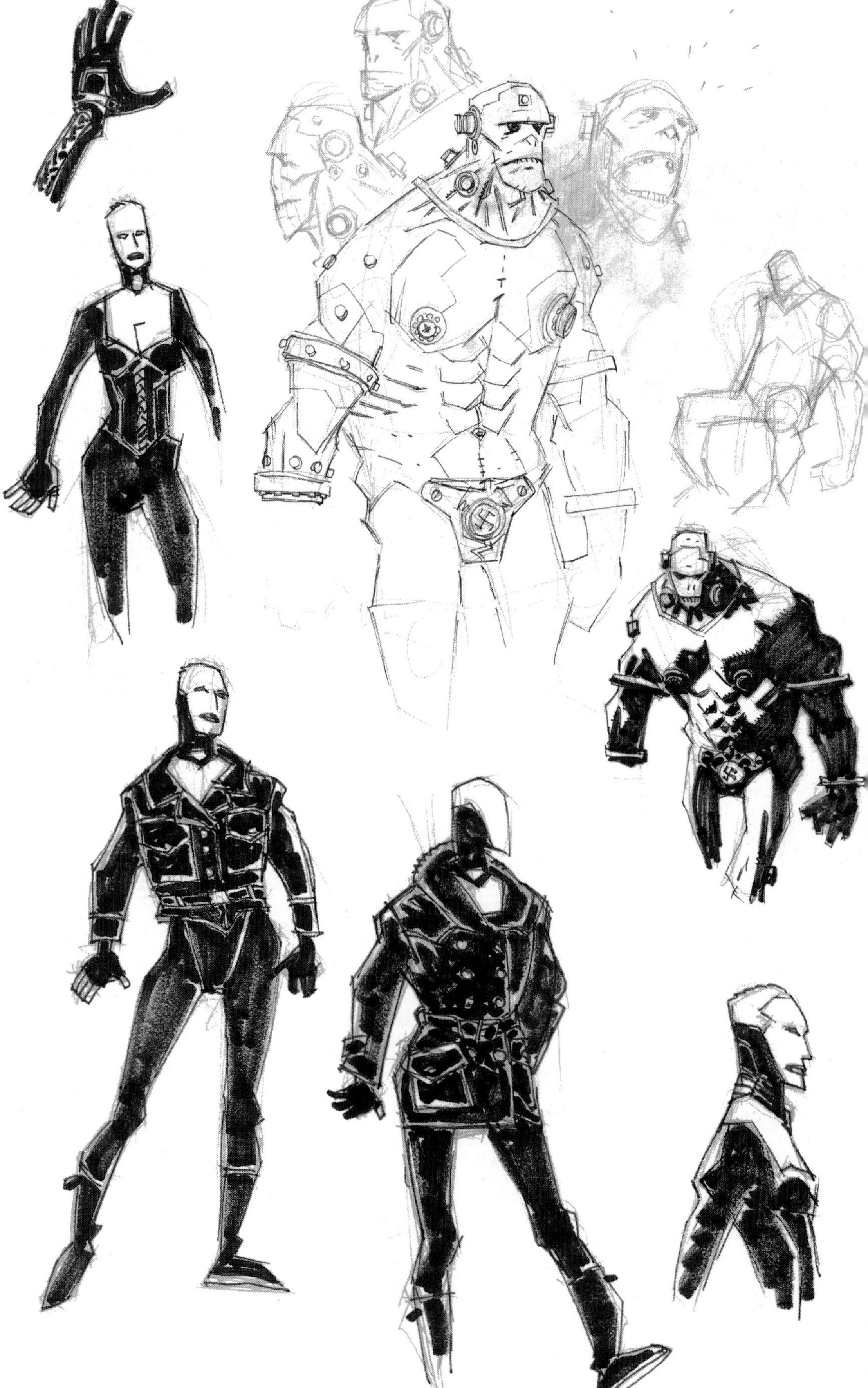

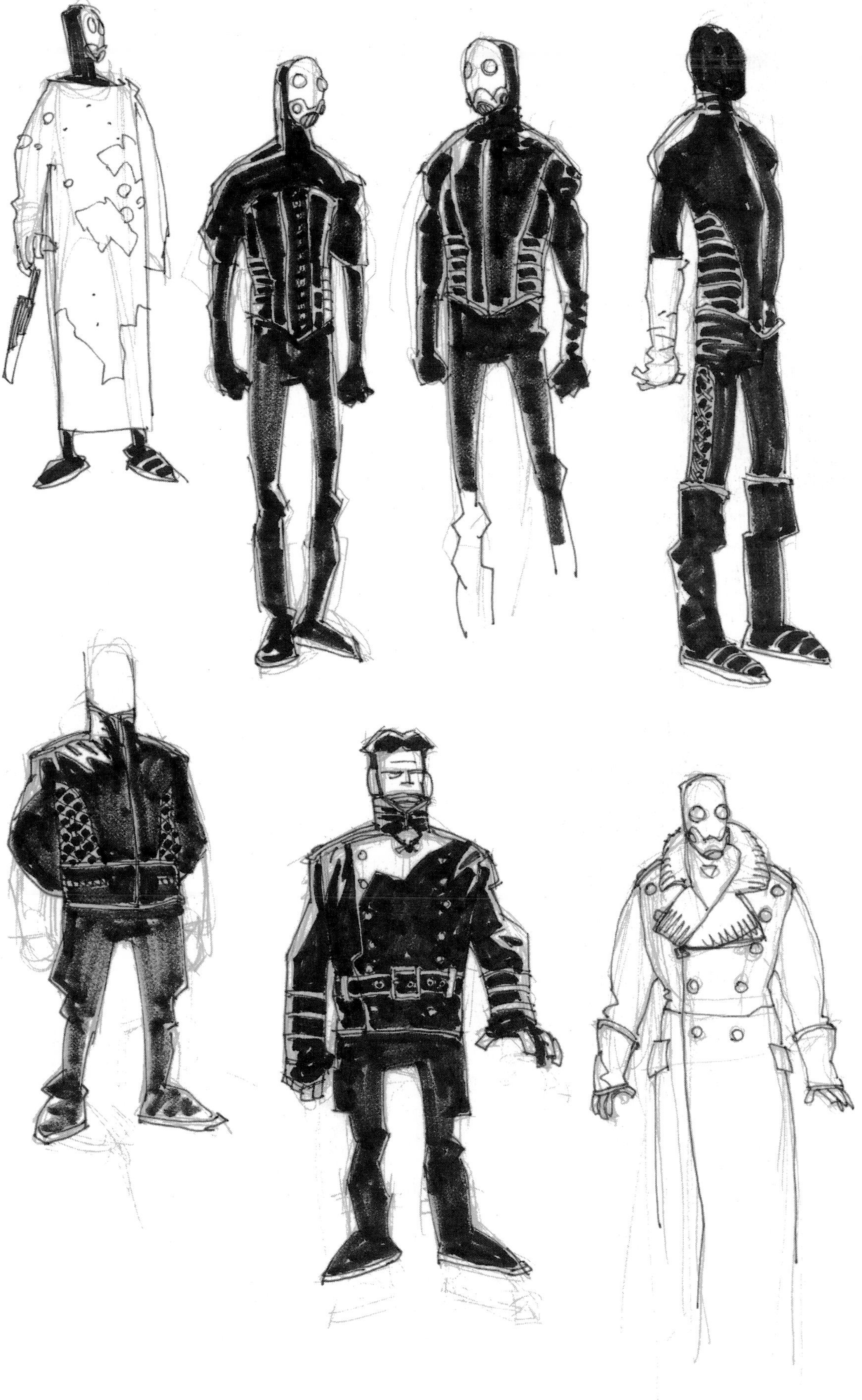

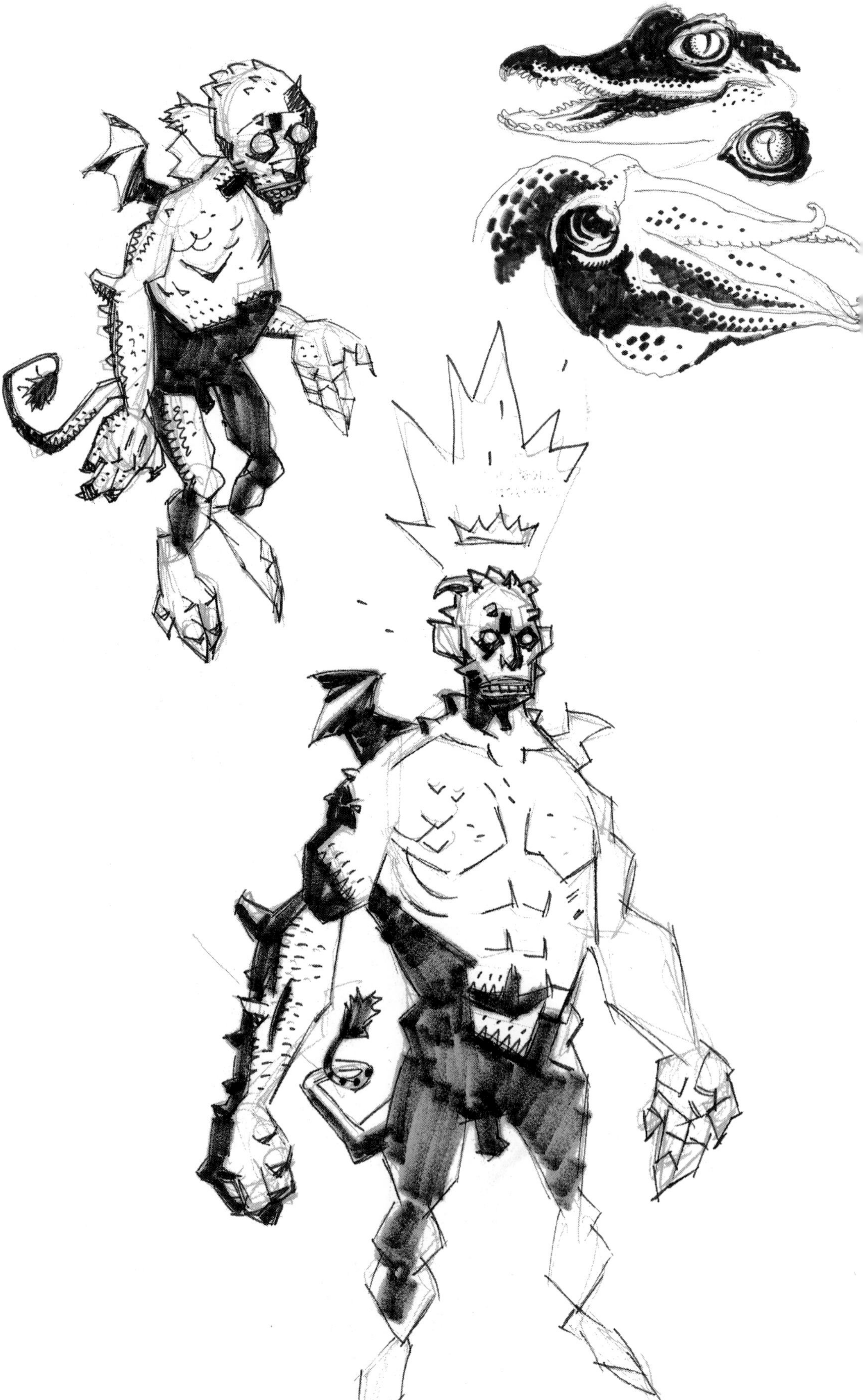

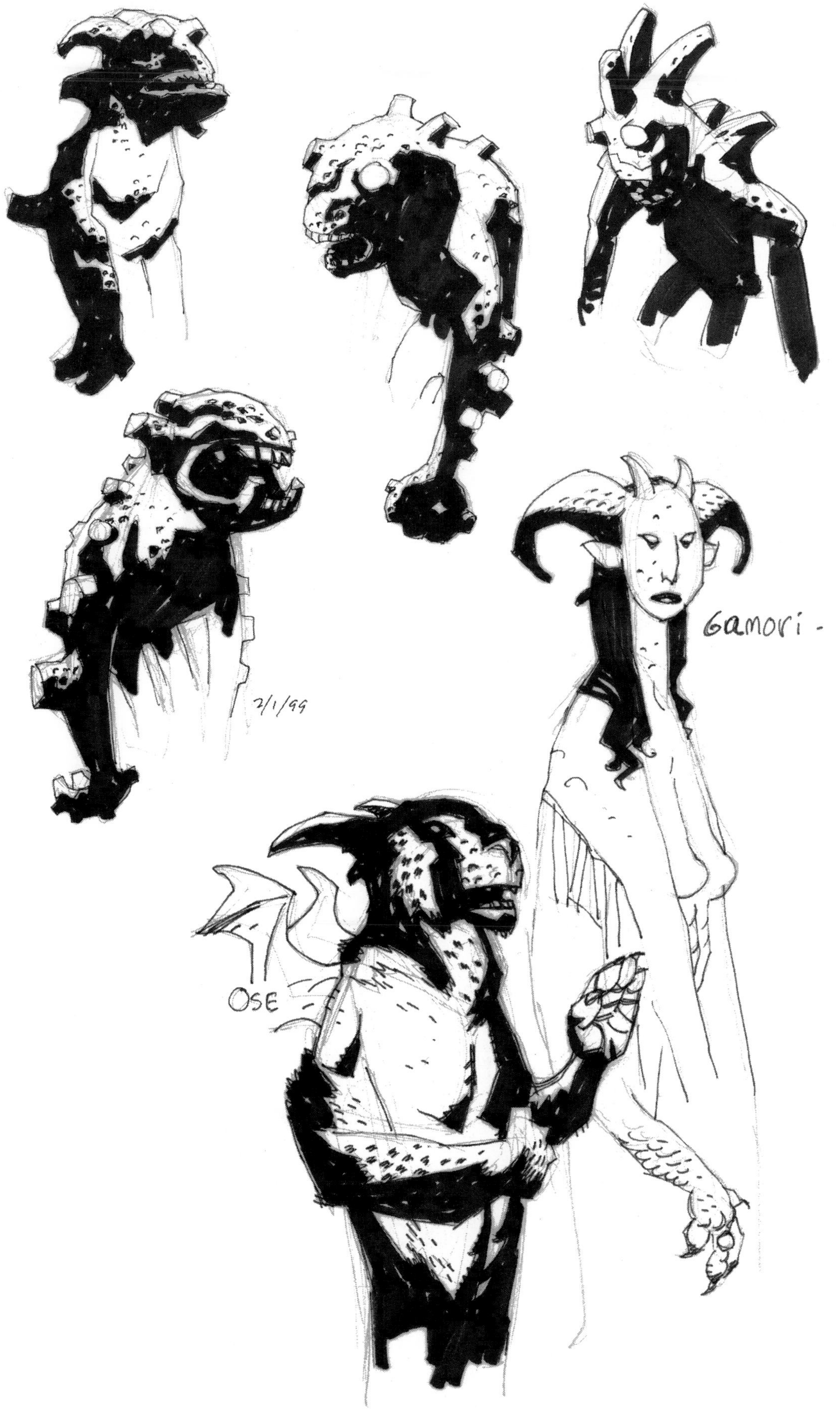
2/1/99
Gamori -
OSE

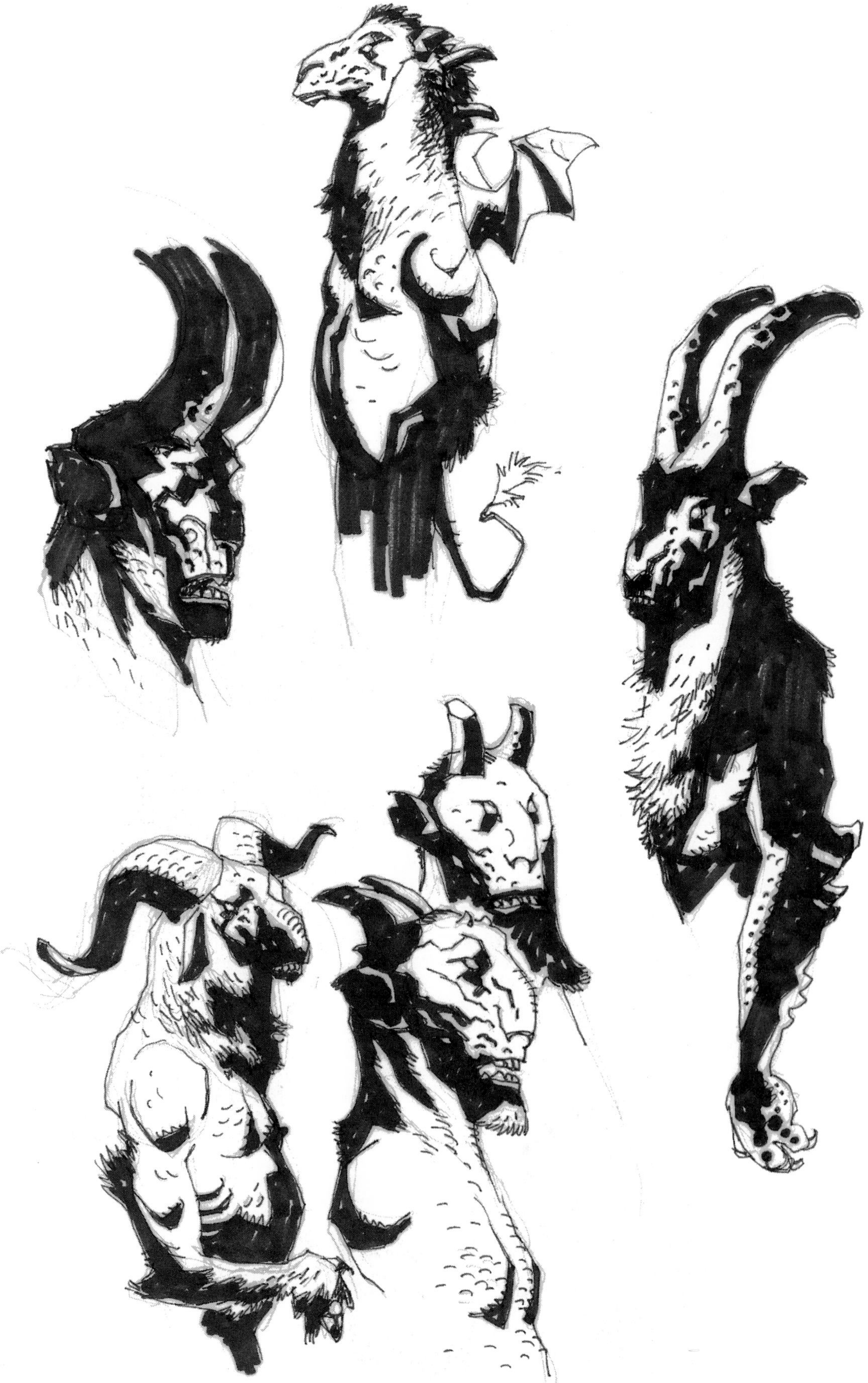

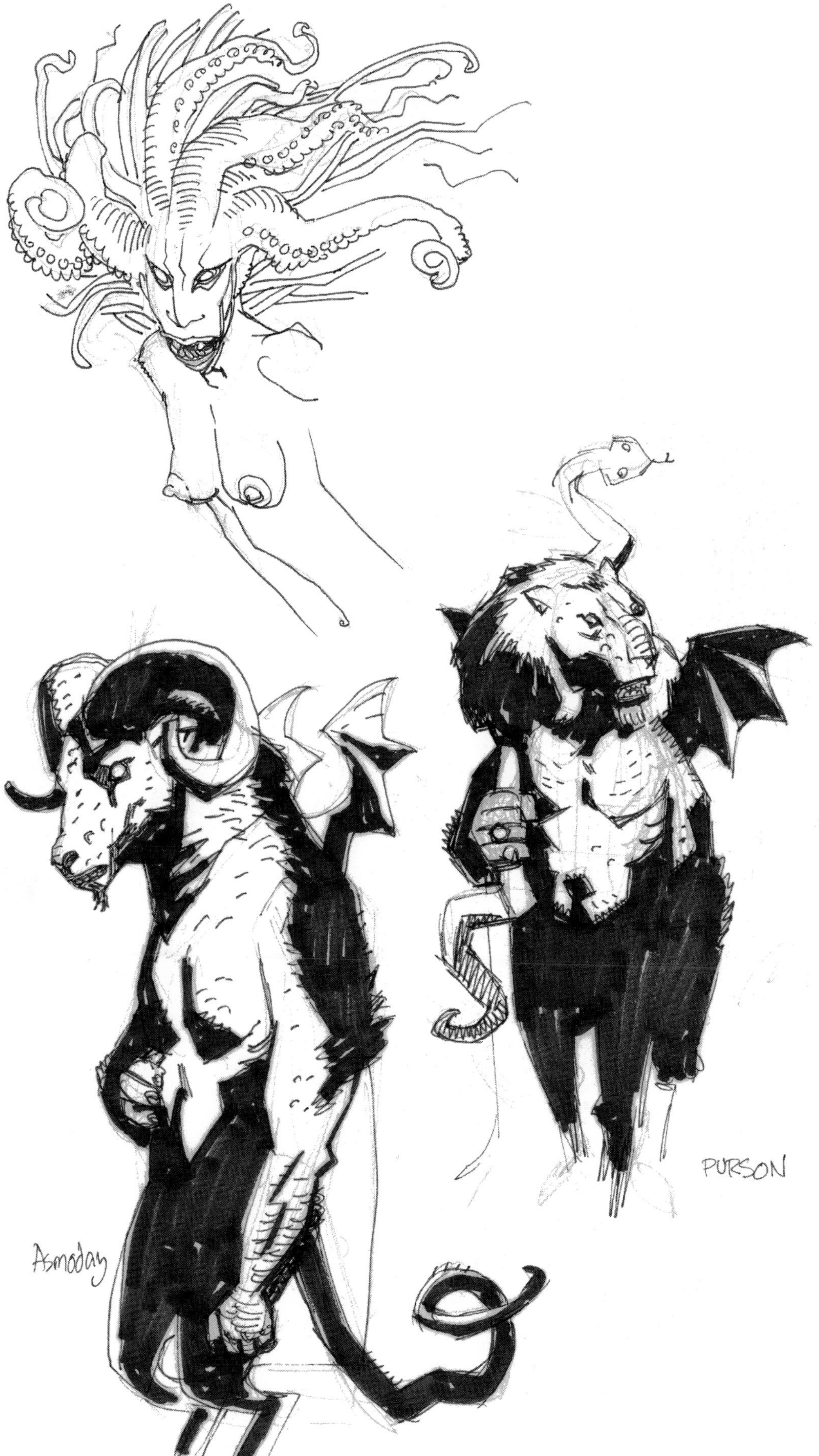
PURSON
Asmoday

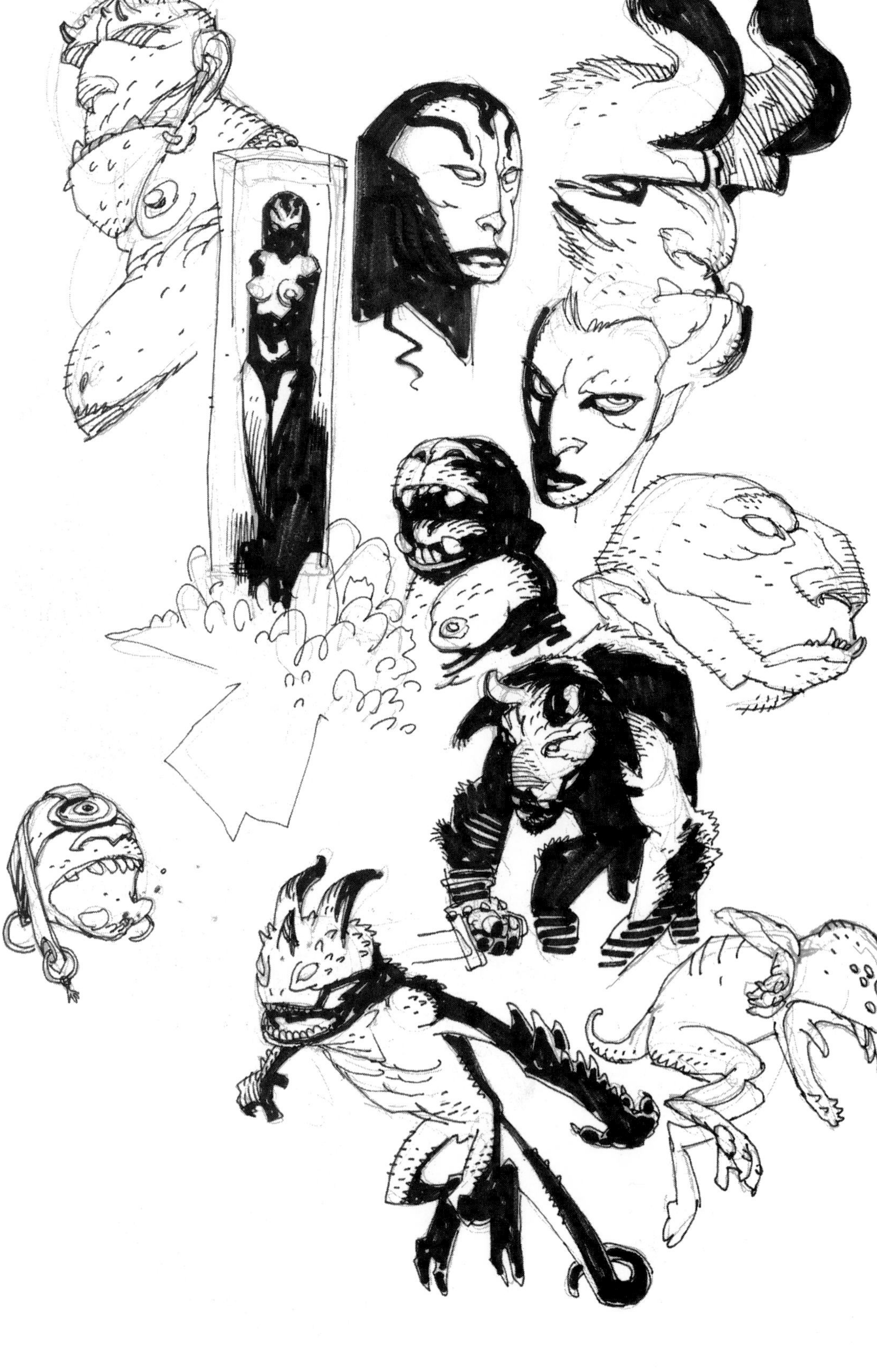

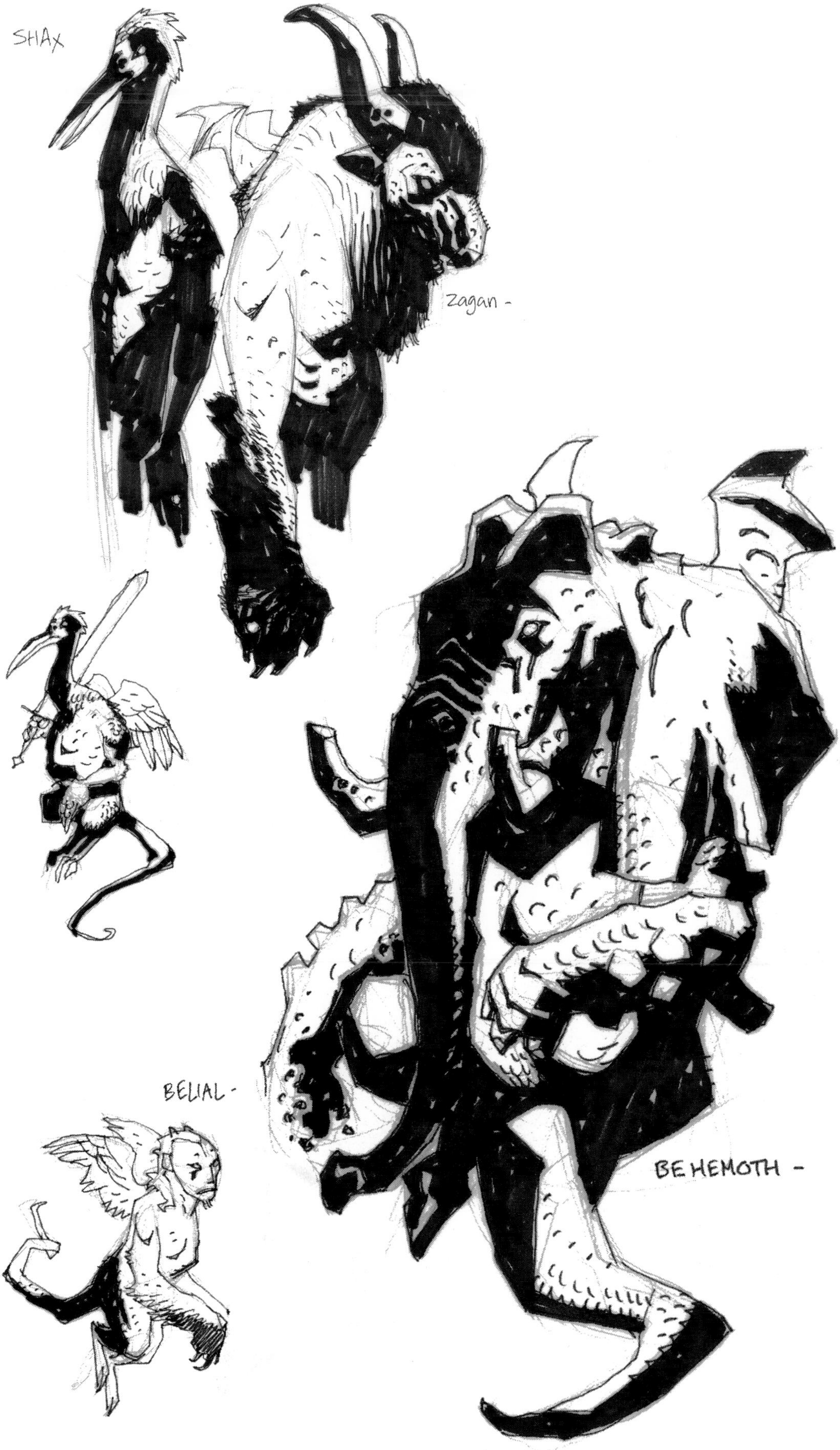
SHAX
Zagan -
BELIAL -
BEHEMOTH -

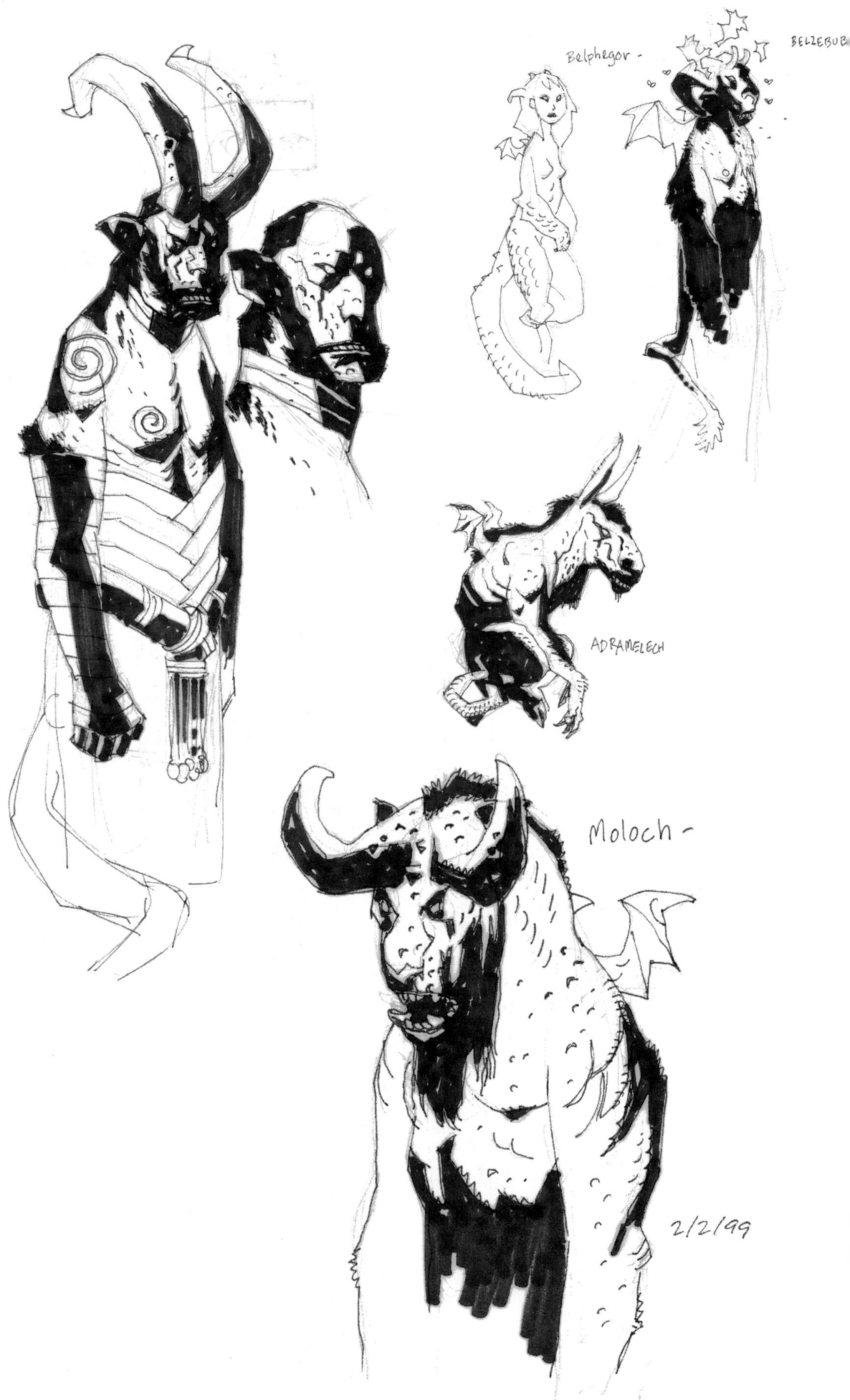
Belphegor -
BELZEBUB
ADRAMELECH
Moloch -
2/2/99

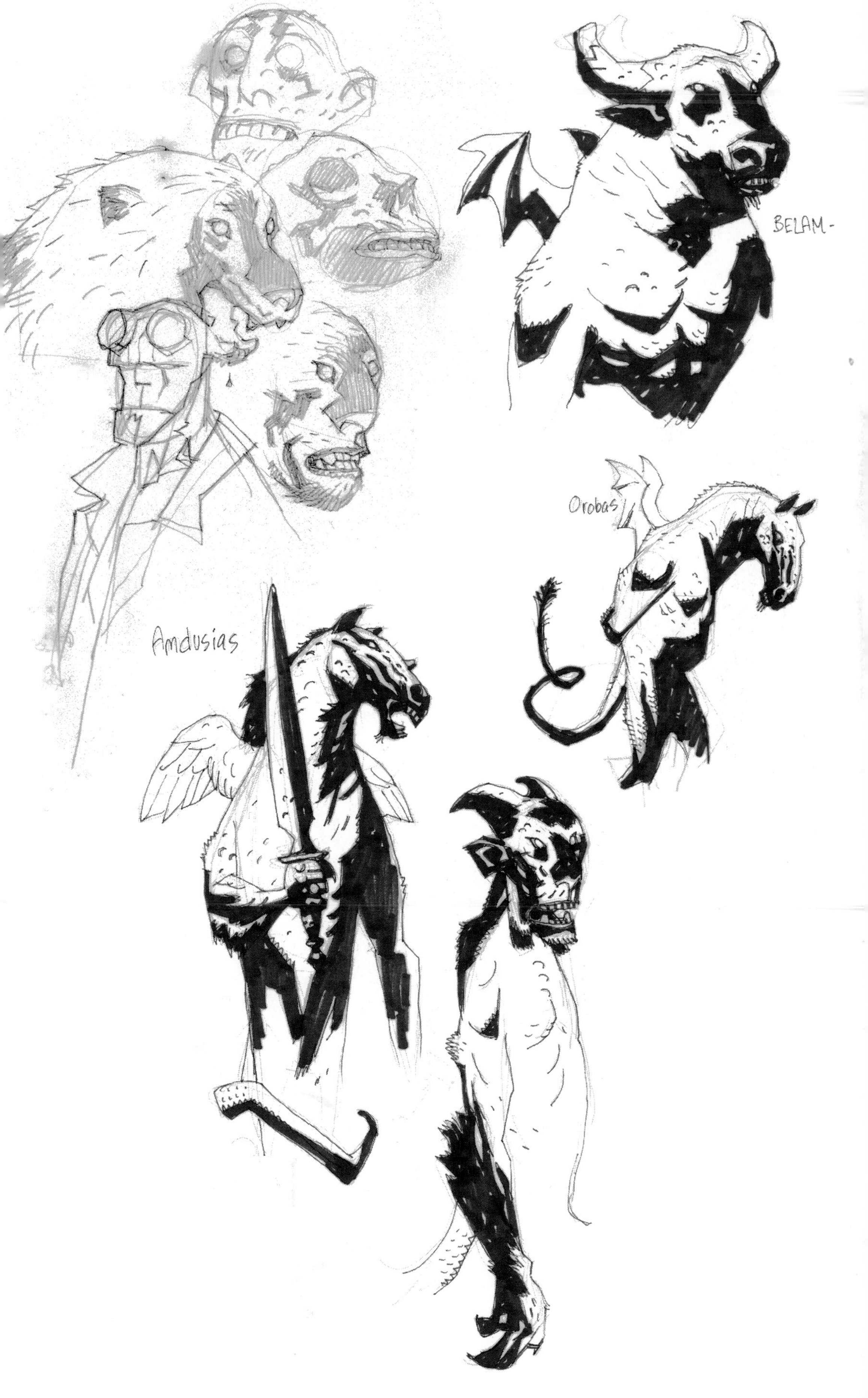
BELAM-
Orobas
Amdusias

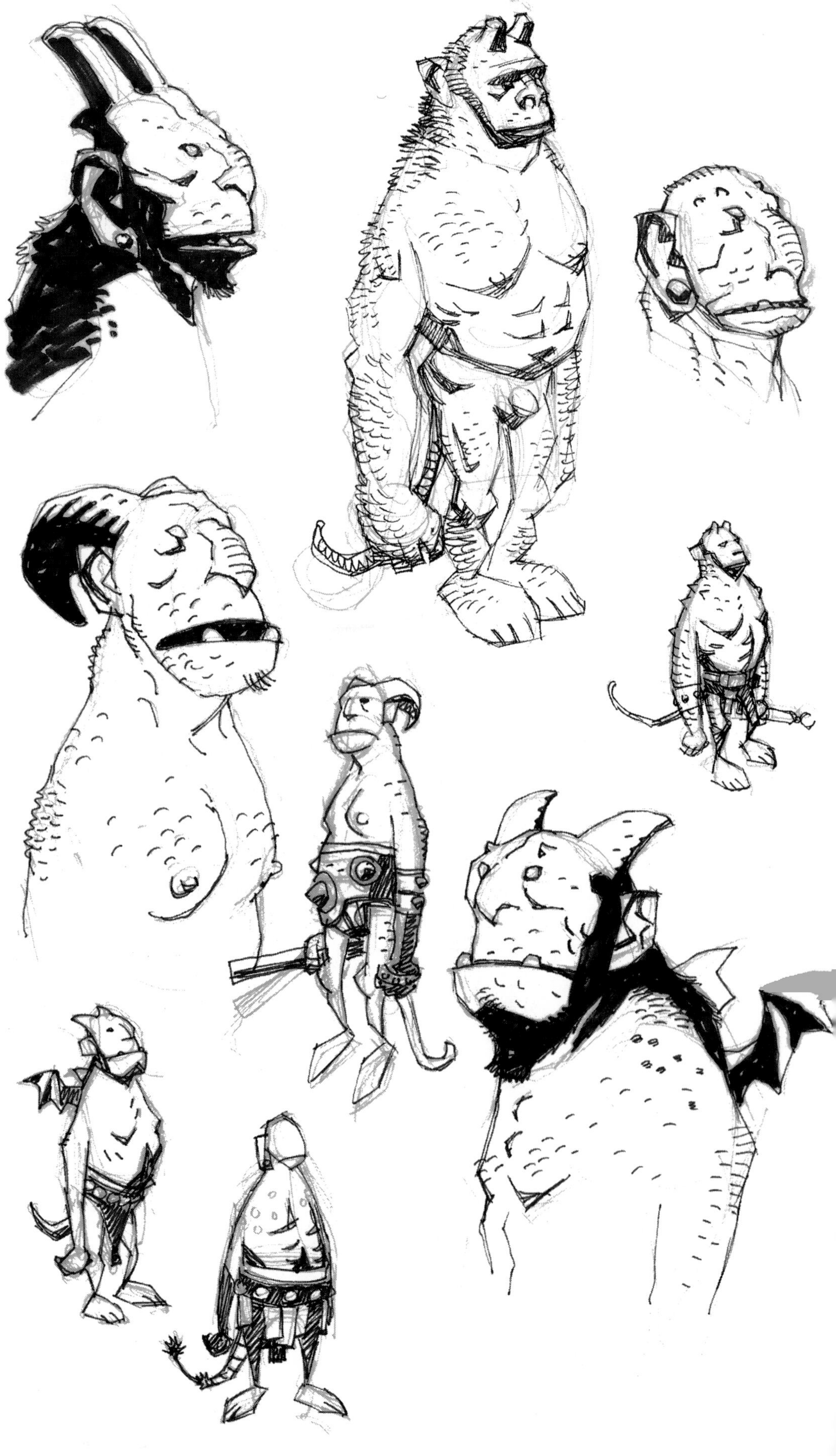

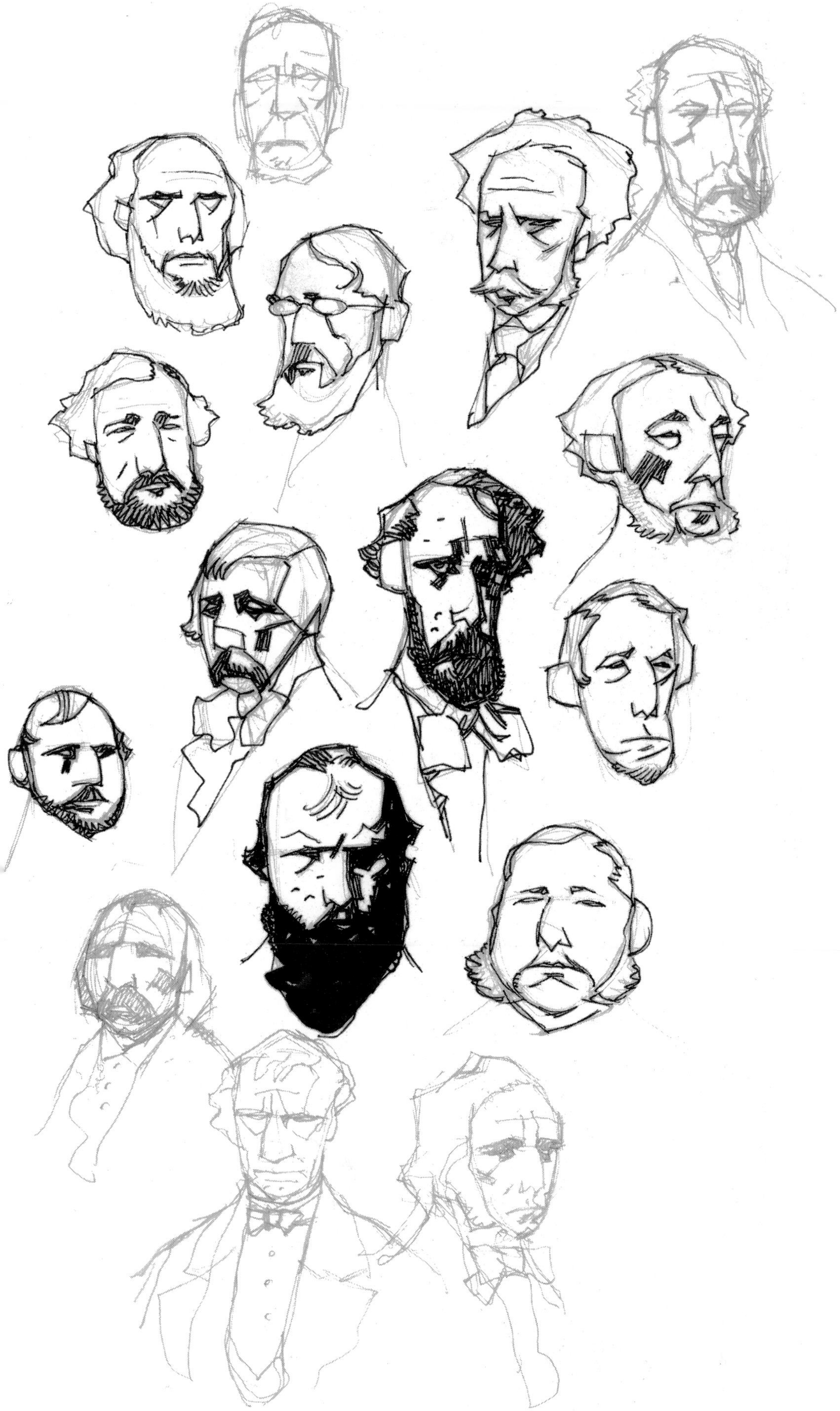

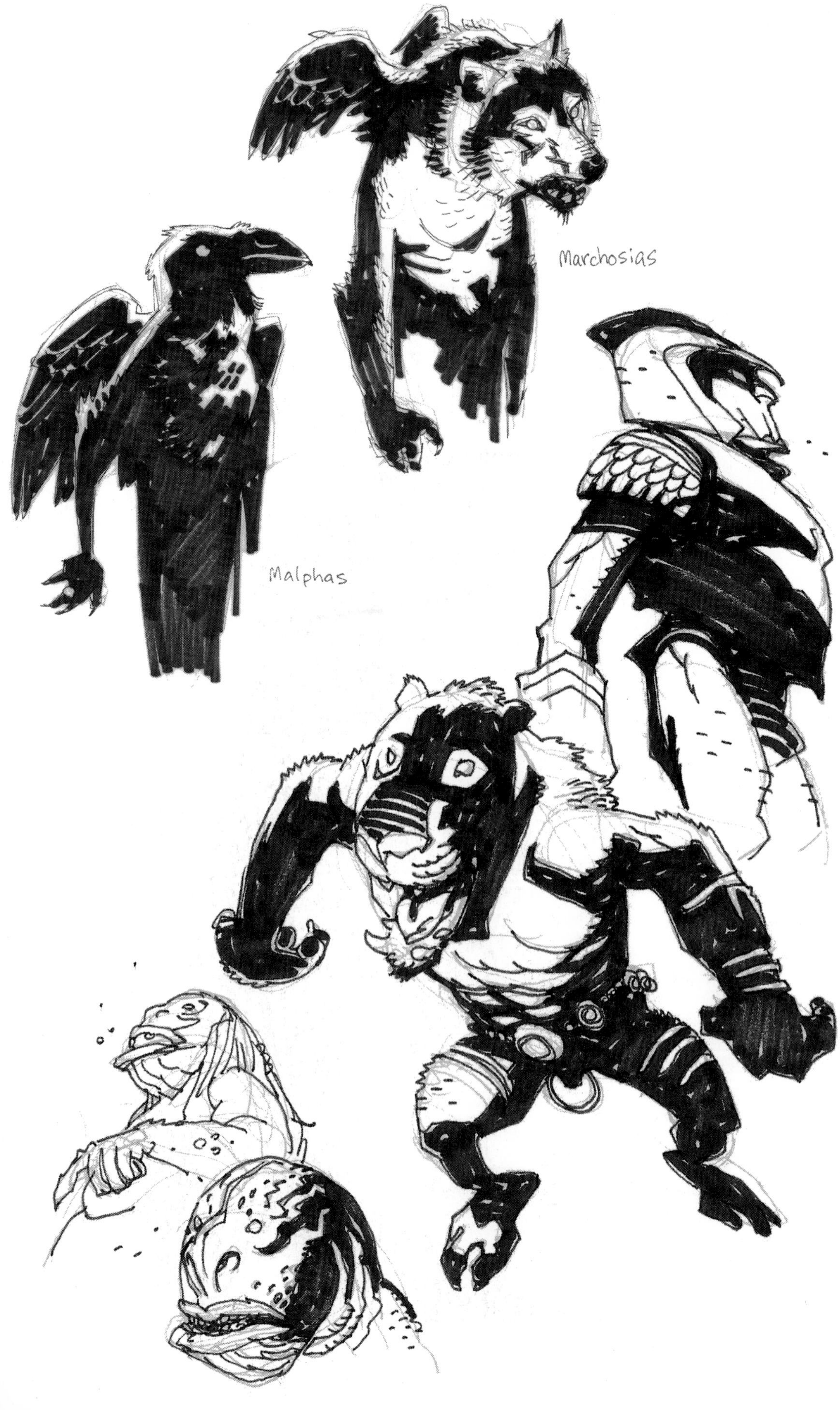
Marchosias
Malphas

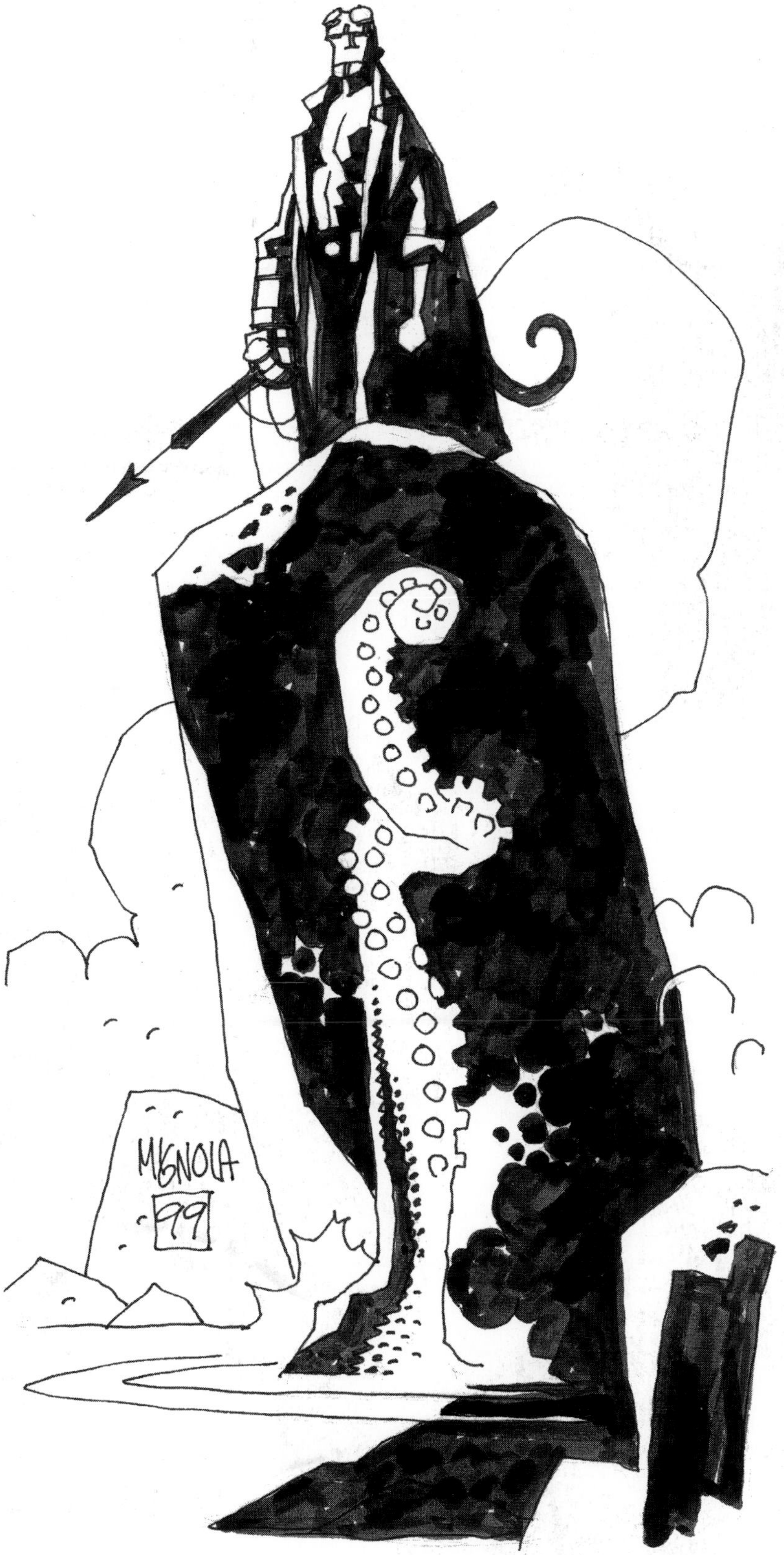
MIGNOLA
99

HELLBOY™

by MIKE MIGNOLA

EED OF DESTRUCTION
vith John Byrne
SBN: 1-59307-094-2 $17.95

VAKE THE DEVIL
SBN: 1-59307-095-0 $17.95

'HE CHAINED COFFIN
ND OTHERS
SBN: 1-59307-091-8 $17.95

THE RIGHT HAND OF DOOM
SBN: 1-59307-093-4 $17.95

CONQUEROR WORM
SBN: 1-59307-092-6 $17.95

'HE ART OF HELLBOY
SBN: 1-59307-089-6 $29.95

HELLBOY WEIRD TALES
Volume 1
By John Cassaday, Jason Pearson,
Eric Powell, Alex Maleev,
Bob Fingerman and others
SBN: 1-56971-622-6 $17.95

HELLBOY WEIRD TALES
Volume 2
By John Cassaday, JH Williams III,
P. Craig Russell, Jim Starlin,
Frank Cho, Evan Dorkin and others
SBN: 1-56971-935-5 $17.95

B.P.R.D. HOLLOW EARTH
AND OTHERS
By Mike Mignola, Chris Golden,
Ryan Sook and others
SBN: 1-56971-862-8 $17.95

B.P.R.D. THE SOUL OF VENICE
AND OTHERS
By Mike Oeming, Guy Davis,
Scott Kolins, Geoff Johns and others
SBN: 1-59307-132-9 $17.95

ODD JOBS
Short stories by Mike Mignola,
Poppy Z. Brite, Chris Golden and others
Illustrations by Mike Mignola
SBN: 1-56971-440-1 $14.95

HELLBOY BASEBALL CAP
#17-106 $14.95

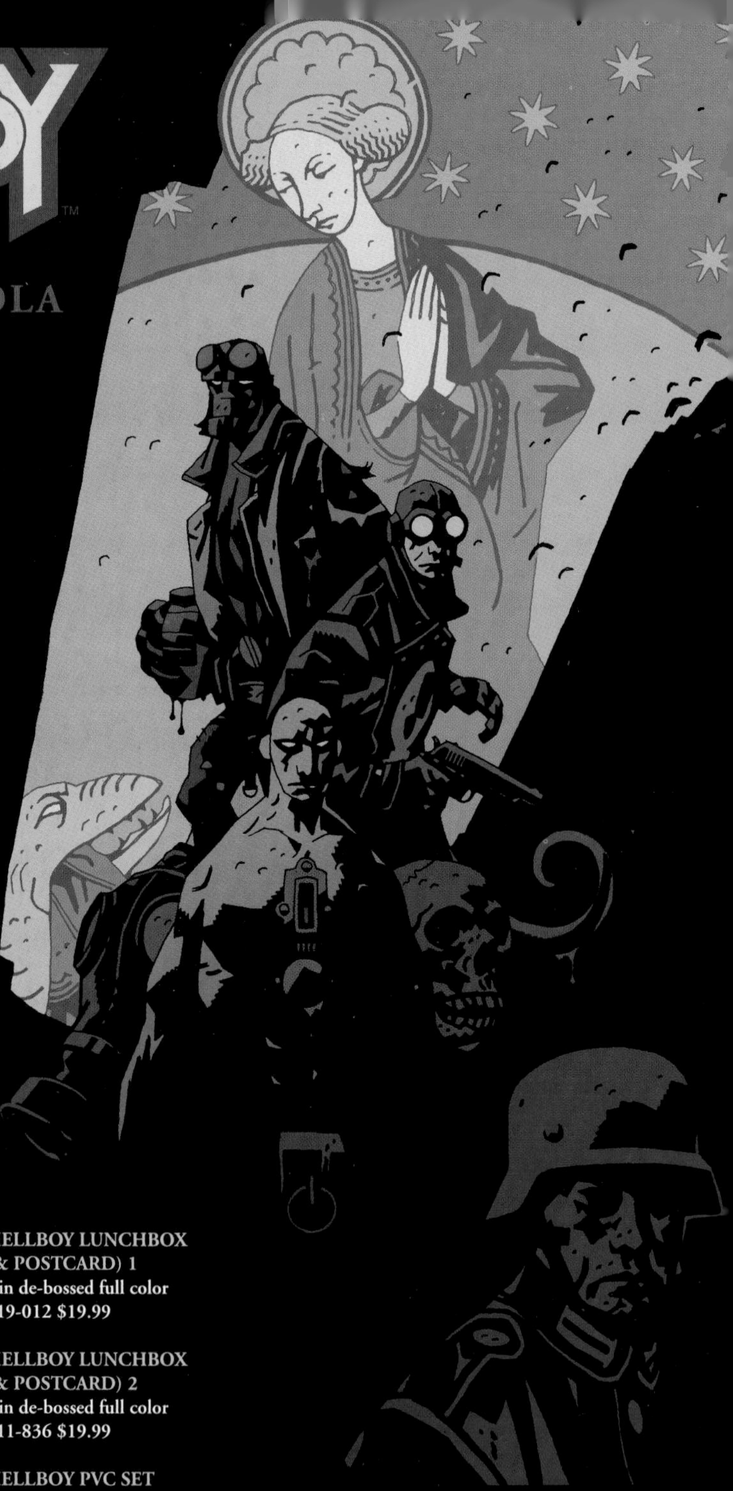

HELLBOY LUNCHBOX
(& POSTCARD) 1
Tin de-bossed full color
#19-012 $19.99

HELLBOY LUNCHBOX
(& POSTCARD) 2
Tin de-bossed full color
#11-836 $19.99

HELLBOY PVC SET
#10-666 $39.99

HELLBOY JOURNAL
#12-309 $9.99

HELLBOY SWEATSHIRT
Red-and-Yellow Hellboy Logo
#12-411 $39.99

HELLBOY ZIPPO LIGHTER
#17-101 $29.95

HELLBOY BOOKS AND MERCHANDISE
CAN BE VIEWED AT www.darkhorse.com

To find a comics shop in your area, call 1-888-266-4226
For more information or to order direct:
•On the web: www.darkhorse.com
•E-mail: mailorder@darkhorse.com
•Phone: 1-800-862-0052 or (503) 652-9701
Mon.-Sat. 9 A.M. to 5 P.M. Pacific Time

DARK HORSE COMICS™ *drawing on your nightmares*